Learning C#

Jesse Liberty

O'REILLY®

Beijing · Cambridge · Farnham · Köln · Paris · Sebastopol · Taipei · Tokyo

Learning C#
by Jesse Liberty

Published by O'Reilly & Associates, Inc., 1005 Gravenstein Highway North, Sebastopol, CA 95472.

O'Reilly & Associates books may be purchased for educational, business, or sales promotional use. Online editions are also available for most titles (*safari.oreilly.com*). For more information, contact our corporate/institutional sales department: (800) 998-9938 or *corporate@oreilly.com*.

Editor:	Valerie Quercia
Production Editor:	Darren Kelly
Cover Designer:	Hanna Dyer
Interior Designer:	David Futato

Printing History:

> September 2002:   First Edition.

ISBN: 0-596-00376-5

[M]

Table of Contents

Preface

In July 2000, Microsoft announced the release of its new .NET platform, which represented a major change in the way people think about programming. .NET facilitates object-oriented Internet development. C# is a programming language that was developed specifically for the purpose of writing applications for the .NET platform. C# builds on lessons learned from other languages, like C (high performance), Java (high security), and Visual Basic (rapid development). And this new language is ideally suited for developing distributed web applications.

About This Book

Learning C# is a primer on the C# language, in the context of the .NET development environment, and also on object-oriented programming. This book focuses on the fundamentals of the C# programming language, both syntactical and semantic. After mastering these concepts, you should be ready to move on to a more advanced programming guide that will help you create large-scale web and Windows applications. Chapter 20, *Afterword*, provides a number of suggestions for your continued study of C# and .NET development.

Who This Book Is For

Learning C# was written for programmers with little or no object-oriented programming experience, as well as for novice programmers. Those coming from another language may have a slight advantage, but I've tried to provide an on-ramp for beginners as well, by defining all terms, demonstrating the relationships among the various constructs, and reviewing key concepts along the way.

How the Book Is Organized

Chapter 1, *C# and .NET Programming*, introduces you to the C# language and the .NET platform.

Chapter 2, *Getting Started with C#*, presents a simple application that prints the words "Hello World" to a console window, and gives a line-by-line analysis of the code.

Chapter 3, *Object-Oriented Programming*, explains the principles behind and goals of this programming methodology, including the three pillars of object-oriented programming: encapsulation, specialization, and polymorphism.

Chapter 4, *Visual Studio .NET*, introduces the Integrated Development Environment (IDE) designed specifically for .NET; using the IDE can greatly simplify how you write applications.

Chapter 5, *C# Language Fundamentals*, introduces the basic syntax and structure of the C# language, including the intrinsic types, variables, statements, and expressions.

Chapter 6, *Branching*, describes some of the ways you can change the order in which methods are called within a program. Statements such as if, switch, goto, and break will be considered, along with the concept of loops, which are created using such keywords as for, while, and do...while.

Chapter 7, *Operators*, describes some of the symbols that cause C# to take an action, such as assigning a value to a variable and arithmetically operating on values (adding, subtracting, and so forth).

Chapter 8, *Classes and Objects*, introduces the key concepts of programmer-defined types (classes) and instances of those types (objects). Classes and objects are the building blocks of object-oriented programming.

Chapter 9, *Inside Methods*, delves into the specific programming instructions you'll write to define the behavior of objects.

Chapter 10, *Basic Debugging*, introduces the debugger integrated into the Visual Studio .NET Integrated Development Environment.

Chapter 11, *Inheritance and Polymorphism*, explores two of the key concepts behind object-oriented programming and demonstrates how you might implement them in your code.

Chapter 12, *Operator Overloading*, explains how to add standard operators to the types you define.

Chapter 13, *Structs*, introduces the structure or struct, a programmer-defined type similar to a class, but with specific and more limited functionality.

Chapter 14, *Interfaces*, explains how you can define a set of behaviors (an interface) that any number of classes might implement.

Chapter 15, *Arrays*, introduces the array, an indexed collection of objects that are all the same type. Arrays are one of the collection types recognized by C#.

Chapter 16, *Collection Interfaces and Types*, describes some of the other C# collections, including stacks and queues.

Chapter 17, *Strings*, discusses the manipulation of strings of characters, the C# string class, and regular expression syntax.

Chapter 18, *Throwing and Catching Exceptions*, explains how to handle errors and abnormal conditions that may arise in relation to your programs.

Chapter 19, *Delegates and Events*, discusses how to write code to respond to programming occurrences like mouse clicks, keystrokes, and other events; event handling is often accomplished by the use of delegates, which are objects that encapsulate any method that matches the delegate's specification.

Chapter 20, *Afterword*, describes where you might go to learn more about C# and .NET programming, including other books, web sites, newsgroups, and so forth.

The book concludes with an appendix of *C# Keywords*.

Conventions Used in This Book

The following font conventions are used in this book:

Italic
> Used for pathnames, filenames, program names, Internet addresses, such as domain names and URLs, and new terms where they are defined.

Constant Width
> Used for command lines and options that should be typed verbatim, C# keywords, and code examples.

Constant Width Italic
> Used for replaceable items, such as variables or optional elements, within syntax lines or code.

Constant Width Bold
> Used for emphasis within program code.

Pay special attention to notes set apart from the text with the following icons:

 This is a tip. It contains useful supplementary information about the topic at hand.

This is a warning. It helps you solve and avoid annoying problems.

Support

As part of my responsibilities as author, I provide ongoing support for my books through my web site:

http://www.LibertyAssociates.com

On this web site, you'll also find the source code for all the examples in *Learning C#*, as well as access to a book-support discussion group with a section set aside for questions about C#. Before you post a question, however, please check the FAQ (Frequently Asked Questions) list and the errata file on my web site. If you check these files and still have a question, then please go ahead and post to the discussion center.

The most effective way to get help is to ask a very precise question or even to create a very small program that illustrates your area of concern or confusion. You may also want to check the various newsgroups and discussion centers on the Internet. Microsoft offers a wide array of newsgroups, and Developmentor (*http://www.develop.com*) has wonderful .NET email discussion list, as does Charles Carroll at *http://www.asplists.com*.

We'd Like to Hear from You

We have tested and verified the information in this book to the best of our ability, but you may find that features have changed (or even that we have made mistakes!). Please let us know about any errors you find, as well as your suggestions for future editions, by writing to:

O'Reilly & Associates, Inc.
1005 Gravenstein Highway North
Sebastopol, CA 95472
(800) 998-9938 (in the U.S. or Canada)
(707) 829-0515 (international/local)
(707) 829-0104 (fax)

We have a web page for this book where we list examples and any plans for future editions. You can access this information at:

http://www.oreilly.com/catalog/learncsharp

You can also send messages electronically. To be put on the mailing list or request a catalog, send email to:

info@oreilly.com

To comment on the book, send email to:

bookquestions@oreilly.com

For more information about this book and others, as well as additional technical articles and discussion on the C# and the .NET Framework, see the O'Reilly & Associates web site:

http://www.oreilly.com

and the O'Reilly .NET DevCenter:

http://www.oreillynet.com/dotnet

ONDotnet.com provides independent coverage of fundamental, interoperable, and emerging Microsoft .NET programming and Web services technologies.

Acknowledgments

To ensure that Learning C# is accurate, complete, and targeted at the needs and interests of programmers, I enlisted the help of some of the brightest people I know, including Dan Hurwitz, Seth Weiss, and Sue Lynch.

John Osborn signed me to O'Reilly, for which I will forever be in his debt. Claire Cloutier and Tatiana Diaz helped make this book better than what I'd written. Rob Romano created a number of the illustrations and improved the others. Tim O'Reilly provided support and resources, and I'm grateful. A special thank you to Val Quercia, who added great value to this book, as she has to many others. If this book is clear and understandable, it is due to her vigilance.

CHAPTER 1

C# and .NET Programming

Learning C# introduces C# specifically, and the .NET development platform more generally, to programmers with little or no object-oriented programming experience. Along the way, you will learn a great deal about writing high-quality, industrial-strength programs for .NET.

This brief introduction will show you how C# fits into the .NET picture, what you can do with the language, and what benefits this language has over its predecessors.

You will also learn some of the concepts integral to object-oriented programming, which has revolutionized how web and Windows applications are developed. Object-oriented programming is closely tied to the semantics of the C# language, that is, the meaning behind the code you write. Obviously, you need to have a basic understanding of the syntax of the C# language, but you also need to understand what you are actually trying to accomplish.

C# and .NET

In the past, you might have learned a language like C or Java without much concern about the platform on which you would be programming. These cross-platform languages were as comfortable on a Unix box as they were on a PC running Windows.

C#, however, was created specifically for .NET. While .NET may become cross-platform some day soon—a Unix port is reportedly in the offing—for now the overwhelming majority of .NET programs will be written to run on a machine running .NET. At the time of this writing, that means a Windows machine.

The .NET Platform

When Microsoft announced C# in July 2000, its unveiling was part of a much larger event: the announcement of the .NET platform. The .NET platform is a development framework that provides a new way to create Windows applications. However, .NET goes beyond traditional Windows programming to facilitate creating web applications quickly and easily.

Microsoft says it is devoting 80% of its research and development budget to .NET and its associated technologies. The results of this commitment are impressive. For one thing, the scope of .NET is huge. The platform consists of three separate product groups:

- A set of languages, including C# and Visual Basic .NET; a set of development tools, including Visual Studio .NET; and powerful tools for building applications, including the *Common Language Runtime* (CLR), a platform for compiling, debugging, and executing .NET applications.
- A set of .NET Enterprise Servers, formerly known as SQL Server 2000, Exchange 2000, BizTalk 2000, and so on, that provide specialized functionality for relational data storage, email, B2B commerce, etc.
- New .NET-enabled non-PC devices, from cell phones to game boxes.

The C# language can be used to develop three types of applications you can run on your Windows computer:

- Console applications, which display no graphics
- Windows applications, which use the standard Windows interface
- Web applications, which can be accessed with a browser

This book will focus primarily on the basics of the C# language, mostly using simple console applications to illustrate language fundamentals.

The .NET Framework

Central to the .NET platform is a development environment known as the *.NET Framework*. The Framework specifies how .NET programming constructs such as intrinsic types, classes, and interfaces are implemented. You will learn about these constructs in the chapters ahead.

The .NET Framework sits on top of any flavor of the Windows operating system. The most important components of the Framework are the Common Language Runtime (CLR), described in the preceding section, and the *Framework Class Library* (FCL), which provides an enormous number of predefined types or classes for you to use in your programs. You will learn how to define your own classes in Chapter 8. Complete coverage of all the FCL classes is beyond the scope of this book. For more information, see *C# in a Nutshell* (O'Reilly & Associates).

The C# Language

The C# language is disarmingly simple, but C# is highly expressive when it comes to implementing modern programming concepts. C# includes all the support for structured, component-based, object-oriented programming that one expects of a modern language built on the shoulders of C++ and Java.

A small team led by two distinguished Microsoft engineers, Anders Hejlsberg and Scott Wiltamuth, developed the C# language. Hejlsberg is also known for creating Turbo Pascal, a popular language for PC programming, and for leading the team that designed Borland Delphi, one of the first successful Integrated Development Environments for client/server programming.

The goal of C# is to provide a simple, safe, object-oriented, Internet-centric, high-performance language for .NET development. C# is simple because there are relatively few *keywords*. This makes it easy to learn and easy to adapt to your specific needs.

> Keywords are special words reserved by the language that have a specific meaning within all C# programs. Keywords include if, while, and for. You'll learn about these keywords in the coming chapters.

C# is considered safe because it provides support in the language to find bugs early in the development process. This makes for code that is easier to maintain and programs that are more reliable.

C# was designed, from the very start, to support object-oriented programming. This book will explain not only how to write object-oriented programs, but also why object-oriented programming has become so popular. The short answer is this: programs are becoming increasingly complex, and object-oriented programming techniques help you manage that complexity.

C# was designed for .NET, and .NET was designed for developing web and web-aware programs. The Internet is a primary resource in most .NET applications.

Finally, C# was designed for professional high-performance programming.

The Structure of C# Applications

At the most fundamental level, a C# application consists of *source code*. Source code is human-readable text written in a text editor. A text editor is like a word processor, but it puts no special characters into the file to support formatting, only the text. A classic text editor is Notepad.

Example 1-1 shows an example of a very simple source code file.

Example 1-1. A source code file

```
namespace NotePad
{
   class HelloWorld
   {
      // every console app starts with Main
      static void Main()
      {
         System.Console.WriteLine("Hello world!");
      }
   }
}
```

This program is explained in detail in Chapter 2. For now, observe that the program itself is readable; it is in normal text. The words may be strange and the layout unusual, but there are no special characters—just the normal text produced by your keyboard.

Once you write your program in an editor, you must compile it. For that you need a compiler. You will learn how to use the C# compiler in Chapter 2. Once compiled, your program must be run and tested.

While you *can* perform all of these tasks using Notepad (or another text editor) and various command-line tools, your programming life will be much easier if you use the Integrated Development Environment (IDE) called Visual Studio .NET. VS.NET was designed with .NET development in mind and greatly simplifies the writing of C# program code.

The Development Environment

The Visual Studio .NET Integrated Development Environment provides enormous advantages to the C# programmer. This book tacitly assumes that you'll use Visual Studio .NET for your work. However, the discussion focuses more on the language and the platform than on the tools.

Nonetheless, Chapter 4 provides a good introduction to the IDE in some detail. Chapter 10 returns to the IDE to examine the debugger, which will help you find and correct problems in your code.

CHAPTER 2

Getting Started with C#

You can use C# to create three different types of programs:

- Web applications
- Windows applications
- Console applications

The .NET platform is web-centric. The C# language was developed to allow .NET programmers to create very large, powerful, high-quality web applications quickly and easily. The .NET technology for creating web applications is called ASP.NET.

ASP.NET, the next generation from ASP (Active Server Pages), is composed of two Microsoft development technologies: Web Forms and Web Services. While the development of fully realized web applications using these technologies is beyond the scope of this book, learning the basics of the C# language will certainly get you started in the right direction. C# is generally acknowledged to be the language of choice for ASP.NET development.

Typically, you'll create an ASP.NET application when you want your program to be available to end users on any platform (e.g., Windows, Mac, Unix). By serving your application over the Web, end users can access your program with any browser.

When you want the richness and power of a native application running directly on the Windows platform, alternatively you might create a desktop-bound Windows application. The .NET tools for building Windows applications are called Windows Forms; a detailed analysis of this technology is also beyond the scope of this book.

However, if you don't need a Graphical User Interface (GUI) and just want to write a simple application that talks to a console window (i.e., what we used to call a DOS box), you might consider creating a console application. This book makes extensive use of console applications to illustrate the basics of the C# language.

Web, Windows, and console applications are described and illustrated in the following pages.

Console applications

A console application runs in a console window, as shown in Figure 2-1. A console window (or DOS box) provides simple text-based output.

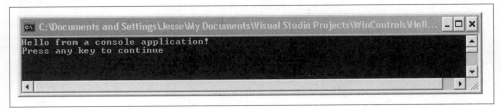

Figure 2-1. A console application

Console applications are very helpful when learning a language because they strip away the distraction of the Graphical User Interface. Rather than spending your time creating complex windowing applications, you can focus on the details of the language constructs, such as how you create classes and methods, how you branch based on runtime conditions, and how you loop. All these topics will be covered in detail in coming chapters.

Windows applications

A Windows application runs on a PC's desktop. You are already familiar with Windows applications such as Microsoft Word or Excel. Windows applications are much more complex than console applications and can take advantage of the full suite of menus, controls, and other widgets you've come to expect in a modern desktop application. Figure 2-2 shows the output of a simple windows application.

Figure 2-2. A Windows application

ASP.NET applications

An ASP.NET application runs on a web server and delivers its functionality through a browser, typically over the Web. ASP.NET technology facilitates developing web applications quickly and easily. Figure 2-3 shows a message from a simple ASP.NET application.

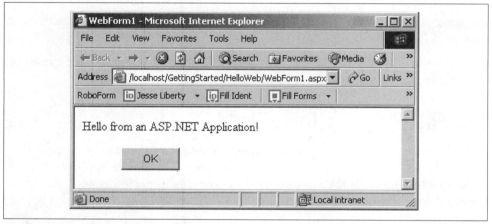

Figure 2-3. An ASP.NET application

Although most commercial applications will be either Windows or ASP.NET programs, console applications have a tremendous advantage in a C# primer. Windows and ASP.NET applications bring a lot more overhead; there is great complexity in managing the window and all the events associated with the window. (Events are covered in Chapter 19.) Console applications keep things simple—allowing you to focus on the features of the language.

> This book does not go into all the myriad details of building robust Windows and ASP.NET applications. For complete coverage of these topics, please see *Programming ASP.NET* and *Programming .NET Windows Applications*, both by Jesse Liberty and Dan Hurwitz (O'Reilly).

What's in a Program?

A program consists of English-language instructions called source code. The syntax for these instructions is strictly defined by the language. Source code consists of a series of statements. A statement is an instruction to the complier. Each instruction must be formed correctly, and one task you'll face when learning C# will be to learn the correct syntax of the language. For example, in C# every statement ends with a semi-colon.

Each instruction has a semantic meaning that expresses what you are trying to accomplish. Although you must follow the syntax, the semantics of the language are far more important in developing effective object-oriented programs. This book will provide insight into both the syntax and the semantics of good C# programs.

Save the source code you write in a text file. You can write this source code file using any simple text editor (such as Notepad), or you can use the Visual Studio .NET Integrated Development Environment (IDE). Visual Studio .NET is described in Chapter 4.

Once you write your program, you compile it using the C# compiler. The end result of compiling the program is an application.

Your First Program: Hello World

In this chapter, you will create a very simple application that does nothing more than display the words "Hello World" to your monitor. This console application is the traditional first program for learning any new language; it demonstrates some of the basic elements of a C# program.

Once you write your "Hello World" program and compile it, this chapter will provide a line-by-line analysis of the source code. This analysis gives something of a preview of the language; Chapter 5 describes the fundamentals much more fully.

As explained earlier, you can create C# programs with any text editor. You can, for example, create each of the three programs shown previously (in Figures 2-1, 2-2, and 2-3) with Notepad. To demonstrate that this is possible, you'll write your very first C# program using Notepad.

Begin by opening Notepad and typing in the program exactly as shown in Example 2-1.

Example 2-1. Hello World in Notepad

```
namespace NotePad
{
   class HelloWorld
   {
      // every console app starts with Main
      static void Main()
      {
          System.Console.WriteLine("Hello world!");
      }
   }
}
```

That is the entire program. Save it to your disk as a file called *helloworld.cs*.

We'll examine this program in some detail in just a moment. First, however, it must be compiled.

The Compiler

Once you save your program to disk, you must compile the code to create your application. Compiling your source code means running a compiler and passing in the source code file. You run the compiler by opening a command prompt (DOS box) and entering the program name *csc*. Then you pass in your source code file by entering the filename on the command line, as in the following:

```
csc HelloWorld.cs
```

The job of the compiler is to turn your source code into a working program. It turns out to be just slightly more complicated than that because .NET uses an intermediate language called Microsoft Intermediate Language (MSIL, sometimes abbreviated to IL). The compiler reads your source code and produces IL. The .NET Just In Time (JIT) compiler then reads your IL code and produces an executable application in memory.

Microsoft provides a command window with the correct environment variables set. Open the command window by selecting the following menu items in this order:

```
Start -> Programs -> Microsoft Visual Studio .NET
-> Visual Studio.NET Tools -> Visual Studio .NET Command Prompt
```

Then navigate to the directory in which you created your code file and enter the following command:

```
csc helloworld.cs
```

The Microsoft C# compiler compiles your code; when you display the directory you'll find the compiler has produced an executable file called *helloworld.exe*. Type *helloworld* at the command prompt, and your program executes, as shown in Figure 2-4.

Presto! You are a C# programmer. That's it, close the book, you've done it. Okay, don't close the book—there are details to examine, but take a moment to congratulate yourself. Have a cookie.

Granted, the program you created is one of the simplest C# programs imaginable, but it is a complete C# program, and it can be used to examine many of the elements common to C# programs.

Examining Your First Program

The single greatest challenge when learning to program is that you must learn everything before you can learn anything. Even this simple "Hello World" program uses many features of the language that will be discussed in coming chapters, including classes, namespaces, statements, static methods, objects, strings, inheritance, blocks, libraries, and even something called polymorphism!

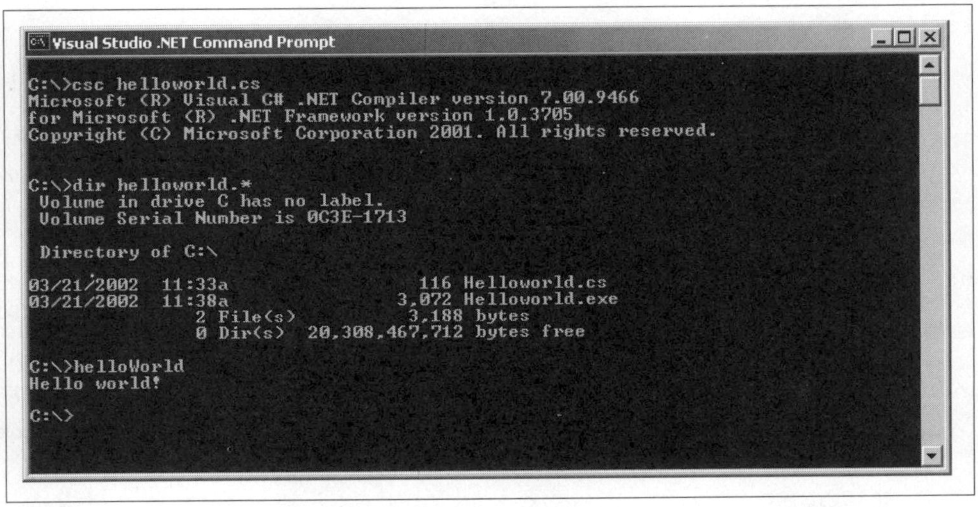

Figure 2-4. Compiling and running Hello World

It is as if you were learning to drive a car. You must learn to steer, accelerate, brake, and understand the flow of traffic. Right now we're going to get you out on the highway and just let you steer for a while. Over time you'll learn how to speed up and slow down. Along the way you'll learn to set the radio and adjust the heat so that you'll be more comfortable. In no time you'll be driving, and then won't your parents begin to worry.

Line-by-Line Analysis

Hang on tight, we're going to zip through this quickly and come back to the details in subsequent chapters.

The first line in the program defines a *namespace*:

```
namespace NotePad
```

You will create many names when programming in C#. Every object and every type of object must be named. It is possible for the names you assign to conflict with the names assigned by Microsoft or other vendors. A namespace is a way to say "these names are mine."

In this program, you've created a namespace called NotePad. Each namespace must be enclosed in braces ({}). Thus, the second line of the Hello World program is an open brace to mark the beginning of the NotePad namespace. The open brace is matched by a closing brace at the end of the program.

Within the braces of the namespace, you write other programming constructs. For instance, you might define what is called an object. Every object named within these braces is implicitly prefixed with the name NotePad. The dot operator (.) separates the namespace from the name of the object within the namespace. Thus, if you were to create an object MyObject within the namespace NotePad, the real name of that object would be NotePad.MyObject. You can read this as either "NotePad dot MyObject" or "NotePad MyObject". Actually, you use the dot operator quite a lot; you'll see various other uses as we proceed.

Classes define a category, or type, of object. In C# there are thousands of classes. A class is a new, user-defined type. Classes are used to define Windows controls (buttons, list boxes, etc.), as well as types of things (employees, students, telephones, etc.) in the program you are writing. Some classes you create yourself, and some you obtain from the .NET Framework. Each class must be named.

Classes are the core of C# and object-oriented programming. You'll learn about classes in detail in Chapter 3, as well as in Chapter 5.

The third line in our Hello World program creates a class named, aptly, HelloWorld. Like a namespace, a class is defined within braces. The following code represents the opening of the HelloWorld class definition:

```
class HelloWorld
{
```

A method is a small block of code that performs an action. The Main() method is the "entry point" for every C# console application; it is where your program begins. The next few lines in Hello World mark the beginning of the Main() method:

```
static void Main()
{
```

Methods are covered in detail in Chapter 9 but are mentioned in virtually every chapter in this book.

A comment (here in bold) appears just before the start of the Main() method:

```
// every console app starts with Main
static void Main()
{
```

A comment is just a note to yourself. You insert comments to make the code more readable to programmers. You can place comments anywhere in your program that you think the explanation will be helpful; they have no effect on the running program.

C# recognizes three styles of comments. The comment in Hello World begins with two slashes (//). The slashes indicate that everything to the right on the same line is a comment.

The second style is to begin your comment with a forward slash followed by an asterisk (/*) and to end your comment with the opposite pattern (*/). These pairs of characters are called the opening C-style comment and the closing C-style comment, respectively.

These comment symbols were inherited from the C language—thus the names used to identify them. They are also used in C++ and Java.

Everything between these comment symbols is a comment. C-style comments can span more than one line, as in the following:

```
/* This begins a comment
This line is still within the comment
Here comes the end of the comment */
```

The third and final style of comments uses three forward slashes ///. This is an XML-style comment and is used for advanced documentation techniques. XML comments are beyond the scope of this book.

Notice that the Main() method is defined with the keywords static and void.

```
static void Main()
```

The static keyword indicates that you can access this method without having an object of your class available. While a class defines a type, each instance of that type is an object (much as Car defines a type of vehicle and your aging rust-bucket is an individual instance of Car). Thus, while Button defines a type of control for a Windows program, any individual program will have many Button objects, each with its own label (e.g., OK, Cancel, Retry).

Normally, methods can be called only if you have an object, but static methods are special and can be called without an object. (The use of static methods, other than Main(), is fairly advanced and won't be covered until Chapter 8.)

The second keyword in the statement defining the Main() method is void:

```
static void Main()
```

Typically, one method calls another. The called method will do work, and it can return a value to the calling method. (You'll see how methods call one another and return values in Chapter 9.) If a method does not return a value, it is declared void. The keyword void is a signal to the compiler that your method will not return a value to the calling method.

The operating system calls Main() (when the program is invoked). It is possible for Main() to return a value (typically an error code) that might be used in a batch file. In this case, you've declared that Main() will not return a value since you will not be calling this program from a batch file. Every method name is followed by parentheses

```
static void Main()
```

It is possible to pass values into a method so that the method can manipulate or use those values. These values are called parameters or arguments. (Method parameters are covered in Chapter 9.) In this case, Main() has no parameters. All methods are enclosed within braces. Within the braces for Main() is a single line of code:

```
System.Console.WriteLine("Hello world!");
```

The Console is an object that represents your screen. The Console class is defined within the System namespace, and so its full identification is System.Console.

The Console class has a static method, WriteLine(), which you access not with an instance of Console, but through the Console class itself. Since you access the method with the dot operator, you write System.Console.WriteLine.

The WriteLine() method declares a single parameter: the string you want to display. When you pass a string in to the method, the string is an argument. The argument ("Hello world") corresponds to the parameter the method expects, and the string is displayed. The complete call to the method is:

```
System.Console.WriteLine("Hello world!");
```

If you will use many objects from the System namespace, you can save typing by telling the compiler that many of the objects you'll refer to are in that namespace. You do so by adding a using declaration to the beginning of your program:

```
using System;
```

Once you add this line, you can use the Console class name without explicitly identifying that it is in the System namespace. If you add the using declaration, you can rewrite the contents of Main() as follows:

```
Console.WriteLine("Hello world!");
```

The final series of lines close the various nested opening braces. The first closes the brace for Main(), the second closes the brace for the class, and the third closes the brace for the namespace. Each open brace must be matched by a closing brace.

The class is defined within the namespace declaration, and thus you do not close the namespace until you've closed the class. Similarly, the method Main() is declared within the class, so you do not close the class until you've closed the method.

Whew! That was a lot to take in all at once! Don't panic, all of the concepts introduced here are explained in detail in coming chapters.

CHAPTER 3
Object-Oriented Programming

Windows and web programs are enormously complex. Programs present information to users in graphically rich ways, offering complicated user interfaces, complete with drop-down and pop-up menus, buttons, listboxes, and so forth. Behind these interfaces, programs model complex business relationships, such as those among customers, products, orders, and inventory. You can interact with such a program in hundreds if not thousands of different ways, and the program must respond appropriately every time.

To manage this enormous complexity, programmers have developed a technique called object-oriented programming. It is based on a very simple premise: you manage complexity by modeling its essential aspects. The closer your program models the problem you are trying to solve, the easier it is to understand (and thus to write and to maintain) that program.

Programmers refer to the problem you are trying to solve and all the information you know that relates to your problem as the *problem domain*. For example, if you are writing a program to manage the inventory and sales of a company, the problem domain would include everything you know about how the company acquires and manages inventory, makes sales, handles the income from sales, tracks sales figures, and so forth. The sales manager and the stock room manager would be problem domain experts who can help you understand the problem domain.

A well-designed object-oriented program is filled with objects from the problem domain. At the first level of design, you'll think about how these objects interact and what their state, capabilities, and responsibilities are.

State
> A programmer refers to the current conditions and values of an object as that object's state. For example, you might have an object representing a customer. The customer's state includes the customer's address, phone number, email, as well as the customer's credit rating, recent purchase history, and so forth.

Capabilities

The customer has many capabilities, but a developer cares only about modeling those that are relevant to the problem domain. Thus a customer object might be able to buy an item, return an item, increase his credit rating, and so forth.

Responsibilities

Along with capabilities come responsibilities. The customer object is responsible for managing its own address. In a well-designed program, no other object needs to know the details of the customer's address. The address might be stored as data within the customer object, or it might be stored in a database, but it is up to the customer object to know how to retrieve and update his own address.

Of course, all of the objects in your program are just *metaphors* for the objects in your problem domain.

Metaphors

Many of the concepts used throughout this book, and any book on programming, are actually metaphors. We get so used to the metaphors that we forget they are metaphors. You are used to talking about a window on your program, but of course there is no such thing; there is just a rectangle with text and images in it. It looks like a window into your document so we call it a window. Of course, you don't actually have a document either, just bits in memory. No folders, no buttons—these are all just metaphors.

There are many levels to these metaphors. When you see a window on the screen, the window itself is just a metaphor enhanced by an image drawn on your screen. That image is created by lighting tiny dots on the screen, called pixels. These pixels are lit in response to instructions written in your C# program. Each instruction is really a metaphor; the actual instructions read by your computer are in *Assembly* language, low-level instructions that are fed to the underlying computer chip. These Assembly instructions map to a series of 1s and 0s that the chip understands. Of course, the 1s and 0s are just metaphors for electricity in wires. When two wires meet, we measure the amount of electricity, and if there is a threshold amount we call it 1, otherwise 0. You get the idea.

Good metaphors can be very powerful. The art of object-oriented programming is really the art of conceiving of good metaphors.

Creating Models

Humans are model-builders. We create models of the world to manage complexity and to help us understand problems we're trying to solve. You see models all the time. Maps are models of roadways. Globes are models of the Earth. Chemical symbols are models of chemical interactions. Atomic models are representations of the interaction of sub-atomic particles.

Models are simplifications. There is little point to a model that is as complex as the object in the problem domain. If you had a map of the United States that had every rock, blade of grass, and bit of dirt in the entire country, the map would have to be as big as the country itself. Your road atlas of the U.S. eschews all sorts of irrelevant detail, focusing only on those aspects of the problem domain (e.g., the country's roads) that are important to solving the problem (e.g., getting from place to place). If you want to drive from Boston to New York City, you don't care where the trees are; you care where the exits and interchanges are located. Therefore, the network of roads is what appears on the atlas.

Albert Einstein once said: "Things should be made as simple as possible, but not any simpler." A model must be faithful to those aspects of the problem domain that are relevant. For example, a road map must provide accurate relative distances. The distance from Boston to New York must be proportional to the actual driving distance. If one inch represents 25 miles at the start of the trip, it must represent 25 miles throughout the trip, or the map will be unusable.

A good object-oriented design is an accurate model of the problem you are trying to solve. Your design choices influence not only how you solve the problem, but in fact they influence how you think about the problem. A good design, like a good model, allows you to examine the relevant details of the problem without confusion.

Classes and Objects

The most important metaphors in object-oriented programming are the *class* and the *object*.

A class defines a new type of thing. The class defines the common characteristics of every object of that new type. For example, you might define a class Car. Every car will share certain characteristics (wheels, brake, accelerator, and so forth). Your car and my car both belong to the class of Cars; they are of type Car.

An object is an individual instance of a class. Each individual car (your particular car, my particular car) is an instance of the class Car, and thus is an object. An object is just a thing.

We perceive the world to be composed of things. Look at your computer. You do not see various bits of plastic and glass amorphously merging with the surrounding environment. You naturally and inevitably see distinct things: a computer, a keyboard, a monitor, speakers, pens, paper. Things.

More importantly, even before you decide to do it, you've categorized these things. You immediately classify the computer on your desk as a specific instance of a type of thing: this computer is one of the type computer. This pen is an instance of a more general type of thing, pens. It is so natural you can't avoid it, and yet the process is so subtle it's difficult to articulate. When I see my dog Milo, I can't help also seeing him *as a dog*, not just as an individual entity. Milo is an instance, Dog is a class.

The theory behind object-oriented programming is that for computer programs to accurately model the world, the programs should reflect this human tendency to think about individual things and types of things. In C# you do that by creating a class to define a type and creating an object to model a thing.

Defining a Class

When you define a class you describe the characteristics and behavior of objects of that type. In C#, you describe characteristics with *member fields*.

```
class Dog
{
    private int weight;  // member field
    private String name; // member field
```

Member fields are used to hold each object's state. For example, the state of the Dog is defined by its current weight and name. The state of an Employee might be defined by (among other things) her current salary, management level, and performance rating. Chapter 8 includes a full discussion of member fields.

You define the behavior of your new type with *methods*. Methods contain code to perform an action.

```
class Dog
{
    private int weight;
    private String name;
    public void bark()
    {
        // code here to bark
    }
```

 The keywords public and private are known as *access modifiers*, which are used to specify what classes can access particular members. For instance, public members can be called from methods in any class, while private members are visible only to the methods of the class that defines the member. Thus, objects of any class can call bark on a Dog, but only methods of Dog have access to the weight and name of the Dog. Access modifiers are discussed in Chapter 8.

A class typically defines a number of methods to do the work of that class. A Dog class might contain methods for barking, eating, napping, and so forth. An Employee class might contain methods for adjusting salary, submitting annual reviews, and evaluating performance objectives.

Methods can manipulate the state of the object by changing the values in member fields, or a method could interact with other objects of its own type or with objects of other types. This interaction among objects is crucial to object-oriented programming.

For example, a Dog method might change the state of the Dog (e.g., weight), interact with other Dogs (e.g., bark and sniff), or interact with People (e.g., beg for food). A Product object might interact with a Customer object, and a Video object might interact with an EditingWindow object.

Designing a good C# program is not unlike forming a good team; you look for players—or objects, in the case of a program—with different skills to whom you can assign the various tasks you must accomplish. Those players cooperate with one another to get the job done.

In a good object-oriented program, you will design objects that represent things in your problem domain. You will then divide the work of the program among your objects, assigning responsibility to objects based on their ability.

Class Relationships

The heart of object-oriented design is establishing relationships among the classes. Classes interact and relate to one another in various ways.

The simplest interaction is when a method in one class is used to call a method in a second class. For example, the Manager class might have a method that calls the UpdateSalary method on an object of type Employee. We then say that the Manager class and the Employee class are *associated*. Association among classes simply means they interact.

Some complicated types are *composed* of other types. For example, an automobile might be composed of wheels, engine, transmission, and so forth. You might model this by creating a Wheel class, an Engine class, and a Transmission class. You could then create an Automobile class, and each automobile would have four instances of the Wheel class and one instance each of the Engine and Transmission class. Another way to view this relationship is to say that the Automobile class *aggregates* the Wheel, Engine, and Transmission classes.

This process of aggregation (or composition) allows you to build very complex classes from relatively simple classes. The .NET Framework provides a String class to handle text strings. You might create your own Address class out of five text strings (address line 1, address line 2, city, state, and zip). You might then create a second class, Employee, which has as one of its members an instance of Address.

The Three Pillars of Object-Oriented Programming

Object-oriented programming is built on three sturdy pillars: *encapsulation*, *specialization*, and *polymorphism*.

Each class should be fully encapsulated, that is, it should fully define the state and responsibilities of that type. For example, if you create an Employee object, that Employee object should fully define all there is to know, from the perspective of your program, about each Employee. You do not, typically, want to have one class that defines the Employee's work information and a second, unrelated class that defines the Employee's contact information. Instead, you want to encapsulate all this information inside the Employee class, perhaps by aggregating the contact information as a member of the Employee class.

Specialization allows you to establish hierarchical relationships among your classes. For example, you can define a Manager to be a specialized type of an Employee and an Employee to be a specialized type of Person. This allows you to leverage the state and abilities of an Employee object in the more specialized form of the Manager.

Polymorphism allows you to treat a group of objects in a similar way and have the objects sort out how to implement the programming instructions. For instance, suppose you have a collection of Employee objects, and you want to tell each Employee to give himself a raise. Employees get a straight 5% raise, while raises for Managers are determined by how well they've fulfilled their annual objectives. With polymorphism, you can tell each object in the collection to give itself a raise, and the "right thing happens" regardless of the real type of the object. That is, each employee gets 5%, while each manager gets the appropriate raise based on objectives.

Encapsulation

The first pillar of object-oriented programming is encapsulation. The idea behind encapsulation is that you want to keep each type or class discreet and self-contained, so you can change the implementation of one class without affecting any other class.

A class that provides a method that other classes can use is called a *server*. A class that uses that method is called a *client*. Encapsulation allows you to change the details of how a server does its work without breaking anything in the implementation of the client.

This is accomplished by drawing a bright and shining line between the *public interface* of a class and its *private implementation*. The public interface is a contract issued by your class that says, "I promise to be able to do this work." Specifically, you'll see that a public interface says, "call this method, with these parameters, and I'll do this work, and return this value." A client can rely on a public interface not to change. If the public interface does change, then the client must be recompiled and perhaps redesigned.

On the other hand, the private implementation is, as its name implies, private to the server. The designer of the server class is free to change *how* it does the work promised in the public interface, so long as it continues to fulfill the terms of its implicit contract: it must take the given parameters, do the promised work, and return the promised value.

For example, you might have a public method that promises as follows: "Give me a dollar amount and a number of years, and I'll return the net present value." How you compute that amount is your business; if a client supplies a dollar amount and a number of years, you must return the net present value. You might implement that initially by keeping a table of values. You might change that at a later time to compute the value using the appropriate algebra. That is your business, and it does not affect the client. As long as you don't change the public interface (i.e., as long as you don't change the number or type of parameters expected or change the type of the return value) your clients will not break while you change the implementation.

Specialization

The second pillar, specialization, is implemented in C# by declaring that a new class derives from an existing class. When you do so, the specialized class inherits the characteristics of the more general class. The specialized class is called a *derived* class, while the more general class is known as a *base* class.

The specialization relationship is referred to as the *is-a* relationship. A dog *is a* mammal, a car *is a* vehicle. (Dog would be derived from the base class Mammal and Car from the base class Vehicle.)

Specialization allows you to create a family of objects. In Windows a button *is a* control. A list box *is a* control. Controls have certain characteristics (color, size, location) and certain abilities (can be drawn, can be selected). These characteristics and abilities are inherited by all of their derived types, which allows for a very powerful form of reuse. Rather than cutting and pasting code from one type to another, the derived type inherits the shared fields and methods. If you change how a shared ability is implemented, you do not have to update code in every derived type; they inherit the changes.

For example, a Manager is a special type of Employee. The Manager adds new capabilities (hiring, firing, rewarding, praising) and a new state (annual objectives, management level, etc.). The Manager, however, also inherits the characteristics and capabilities common to all Employees. Thus a Manager has an address, a name, and an employee ID, and Managers can be given raises, can be laid off, and so forth. You'll see specialization at work in Chapter 11.

Polymorphism

Polymorphism, the third pillar of object-oriented programming, is closely related to inheritance. The prefix *poly* means many; *morph* means form. Thus, polymorphism refers to the ability of a single type or class to take many forms.

There are times that you will know you have a collection of a general type, for example a collection of Controls, but you do not know (or care) what the specific subtype each of your controls is (one may be a button, another a list box, etc.). The important thing is that you know they all inherit shared abilities (e.g., the draw method) and that you can treat them all as controls. If you write a programming instruction that tells each control to draw itself, this is implemented properly on a per-control basis (i.e., buttons draw as buttons, listboxes draw as listboxes). You do not need to know how each subtype accomplishes this; you only need to know that each type is defined to be able to draw.

Polymorphism allows you to treat a collection of disparate derived types (buttons, list boxes, etc.) as a group. You treat the general group of controls the same way, and each individual control does the right thing according to its specific type. Chapter 11 provides more concrete examples.

Object-Oriented Analysis and Design

The steps before programming anything, other than a trivial demonstration program, are analysis and design. Analysis is the process of understanding and detailing the problem you are trying to solve. Design is the actual planning of your solution.

With trivial problems (such as computing the Fibonacci series*), you may not need an extensive analysis period, but with complex business problems the analysis process can take weeks, or even months. One powerful analysis technique is to create what are called use-case scenarios, in which you describe in some detail how the system will be used. Among the other considerations in the analysis period are determining your success factors (how do you know if your program works) and writing a specification of your program's requirements.

Once you've analyzed the problem, you design the solution. Imagining the classes you will use and their inter-relationships is key to the design process. You might design a simple program on the fly, without this careful planning; but in any serious business application, you will want to take some time to think through the issues.

---

* The Fibonacci series is the values 0,1,1,2,3,5,8,13.... The series is named for Fibonacci, who in 1202 investigated how fast rabbits could breed in ideal circumstances. The series works by adding the previous two numbers to get the next (thus 8 is the sum of 5+3).

There are many powerful design techniques, you might use. One interesting controversy that has arisen recently is between traditional object-oriented design on the one hand* and eXtreme programming on the other.†

There are other competing approaches as well. How much time you'll put into these topics will depend, in large measure, on the complexity of the problems you are trying to solve and the size of your development team.

 My personal approach to managing complexity is to keep team size very small. I have worked on large development teams, and over the years I've come to believe that the ideal size is three. Three highly skilled programmers can be incredibly productive and with three you don't need a manager. Three people can have only one conversation at a time. Three people can never be evenly split on a decision. One day I'll write a book on programming in teams of three, but this isn't it, and so we'll stay focused on C# programming, rather than on design debates.

About the Examples in This Book

Object-oriented programming is designed to help you manage complex programs. Unfortunately, it is very difficult to show complex problems and their solutions in a primer on C#. The complexity of these problems gets in the way of what you're trying to learn about. Because of necessity, the examples in this book will be extremely simple. The simplicity may hide some of the motivation for the technique, but the simplicity makes the technique clearer. You'll have to take it on faith, for now, that these techniques scale up well to very complex problems.

Most of the chapters of this book focus on the syntax of C#. You need the syntax of the language to be able to write a program at all, but it's important to keep in mind that the syntax of any language is less important than its semantics. The meaning of what you are writing and why you're writing it are the real focus of object-oriented programming and thus of this book.

Don't let concern with syntax get in the way of understanding the semantics. The compiler can help you get the syntax right (if only by complaining when you get it wrong), and the documentation can remind you of the syntax, but understanding the semantics, the meaning of the construct, is the hard part. Throughout this book, I work hard to explain not only *how* you do something, but *why* and *when* you do it.

---

* See *The Unified Modelling Language User Guide*, *The Unified Software Development Process*, and *The Unified Modelling Language (UML) Reference Manual*, by Grady Booch, Ivar Jacobson, and James Rumbaugh (Addison Wesley).

† See *Planning Extreme Programming* by Kent Beck and Martin Fowler (Addison Wesley).

CHAPTER 4

Visual Studio .NET

In Chapter 2 you learned that you *can* create your C# applications using Notepad. In this chapter, you'll learn why you never *will*. Microsoft developed Visual Studio .NET (VS.NET) to facilitate the creation of Windows and web applications. You will find that this Integrated Development Environment (IDE) is a *very* powerful tool that will greatly simplify your work.

Visual Studio .NET offers many advantages to the .NET developer. The following features are discussed in this chapter:

- A modern interface using a tabbed document metaphor for source code and layout screens, and toolbars and informational windows that dock where you want them

- Code completion, which allows you to enter code with fewer errors and much less typing

- IntelliSense, which pops up help on every method and function call as you type

- Dynamic, context-sensitive help, which allows you to view topics and samples relevant to the code you are writing at the moment

- Immediate flagging of syntax errors (e.g., missing characters, misplaced braces, etc.), which allows you to fix problems as they are entered

- The ability to compile and test programs right in the IDE

- A built-in task list to keep track of changes you need to make

- A Start Page that provides easy access to new and existing projects

- Customization capability, which allows you to set user preferences for IDE appearance and behavior

One VS.NET feature will be so important to you, even as a C# novice, that it actually merits its own chapter: an integrated debugger, which allows you to step through code, observe program run-time behavior, and set breakpoints, even across multiple languages. The debugger is considered in detail in Chapter 10.

In addition to these basic capabilities, VS.NET provides a number of advanced features that will simplify the development process. These features include:

- Convenient access to multiple design and code windows
- WYSIWYG (What You See Is What You Get) visual design of Windows forms and web forms
- An HTML editor which provides both Design and HTML views that update each other in real time
- A Solution Explorer, which displays all the files comprising your solution (a collection of projects) in a hierarchical format
- A Server Explorer, which allows you to log on to servers to which you have network access, access the data and services on those servers, and perform a variety of other chores
- Integrated support for source control software

Many of these advanced features are covered in detail in *Programming ASP.NET* and *Programming .NET Windows Applications* (both books cowritten by Jesse Liberty and Dan Hurwitz, published by O'Reilly).

Robert Heinlein said "TANSTAAFL: There ain't no such thing as a free lunch."* While Visual Studio .NET can save you a lot of grunt typing (and in general greatly facilitate and accelerate the development process), the automatically generated code can obscure what is really necessary to create good working applications. It is sometimes difficult to know how Visual Studio .NET accomplishes its legerdemain. Similarly, the proliferation of mysteriously named files across your filesystem can be disconcerting when all you want to do is a simple housekeeping chore, like rename a minor part of the project.

Since most of the applications we'll build in this book are console applications designed to illustrate the basics of the language, there will be very little obscuring code produced. When you create Windows and web applications, however, you'll want to learn to sort through the code Visual Studio .NET generates in order to focus on the logic of your program.

The current chapter cannot possibly teach you everything about Visual Studio .NET; it is far too large and complex an application. What this chapter does is give you the basics for getting started and also point out some of the possible pitfalls.

 Keep in mind that there's no way to familiarize you with some of these features without wading into some slightly deeper waters of C# programming, which will likely be a bit cloudy to you at this stage. As you get deeper into the book and learn more about the language, your understanding of VS.NET will become clearer.

---

* Robert A. Heinlein, *The Moon Is a Harsh Mistress* (St. Martin's Press).

Start Page

The Start Page is the first thing you see when you open Visual Studio .NET (unless you configure it otherwise). From here you can create new projects or open a project you worked on in a previous session. You can also find out what is new in .NET, access .NET newsgroups and web sites, search for help online, download useful code, or adjust Visual Studio .NET to your personal requirements. Figure 4-1 shows a typical Start Page.

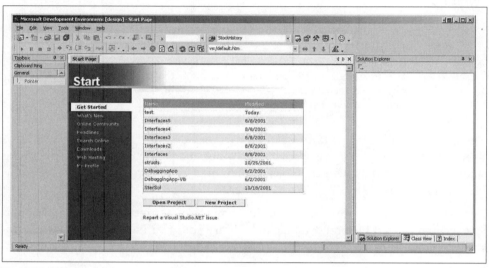

Figure 4-1. Start Page

Along the top of the application window is a set of menus and buttons. These menus and buttons are context-sensitive (i.e., they will change as the current window changes).

Along the left side of the window is a series of links to other resources, such as new developments and events in the .NET community, the MSDN online library, and free sample applications.

Projects and Solutions

A C# program is built from source files, which are text files containing the code you write. Source code files are named with the *.cs* extension. The *HelloWorld.cs* file you created in Chapter 2 is an example.

A typical Visual Studio .NET application can have a number of other files (e.g., assembly information files, references, icons, data connections, etc.). VS.NET organizes these files into a container called a *project*.

Visual Studio .NET provides two types of containers for your source code, folders, files, and related material: the project and the solution. A project is a set of files that work together to create an executable program (*.exe*) or a dynamic link library (*.dll*). Large, complex projects may consist of multiple .dll files called modules.

A solution is a set of one or more related projects. Each time you create a new project, Visual Studio .NET either adds it to an existing solution or creates a new solution.

Solutions are defined within a file named for the solution and have the extension *.sln*.

 The *.sln* file contains metadata, which is basically information about the data. The metadata describes the projects that compose the solution and information about building the solution. Visual Studio .NET also creates a file with the same base name as the *.sln* file, but with the filename extension *.sou* (e.g., *mySolution.sln* and *mySolution.sou*). The *.sou* file contains metadata used to customize the IDE.

There are a number of ways to open an existing solution. The simplest way is to select Open Project from the Start menu (which opens a project and its enclosing solution). Alternatively, you can open a solution in Visual Studio .NET just by double-clicking the *.sln* file in Windows Explorer.

Typically, the build process results in the contents of a project being compiled into an executable (*.exe*) file or a dynamic link library (*.dll*) file. This book focuses on creating executable files.

 The metadata describing the project is contained in a file named after the project with the extension *.csproj*. The project file contains version information, build settings, and references to other source files to include as part of the project.

Templates

When you create a new project, you get the New Project dialog box, shown in Figure 4-2.

In the New Project dialog, you select the project type (in the left-hand pane) and the template (in the right). There are a variety of templates for each project type. A template is a file that Visual Studio .NET uses to set up the initial state of your project.

For the examples in this book, you'll always choose Visual C# Project for the project type, and in most cases, you'll choose Console Application as the template. Specify the name of the directory in which your project will be stored (any directory you like). At this point, you can also name your project. For the purposes of example, enter the name HelloWorld.

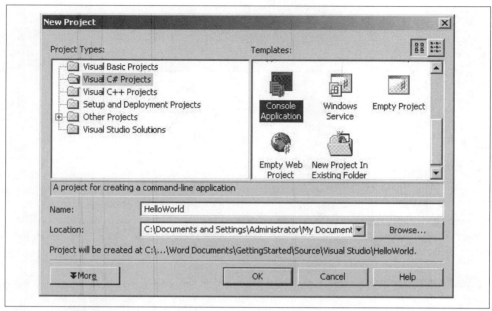

Figure 4-2. New Project dialog lets you choose a project template

Project names can contain any standard characters, except leading or trailing spaces, Windows or DOS keywords, and any of the following special characters:

% & * | \ : " < > ? /

Inside the Integrated Development Environment (IDE)

The Visual Studio .NET Integrated Development Environment (IDE) is centered around an editor. An editor is much like a word processor, except that it produces simple text (without formatting, such as bold and italics). As you may recall, source code files are simple text files.

The Visual Studio .NET IDE also provides support for building Graphical User Interfaces (GUIs), which are integral to Windows and web projects. The following pages introduce some of the key features of the IDE.

Layout

The IDE is a Multiple Document Interface (MDI) application. There is a main window, and within the main window are a number of smaller windows. The central window is the text editing window. Figure 4-3 shows the basic layout.

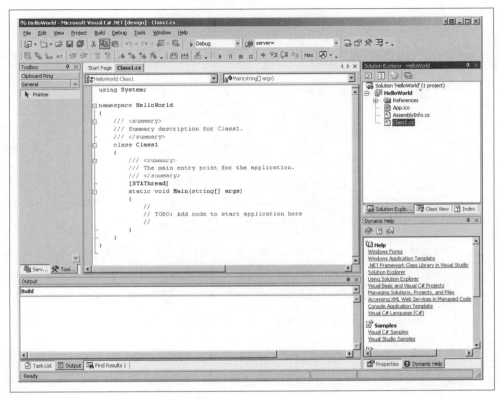

Figure 4-3. The IDE

To the left of the editing window are a number of tabbed windows that contain tools used when creating Windows and web applications. To the right of the editing window is a window called the Solution Explorer. This window shows the files in the current project and the solution to which the project belongs.

In the lower-right corner is the dynamic help window. In the lower-left corner are a number of tabbed windows, including the task list. The IDE will add tasks to this list when your program has errors that must be fixed, and you can add tasks of your own to assist you in remembering what work remains to be done.

All of these windows are resizable and dockable, and many windows share space by using tabs. They can be resized by placing the mouse cursor over the edge you want to move. The cursor will change to a double arrow resizing cursor, at which point you can drag the window edge one way or the other.

The Visual Studio .NET window has a titlebar across the top, with menus below. Under the menus are toolbars with buttons that duplicate many of the common menu commands. Nearly everything that can be done through menus can also be done with context-sensitive pop-up menus, as described shortly.

By default, the toolbars are docked along the top of the window. As with many Windows applications, they can be undocked and moved to other locations, either left free-floating or docked along other window edges. You move the toolbars by grabbing them with the mouse and dragging them where you want.

Right-clicking on the titlebar of a dockable window pops up a menu with three mutually exclusive check items that let you customize the behavior of the window:

Dockable
> Specifies that the window can be dragged and docked along any side of the Visual Studio .NET window.

Hide
> Makes the window disappear, temporarily. To see the window again, i.e., to unhide it, use the View item on the main menu. (The Pushpin icon, described shortly, also affects this behavior.)

Floating
> Specifies that the window will not dock when dragged against the edge of the VS.NET window. Then the floating window can be placed anywhere on the desktop, even outside the Visual Studio .NET window.

In the upper-right corner of the main IDE window are two icons:

Pushpin
> This icon toggles the AutoHide property of the window. When the pushpin is pointing down, the window is pinned in place (AutoHide is turned off). Moving the cursor off the window will not affect its visibility.
>
> When the pushpin is pointing sideways, AutoHide is turned on. Moving the cursor off the window hides the window. To see the window again, hover (or click) on the tab that is now visible along the edge where the window had been docked.

X
> The standard "close window" icon.

IntelliSense

Underlying the IDE is Microsoft's IntelliSense technology, which puts help and editing assistance (including code completion) instantly at your disposal. IntelliSense makes programmers' lives much easier. It provides real-time, context-sensitive help that appears right under your cursor.

For example, in the Hello World code shown in Chapter 2, you called the WriteLine() method for the Console object. If you write this code in Visual Studio .NET, the pop-up help will show you every available method of the Console object as soon as you type the dot (.), as shown in Figure 4-4. And if you begin to type a method—

say you enter the letters "Wr"—IntelliSense jumps to the first method that matches what you've typed so far.

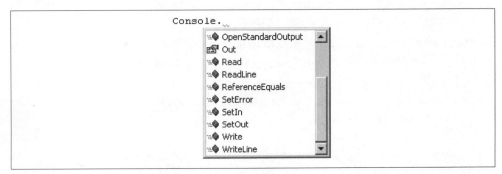

Figure 4-4. Pop-up code completion

Once you enter the method you want to call, Microsoft's pop-up help will show you the various versions of the method and help you determine the parameters you'll need, as illustrated in Figure 4-5.

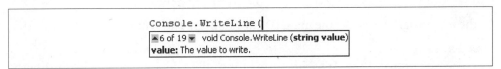

Figure 4-5. Pop-up help

Code completion automatically completes your thoughts for you, drastically reducing your typing. Drop-down lists provide all methods and properties possible in the current context, making them available at a keystroke or mouse click.

Building and Running

You can run your application at any time by selecting either Start or Start Without Debugging from the Debug menu, or you can accomplish the same results by pressing either F5 or Ctrl+F5, respectively. You can also start the program by clicking the Start icon (pictured in Figure 4-6) on the Standard toolbar.

Figure 4-6. The Start icon

For console applications, the advantage of running the program with Ctrl+F5 is that Visual Studio .NET will open your application in a console window, display its results, and then add a line to press a key when you are ready, as shown in

Figure 4-7. This keeps the window open until you've seen the results and pressed a key, at which point the window will close.

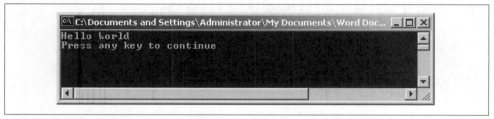

Figure 4-7. Running the application

For More Information

This brief overview of Visual Studio .NET was intended to familiarize you with the tool. There is a great deal more to know about this tool, but most of it will not be relevant to creating the simple applications in this book.

The best way to learn about the power and scope of Visual Studio .NET is to use it and to explore its various nooks and crannies. Try right-clicking in various places and explore the context-sensitive pop-up menus as well.

As you make your way through the book, you'll see various helpful features of Visual Studio .NET highlighted. All of these tips should make programming in C# easier for you. The application's online help files (MSDN) provide extensive additional support.

CHAPTER 5

C# Language Fundamentals

Chapter 2 demonstrates a very simple C# program that prints the text string "Hello world!" to the console screen and provides a line-by-line analysis of that program. However, even that very simple program was complex enough that some of the details had to be skipped over. The current chapter begins an in-depth exploration of the syntax and structure of the C# language.

Types

C# is a *strongly typed* language. That means that every object you create or use in a C# program must have a specific *type* (e.g., you must declare the object to be an integer or a string or a Dog or a Button). The type tells the compiler how big the object is and what it can do.

Types come in two flavors: those that are built into the language (intrinsic types) and those you create (classes, structs, and interfaces, discussed in Chapters 8, 13, and 14, respectively). C# offers a number of intrinsic types, shown in Table 5-1.

Table 5-1. The intrinsic types

Type	Size (in bytes)	.NET type	Description
byte	1	Byte	Unsigned (values 0–255).
char	2	Char	Unicode characters.
bool	1	Boolean	True or false.
sbyte	1	SByte	Signed (values–128 to 127).
short	2	Int16	Signed (short) (values–32,768 to 32,767).
ushort	2	UInt16	Unsigned (short) (values 0 to 65,535).
int	4	Int32	Signed integer values between −2,147,483,648 and 2,147,483,647.
uint	4	UInt32	Unsigned integer values between 0 and 4,294,967,295.

Table 5-1. The intrinsic types (continued)

Type	Size (in bytes)	.NET type	Description
float	4	Single	Floating point number. Holds the values from approximately +/−1.5 * 10⁻⁴⁵ to approximately +/−3.4 * 10³⁸ with 7 significant figures.
double	8	Double	Double-precision floating point; holds the values from approximately +/−5.0 * 10⁻³²⁴ to approximately +/−1.8 * 10³⁰⁸ with 15–16 significant figures.
decimal	12	Decimal	Fixed-precision up to 28 digits and the position of the decimal point. This is typically used in financial calculations. Requires the suffix "m" or "M."
long	8	Int64	Signed integers ranging from −9,223,372,036,854,775,808 to 9,223,372,036,854,775,807.
ulong	8	UInt64	Unsigned integers ranging from 0 to 0xffffffffffffffff.

Each type has a name (e.g., int) and a size (e.g., 4 bytes). The size tells you how many bytes each object of this type occupies in memory. (Programmers generally don't like to waste memory if they can avoid it, but with the cost of memory these days, you can afford to be mildly profligate if doing so simplifies your program.) The description field of Table 5-1 tells you the minimum and maximum values you can hold in objects of each type.

> Each C# type corresponds to an underlying .NET type. Thus, what C# calls an int, .NET calls an INT32. This is interesting only if you care about sharing objects across languages.

Intrinsic types can't do much. You can use them to add two numbers together, and they can display their values as strings. User-defined types can do a lot more; their abilities are determined by the methods you create, as discussed in detail in Chapter 9.

Objects of an intrinsic type are called variables. Variables are discussed in detail later in this chapter.

Numeric Types

Most of the intrinsic types are used for working with numeric values (byte, sbyte, short, ushort, int, uint, float, double, decimal, long, and ulong).

The numeric types can be broken into two sets: unsigned and signed. An unsigned value (byte, ushort, uint, ulong) can hold only positive values. A signed value (sbyte, short, int, long) can hold positive or negative values but the highest value is only half as large. That is, a ushort can hold any value from 0 through 65,535, but a short can hold only –32,768 through 32,767. Notice that 32,767 is nearly half of 65,535 (it is off by one to allow for holding the value zero). The reason a ushort can hold up to 65,535 is that 65,535 is a round number in binary arithmetic (2^{16}).

Another way to divide the types is into those used for integer values (whole numbers) and those used for floating-point values (fractional or rational numbers). The byte, sbyte, ushort, uint, ulong, short, int, and long types all hold whole number values.[*]

The double and float types hold fractional values. For most uses, float will suffice, unless you need to hold a really big fractional number, in which case you might use a double. The decimal value type was added to the language to support accounting applications.

Typically you decide which size integer to use (short, int, or long) based on the magnitude of the value you want to store. For example, a ushort can only hold values from 0 through 65,535, while a uint can hold values from 0 through 4,294,967,295.

That said, memory is fairly cheap, and programmer time is increasingly expensive; most of the time you'll simply declare your variables to be of type int, unless there is a good reason to do otherwise.

Most programmers choose signed types unless they have a good reason to use an unsigned value. This is, in part, just a matter of tradition.

Suppose you need to keep track of inventory. You expect to house up to 40,000 or even 50,000 copies of each book. A signed short can only hold up to 32,767 values. You might be tempted to use an unsigned short (which can hold up to 65,535 values), but it is easier and preferable to just use a signed int (with a maximum value of 2,147,483,647). That way, if you have a runaway best seller, your program won't break (if you anticipate selling more than 2 billion copies of your book, perhaps you'll want to use a long!).[†]

It is better to use an unsigned variable when the fact that the value *must* be positive is an inherent characteristic of the data. For example, if you had a variable to hold a person's age, you would use an unsigned int because an age cannot be negative.

Float, double, and decimal offer varying degrees of size and precision. For most small fractional numbers, float is fine. Note that the compiler assumes that any number with a decimal point is a double unless you tell it otherwise. (The section "Variables" discusses how you tell it otherwise.)

---

[*] The byte and sbyte types are not used very often and won't be described in this book.

[†] Remember, the Y2K problem was caused by programmers who couldn't imagine needing a year later than 1999.

Non-Numeric Types: char and bool

In addition to the numeric types, the C# language offers two other types: char and bool.

The char type is used from time to time when you need to hold a single character. The char type can represent a simple character (A), a Unicode character (\u0041), or an escape character enclosed by single quote marks ('\n'). You'll see chars used in this book, and their use will be explained in context.

The one remaining type of importance is bool, which holds a Boolean value. A Boolean value is a one that is either true or false.* Boolean values are used frequently in C# programming as you'll see throughout this book. Virtually every comparison (e.g., is myDog bigger than yourDog?) results in a Boolean value.

Types and Compiler Errors

The compiler will help you by complaining if you try to use a type improperly. The compiler complains in one of two ways: it issues a warning or it issues an error.

You are well advised to treat warnings as errors. Stop what you are doing and figure out why there is a warning and fix the problem. Never ignore a compiler warning.

Programmers talk about design-time, compile-time, and runtime. Design-time is when you are designing the program, compile-time is when you compile the program, and runtime is (surprise!) when you run the program.

The earlier you unearth a bug, the better. It is better (and cheaper) to discover a bug in your logic at design-time rather than later. Likewise, it is better (and cheaper) to find bugs in your program at compile-time than at run-time. Not only is it better; it is more reliable. A compile-time bug will fail every time you run the compiler, but a run-time bug can hide. Run-time bugs slip under a crack in your logic and lurk there (sometimes for months), biding their time, waiting to come out when it will be most expensive (or most embarrassing) to you.

It will be a constant theme of this book that you *want* the compiler to find bugs. The compiler is your friend. The more bugs the compiler finds, the fewer bugs your users will find. A strongly typed language like C# helps the compiler find bugs in your code. Here's how: suppose you tell the compiler that Milo is of type Dog. Sometime

---

* The bool type was named after George Boole (1815–1864), an English mathematician who published *An Investigation into the Laws of Thought, on Which Are Founded the Mathematical Theories of Logic and Probabilities* and thus created the science of Boolean algebra.

later you try to use Milo to display text. Oops, Dogs don't display text. Your compiler will stop with an error:

```
Dog does not contain a definition for 'showText'
```

Very nice. Now you can go figure out if you used the wrong object or you called the wrong method.

Visual Studio .NET actually finds the error even before the compiler does. When you try to add a method, IntelliSense pops up a list of valid methods to help you, as shown in Figure 5-1.

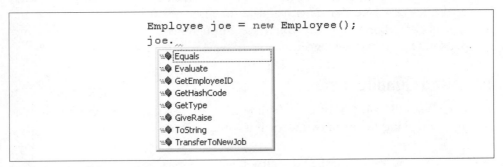

Figure 5-1. IntelliSense

When you try to add a method that does not exist, it won't be in the list. That is a pretty good clue that you are not using the object properly.

Variables

A variable is an object that can hold a value:

```
int myVariable = 15;
```

You *initialize* a variable by writing its type, its *identifier*, and then assigning a value to that variable. The previous section explained types. In this example, the variable's type is int (which is, as you've seen, a type of integer).

An identifier is just an arbitrary name you assign to a variable, method, class, or other element. In this case, the variable's identifier is myVariable.

You can define variables without initializing them:

```
int myVariable;
```

You can then assign a value to myVariable later in your program:

```
int myVariable;
// some other code here
myVariable = 15;  // assign 15 to myVariable
```

You can also change the value of a variable later in the program. That is why they're called variables; their values vary.

```
int myVariable;
// some other code here
myVariable = 15;  // assign 15 to myVariable
// some other code here
myVariable = 12;  // now it is 12
```

Technically, a variable is a named storage location (i.e., stored in memory) with a type. After the final line of code in the previous example, the value 12 is stored in the named location myVariable.

WriteLine( )

The .NET Framework provides a useful method for displaying output on the screen in console applications: System.Console.WriteLine(). How you use this method will become clearer as you progress through the book, but the fundamentals are straightforward. You call the method, passing in a string that you want printed to the console (the screen), as in the Hello World application in Chapter 2.

You can also pass in substitution parameters. A substitution parameter is just a place holder for a value you want to display. For example, you might pass in the substitution parameter {0} and then when you run the program you'll substitute the value held in the variable myInt, so that its value is displayed where the parameter {0} appears in the WriteLine() statement.

Here's how it works. You place a number between braces:

```
System.Console.WriteLine("After assignment, myInt: {0}", myInt);
```

Notice that you follow the quoted string with a comma and then a variable name. The value of the variable will be substituted into the parameter. Assuming myInt has the value 15, the statement shown previously causes the following to display:

```
After assignment, myInt: 15
```

If you have more than one parameter, the variable values will be substituted in order, as in the following:

```
System.Console.WriteLine("After assignment, myInt: {0} and myOtherInt: {1}",
myInt, myOtherInt);
```

Assuming myInt has the value 15, and myOtherInt has the value 20, this will cause the following to display:

```
After assignment, myInt: 15 and myOtherInt: 20.
```

You'll see a great deal more about WriteLine() in coming chapters.

Example 5-1 illustrates the use of variables. To test this program, open Visual Studio .NET and create a console application. Type in the code as shown.

Example 5-1. Using variables

```
class Values
{
    static void Main()
    {
        int myInt = 7;
        System.Console.WriteLine("Initialized, myInt: {0}",
            myInt);
        myInt = 5;
        System.Console.WriteLine("After assignment, myInt: {0}",
            myInt);
    }
}
```

Output:
```
Initialized, myInt: 7
After assignment, myInt: 5
```

Example 5-1 initializes the variable myInt to the value 7, displays that value, reassigns the variable with the value 5, and displays it again.

Definite Assignment

C# requires *definite assignment*; that is, variables must be initialized (or assigned to) before they are used. To test this rule, change the line that initializes myInt in Example 5-1 to:

```
    int myInt;
```

and save the revised program shown in Example 5-2.

Example 5-2. Uninitialized variable

```
class Values
{
    static void Main()
    {
        int myInt;
        System.Console.WriteLine
        ("Uninitialized, myInt: {0}",myInt);
        myInt = 5;
        System.Console.WriteLine("Assigned, myInt: {0}", myInt);
    }
}
```

When you try to compile Example 5-2, the C# compiler will display the following error message:

```
    5.2.cs(6,55): error CS0165: Use of unassigned local
    variable 'myInt'
```

It is not legal to use an uninitialized variable in C#; doing so violates the rule of definite assignment. In this case, "using" the variable myInt means passing it to WriteLine().

So does this mean you must initialize every variable? No, but if you don't initialize your variable then you must assign a value to it before you attempt to use it. Example 5-3 illustrates a corrected program.

Example 5-3. Definite assignment

```
class Values
{
   static void Main()
   {
      int myInt;
      //other code here...
      myInt = 7;   // assign to it
      System.Console.WriteLine("Assigned, myInt: {0}", myInt);
      myInt = 5;
      System.Console.WriteLine("Reassigned, myInt: {0}", myInt);
   }
}
```

Constants

Variables are a powerful tool, but there are times when you want to manipulate a defined value, one whose value you want to ensure remains constant. A *constant* is like a variable in that it can store a value. However, unlike a variable, you cannot change the value of a constant while the program runs.

For example, you might need to work with the Fahrenheit freezing and boiling points of water in a program simulating a chemistry experiment. Your program will be clearer if you name the variables that store these values FreezingPoint and Boiling-Point, but you do not want to permit their values to be changed while the program is executing. The solution is to use a constant. Constants come in three flavors: *literals*, *symbolic constants*, and *enumerations*.

Literal Constants

A literal constant is just a value. For example, 32 is a literal constant. It does not have a name; it is just a literal value. And you can't make the value 32 represent any other value. The value of 32 is always 32. You can't assign a new value to 32, and you can't make 32 represent the value 99 no matter how hard you might try.

Symbolic Constants

Symbolic constants assign a name to a constant value. You declare a symbolic constant using the following syntax:

```
const type identifier = value;
```

The const keyword is followed by a type, an identifier, the assignment operator (=), and the value with which you'll initialize the constant.

This is similar to declaring a variable, except that you start with the keyword const and symbolic constants *must* be initialized. Once initialized, a symbolic constant cannot be altered. For example, in the following declaration, 32 is a literal constant and FreezingPoint is a symbolic constant of type int:

```
const int FreezingPoint = 32;
```

Example 5-4 illustrates the use of symbolic constants.

Example 5-4. Using symbolic constants

```
class Values
{
   static void Main()
   {
      const int FreezingPoint = 32;    // degrees Farenheit
      const int BoilingPoint = 212;

      System.Console.WriteLine("Freezing point of water: {0}",
            FreezingPoint );
      System.Console.WriteLine("Boiling point of water: {0}",
            BoilingPoint );
      //BoilingPoint = 21;

   }
}
```

Example 5-4 creates two symbolic integer constants: FreezingPoint and BoilingPoint. See the sidebar "Naming Conventions" for a discussion of how to name symbolic constants.

Naming Conventions

Microsoft has promulgated white papers on how you should name the variables, constants, and other objects in your program. They define two types of naming conventions: Camel notation and Pascal notation.

In Camel notation, names begin with a lowercase letter. Multi-word names (such as "my button") are written with no spaces and no underscore and with each word after the first capitalized. Thus, the correct name for "my button" is myButton.

Pascal notation is just like Camel notation except that the first letter is also uppercase (FreezingPoint).

Microsoft suggests that variables be written with Camel notation and constants with Pascal notation. In later chapters, you'll learn that member variables are named using Camel notation, while methods and classes are named using Pascal notation.

These constants serve the same purpose as using the literal values 32 and 212 for the freezing and boiling points of water, respectively, in expressions that require them. However, because the constants have names, they convey far more meaning. Also, if you decide to switch this program to Celsius, you can reinitialize these constants at compile time to 0 and 100, respectively, and all the rest of the code should continue to work.

To prove to yourself that the constant cannot be reassigned, try un-commenting the last line of the preceding program, by removing the two slash marks.

```
BoilingPoint = 21;
```

When you recompile, you receive this error:

```
error CS0131: The left-hand side of an assignment must be
a variable, property or indexer
```

Enumerations

Enumerations provide a powerful alternative to literal or simple symbolic constants. An enumeration is a distinct value type, consisting of a set of named constants (called the *enumerator list*).

In Example 5-4, you created two related constants:

```
const int FreezingPoint = 32;
const int BoilingPoint = 212;
```

You might want to add a number of other useful constants to this list as well, such as:

```
const int LightJacketWeather = 60;
const int SwimmingWeather = 72;
const int WickedCold = 0;
```

Notice, however, that this process is somewhat cumbersome; also this syntax shows no logical connection among these various constants. C# provides an alternate construct, the enumeration, which allows you to group logically related constants, as in the following:

```
enum Temperatures
{
    WickedCold = 0,
    FreezingPoint = 32,
    LightJacketWeather = 60,
    SwimmingWeather = 72,
    BoilingPoint = 212,
}
```

The complete syntax for specifying an enumeration uses the enum keyword, as follows:

```
[attributes] [modifiers] enum identifier
[:base-type] {enumerator-list};
```

In a specification statement like the preceding example, anything in square brackets is optional. Thus, you can declare an enum with no attributes, modifiers, or base-type.

The optional attributes and modifiers are considered later in this book. For now, let's focus on the rest of this declaration. An enumeration begins with the keyword enum, which is generally followed by an identifier, in this case "Temperatures":

```
enum Temperatures
```

The base-type is the underlying type for the enumeration. You might specify that you are declaring constant ints, constant longs, etc. If you leave out this optional value (and often you will), it defaults to int, but you are free to use any of the integral types (e.g., ushort, long) except for char. For example, the following fragment declares an enumeration with unsigned integers (uint) as the base-type:

```
enum ServingSizes : uint
{
    Small = 1,
    Regular = 2,
    Large = 3
}
```

Notice that an enum declaration ends with the enumerator list, which contains the constant assignments for the enumeration, each separated by a comma. Example 5-5 rewrites Example 5-4 to use an enumeration.

Example 5-5. Using an enumeration

```
class Values
{
    // declare the enumeration
    enum Temperatures
    {
        WickedCold = 0,
        FreezingPoint = 32,
        LightJacketWeather = 60,
        SwimmingWeather = 72,
        BoilingPoint = 212,
    }

    static void Main()
    {

        System.Console.WriteLine("Freezing point of water: {0}",
            (int) Temperatures.FreezingPoint );
        System.Console.WriteLine("Boiling point of water: {0}",
            (int) Temperatures.BoilingPoint );
    }
}
```

In Example 5-5, you declare an enumerated constant called Temperatures. When you want to use any of the values in an enumeration in a program, the values of the enumeration must be qualified by the enumeration name.

You cannot just refer to FreezingPoint; instead, you use the enumeration identifier (Temperature) followed by the dot operator and then the enumerated constant (FreezingPoint). This is called qualifying the identifier FreezingPoint. Thus, to refer to the FreezingPoint, you use the full identifier Temperature.FreezingPoint.

You might want to display the value of an enumerated constant to the console, as in the following:

```
Console.WriteLine("The freezing point of water is {0}",
    (int) Temperature.FreezingPoint);
```

To make this work properly, you must cast the constant to its underlying type (int). When you cast a value you tell the compiler "I know that this value is really of the indicated type." In this case you are saying "treat this enumerated constant as an int." Since the underlying type is int, this is safe to do. See the sidebar "Casting."

In Example 5-5, the values in the two enumerated constants FreezingPoint and BoilingPoint are both cast to type integer; then that integer value is passed to WriteLine() and displayed.

Each constant in an enumeration corresponds to a numerical value. In Example 5-5, each enumerated value is an integer. If you don't specifically set it otherwise, the enumeration begins at 0 and each subsequent value counts up from the previous. Thus, if you create the following enumeration:

```
enum SomeValues
{
    First,
    Second,
    Third = 20,
    Fourth
}
```

the value of First will be 0, Second will be 1, Third will be 20, and Fourth will be 21.

Strings

It is nearly impossible to write a C# program without creating strings. A string object holds a series of characters.

You declare a string variable using the string keyword much as you would create an instance of any type:

```
string myString;
```

You specify a *string literal* by enclosing it in double quotes:

```
"Hello World"
```

Casting

Objects of one type can be converted into objects of another type. This is called casting. Casting can be either implicit or explicit.

An implicit conversion happens automatically; the compiler takes care of it for you. If you have a short, and you assign it to a variable of type int, the compiler automatically (and silently) casts it for you. You don't have to take any action. This is safe, because an int variable can hold any value that might have been in a short variable.

```
short myShort = 5;
// other code here…
int   myint = myShort; // implicit conversion
```

Explicit conversions happen when you specifically cast a value to a different type by writing the new type in parentheses. The semantics of an explicit conversion are "Hey! Compiler! I know what I'm doing." This is sometimes called "hitting it with the big hammer" and can be very useful or very painful, depending on whether your thumb is in the way.

If you convert from int to short you *can* lose information. If the value in the int is greater than 32,767, it will be truncated in the conversion to a short. The compiler will not perform an implicit conversion from int to short:

```
short myShort;
int myInt = 500;
myShort = myInt;  // won't compile
```

Instead, you must explicitly cast the value:

```
short myShort;
int myInt = 500;
myShort = (short) myInt;  // explicit cast
```

It is common to initialize a string variable that contains a string literal:

```
string myString = "Hello World";
```

Strings will be covered in much greater detail in Chapter 17.

Statements

In C#, a complete program instruction is called a *statement*. Programs consist of sequences of C# statements, each of which must end with a semicolon (;). Here are three statements:

```
int myVariable;                        // a statement
myVariable = 23;                       // another statement
int anotherVariable = myVariable;      // yet another statement
```

C# statements are evaluated in order. The compiler starts at the beginning of a statement list and makes its way to the bottom. This would be entirely straightforward, and terribly limiting, were it not for branching. Branching allows you to change the order in which statements are evaluated. See Chapter 6 for more information about branching.

Expressions

Statements that evaluate to a value are called *expressions*. You may be surprised how many statements do evaluate to a value. For example, an assignment such as:

```
myVariable = 57;
```

is an expression; it evaluates to the value assigned, in this case, 57.

 Note that the preceding statement assigns the value 57 to the variable myVariable. The assignment operator (=) does not test equality; rather it causes whatever is on the right side (57) to be assigned to whatever is on the left side (myVariable). Chapter 7 discusses some of the more useful C# operators (including assignment and equality).

Because myVariable = 57 is an expression that evaluates to 57, it can be used as part of another assignment, such as:

```
mySecondVariable = myVariable = 57;
```

What happens in this statement is that the literal value 57 is assigned to the variable myVariable. The value of that assignment (57) is then assigned to the second variable, mySecondVariable. Thus, the value 57 is assigned to both variables. You can assign a value to any number of variables with one statement using the assignment operator (=), as in the following:

```
int a,b,c,d,e;
a = b = c = d = e = 20;
```

Whitespace

In the C# language, spaces, tabs, and newlines are considered to be "whitespace" (so named because you see only the white of the underlying "page"). Extra whitespace is generally ignored in C# statements. Thus, you can write:

```
myVariable = 5;
```

or:

```
myVariable    =              5;
```

and the compiler will treat the two statements as identical. The key is to use whitespace to make the program more readable to the programmer; the compiler is indifferent.

The exception to this rule is that whitespace within a string is treated as literal; it is not ignored. If you write:

```
Console.WriteLine("Hello World")
```

each space between "Hello" and "World" is treated as another character in the string. (In this case there is only one space character.)

Problems arise only when you do not leave space between logical program elements that require it. For instance, although the expression:

```
int myVariable = 5;
```

is the same as:

```
int myVariable =5;
```

it is not the same as:

```
intmyVariable =5;
```

The compiler knows that the whitespace on either side of the assignment operator is extra, but the whitespace between the type declaration int and the variable name myVariable is *not* extra; it is required.

This is not surprising; the whitespace allows the compiler to *parse* the keyword int rather than some unknown term intmyVariable. You are free to add as much or as little whitespace between int and myVariable as you care to, but there must be at least one whitespace character (typically a space or tab).

 Visual Basic programmers take note: in C#, the end-of-line has no special significance. Statements are ended with semicolons, not new-line characters. There is no line continuation character because none is needed.

CHAPTER 6

Branching

A method is, essentially, a mini-program within your larger program. It is a set of statements that execute one after the other, as in the following:

```
void MyMethod()
{
    int a;  // declare an integer
    a = 5;  // assign it a value
    console.WriteLine("a: {0}", a);  // display the value
}
```

Methods are executed from top to bottom. The compiler reads each line of code in turn and executes one line after another. This continues in sequence until the method *branches*. Branching means that the current method is interrupted temporarily and a new method or routine is executed; when that new method or routine finishes, the original method picks up where it left off. A method can branch in either of two ways: unconditionally or conditionally.

As the name implies, unconditional branching happens every time the program is run. An unconditional branch happens, for example, whenever the compiler encounters a new method call. The compiler stops execution in the current method and branches to the newly called method. When the newly called method returns (i.e., completes its execution), execution picks up in the original method on the line just below the line where the new method was called.

Conditional branching is more complicated. Methods can branch based on the evaluation of certain conditions that occur at runtime. For instance, you might create a branch that will calculate an employee's federal withholding tax only when their earnings are greater than the minimum taxable by law. C# provides a number of statements that support conditional branching, such as if, else, and switch. The use of these statements is discussed later in this chapter.

A second way that methods break out of their mindless step-by-step processing of instructions is by looping. A loop causes the method to repeat a set of steps until some condition is met (e.g., "Keep asking for input until the user tells you to stop or until you receive ten values"). C# provides many statements for looping, including for, while, and do...while, which are also discussed in this chapter.

Unconditional Branching Statements

The simplest example of an unconditional branch is a method call. When a method call is reached, there is no test made to evaluate the state of the object; the program execution branches immediately (and unconditionally) to the start of the new method.

You call a method by writing its name, for example:

```
UpdateSalary()  // invokes the method UpdateSalary
```

As explained in the introduction, when the compiler encounters a method call, it stops execution of the current method and branches to the new method. When that new method completes its execution, the compiler picks up where it left off in the original method. This process is illustrated schematically in Figure 6-1.

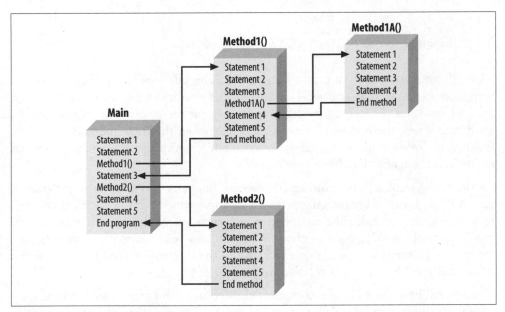

Figure 6-1. How branching works

As Figure 6-1 suggests, it is actually quite common for there to be unconditional branching several methods deep. In Figure 6-1, execution begins in a method called Main(). Statement1 and Statement2 execute; then the compiler sees a call to Method1(). Program execution branches unconditionally to the first line of Method1(), where its first three statements are executed. At the call to Method1A(), execution again branches, this time to the start of Method1A().

The four statements in Method1A() are executed, and Method1A() returns. Execution resumes on the first statement after the method call in Method1() (Statement 4). Execution continues until Method1() ends, at which time execution resumes back in Main() at Statement3. At the call to Method2(), execution again branches; all the statements in Method2() execute, and then Main() resumes at Statement4. When Main() ends, the program itself ends.

You can see the effect of method calls in Example 6-1. Execution begins in Main(), but branches to a method named SomeMethod(). The WriteLine() statements in each method assist you in seeing where you are in the code as the program executes.

Example 6-1. Branching to a method

```
using System;
class Functions
{
    static void Main()
    {
        Console.WriteLine("In Main! Calling SomeMethod()...");
        SomeMethod();
        Console.WriteLine("Back in Main().");

    }
    static void SomeMethod()
    {
        Console.WriteLine("Greetings from SomeMethod!");
    }
}
```

Output:
```
In Main! Calling SomeMethod()...
Greetings from SomeMethod!
Back in Main().
```

Program flow begins in Main() and proceeds until SomeMethod() is invoked. (Invoking a method is sometimes referred to as "calling" the method.) At that point, program flow branches to the method. When the method completes, program flow resumes at the next line after the call to that method.

 You can instead create an unconditional branch by using one of the unconditional branch keywords: goto, break, continue, return, or throw. The first four of these are discussed later in this chapter, while the final statement, throw, is discussed in Chapter 18.

Methods and their parameters and return values are discussed in detail in Chapter 9.

Conditional Branching Statements

While methods branch unconditionally, often you will want to branch within a method depending on a condition that you evaluate while the program is running. This is known as conditional branching. Conditional branching statements allow you to write logic such as "If you are over 25 years old, then you may rent a car."

C# provides a number of constructs that allow you to write conditional branches into your programs; these constructs are described in the following sections.

if Statements

The simplest branching statement is if. An if statement says, "if a particular condition is true, then execute the statement; otherwise skip it." The condition is a Boolean expression. An expression is a statement that evaluates to a value, and a Boolean expression evaluates to either true or false.

The formal description of an if statement is:

```
if (expression)
    Statement1
```

This is the kind of description of the if statement you are likely to find in your compiler documentation. It shows you that the if statement takes an expression (a statement that returns a value) in parentheses, and executes Statement1 if the expression evaluates true. Note that Statement1 can actually be a block of statements within braces, as illustrated in Example 6-2.

 Anywhere in C# that you are expected to provide a statement, you can instead provide a block of statements within braces. (See the sidebar "Brace Styles" later in this chapter.)

Example 6-2. The if statement

```
using System;

namespace Branching
{
    class Test
    {
        static void Main()
        {
            int valueOne = 10;
            int valueTwo = 20;
            int valueThree = 30;

            Console.WriteLine("Testing valueOne against valueTwo...");
            if ( valueOne > valueTwo )
            {
                Console.WriteLine(
                "ValueOne: {0} larger than ValueTwo: {1}",
```

Example 6-2. The if statement (continued)

```
                valueOne, valueTwo);
        }

        Console.WriteLine("Testing valueThree against valueTwo...");
        if ( valueThree > valueTwo )
        {
            Console.WriteLine(
                "ValueThree: {0} larger than ValueTwo: {1}",
                valueThree, valueTwo);
        }   // end if

    }           // end Main
  }             // end class
}               // end namespace
```

In this simple program, you declare three variables, valueOne, valueTwo, and valueThree, with the values 10, 20, and 30, respectively. In the first if statement, you test whether valueOne is greater than valueTwo.

```
if ( valueOne > valueTwo )
{
    Console.WriteLine(
    "ValueOne: {0} larger than ValueTwo: {1}",
    valueOne, valueTwo);
}
```

Because valueOne (10) is less than valueTwo (20), this if statement fails (the condition returns false), and thus the body of the if statement (the statements within the braces) doesn't execute.

> The test for greater-than uses the greater-than operator (>), which is discussed in detail in Chapter 7.

You then test whether valueThree is greater than valueTwo:

```
if ( valueThree > valueTwo )
{
    Console.WriteLine(
        "ValueThree: {0} larger than ValueTwo: {1}",
        valueThree, valueTwo);
}
```

Since valueThree (30) *is* greater than valueTwo (20), the test returns true, and thus the statement executes. The statement in this case is the block in which you call the WriteLine() method, shown in bold. The output reflects that the first if fails but the second succeeds:

```
Testing valueOne against valueTwo...
Testing valueThree against valueTwo...
ValueThree: 30 larger than ValueTwo: 20
```

Single Statement if Blocks

Notice that the `if` statement blocks shown in Example 6-2 each contain only a single statement, one call to WriteLine(). In such cases, you can leave out the braces enclosing the `if` block. Thus you might rewrite Example 6-2 as shown in Example 6-3.

Example 6-3. Single statements with if

```
using System;

namespace Branching
{
    class Test
    {
        static void Main()
        {
            int valueOne = 10;
            int valueTwo = 20;
            int valueThree = 30;

            Console.WriteLine("Testing valueOne against valueTwo...");
            if ( valueOne > valueTwo )
                Console.WriteLine(
                "ValueOne: {0} larger than ValueTwo: {1}",
                valueOne, valueTwo);

            Console.WriteLine("Testing valueThree against valueTwo...");
            if ( valueThree > valueTwo )
                Console.WriteLine(
                    "ValueThree: {0} larger than ValueTwo: {1}",
                    valueThree, valueTwo);

        }        // end Main
    }            // end class
}                // end namespace
```

It is generally a good idea, however, to use the braces even when your `if` block has only a single statement. There are two reasons for this advice. First, the code is somewhat easier to read and understand with the braces. Code that is easier to read is easier to maintain.

 When programmers talk about maintaining code, they mean either adding to the code as requirements change or fixing the code as bugs arise.

The second reason for using braces is to avoid a common error: adding a second statement to the `if` and forgetting to add the braces. Consider the code shown in Example 6-4. The programmer has changed the value of valueThree to 10 and added a second statement to the second `if` block, as shown in bold.

Example 6-4. Adding a second statement to if

```csharp
using System;

namespace Branching
{
    class Test
    {
        static void Main()
        {
            int valueOne = 10;
            int valueTwo = 20;
            int valueThree = 10;

            Console.WriteLine("Testing valueOne against valueTwo...");
            if ( valueOne > valueTwo )
                Console.WriteLine(
                "ValueOne: {0} larger than ValueTwo: {1}",
                valueOne, valueTwo);

            Console.WriteLine("Testing valueThree against valueTwo...");
            if ( valueThree > valueTwo )
                Console.WriteLine(
                    "ValueThree: {0} larger than ValueTwo: {1}",
                    valueThree, valueTwo);
                Console.WriteLine("Good thing you tested again!");

        }       // end Main
    }           // end class
}               // end namespace
```

Now, before reading any further, review the code and decide for yourself what the output should be. Don't cheat by looking past this paragraph. Then, when you think you know what the output will be, take a look at this:

```
Testing valueOne against valueTwo...
Testing valueThree against valueTwo...
Good thing you tested again!
```

Were you surprised?

The programmer was fooled by the lack of braces and the indentation. Remember that indentation is whitespace and is ignored by the compiler. From the perspective of the programmer, the second statement ("Good thing...") is part of the if block:

```csharp
if ( valueThree > valueTwo )
    Console.WriteLine(
        "ValueThree: {0} larger than ValueTwo: {1}",
        valueThree, valueTwo);
    Console.WriteLine("Good thing you tested again!");
```

The compiler, however, considers only the first statement after the if test to be part of the if statement. The second statement is not part of the if statement. To the compiler, the if statement looks like this:

```
if ( valueThree > valueTwo )
    Console.WriteLine(
        "ValueThree: {0} larger than ValueTwo: {1}",
        valueThree, valueTwo);

Console.WriteLine("Good thing you tested again!");
```

If you want the second statement to be part of the if statement, you must use braces, as in the following:

```
if ( valueThree > valueTwo )
{
    Console.WriteLine(
        "ValueThree: {0} larger than ValueTwo: {1}",
        valueThree, valueTwo);
    Console.WriteLine("Good thing you tested again!");
}
```

Because of this potential for confusion, many C# programmers use braces with every if statement, even if the statement is only one line.

Brace Styles

There are many ways you can form braces around an if statement (and around other blocks of code), but most C# programmers will use one of three styles:

```
if (condition)
{
    // statement
}

if (condition)
    {
    // statement
    }

if (condition){
    // statement
}
```

The first style, used throughout this book, is to put the braces under the keyword if and to indent the contents of the if block. The second style, not very popular any more, is to indent the braces with the contents of the if block. The third style is to put the opening brace on the same line as the if statement and the closing brace under the if statement.

The third style is called K&R style, after Kernighan and Ritchie, the authors of the seminal book *The C Programming Language* (Prentice Hall). Their book was so influential that many programmers feel a strong commitment to this style of braces. While it does save room in a book, the K&R style is a bit less clear, and so this book will use the first style.

---

if...else Statements

Often, you will find that you want to take one set of actions when the condition tests true and a different set of actions when the condition tests false. This allows you to write logic such as "If you are over 25 years old, then you may rent a car; *otherwise*, you must take the train."

The *otherwise* portion of the logic is executed in the else statement. For example, you can modify Example 6-2 to print an appropriate message whether or not valueOne is greater than valueTwo, as shown in Example 6-5.

Example 6-5. The else statement

```
using System;

namespace Branching
{
    class Test
    {
        static void Main()
        {
            int valueOne = 10;
            int valueTwo = 20;

            Console.WriteLine("Testing valueOne against valueTwo...");
            if ( valueOne > valueTwo )
            {
                Console.WriteLine(
                    "ValueOne: {0} larger than ValueTwo: {1}",
                    valueOne, valueTwo);
            }        // end if
            else
            {
                Console.WriteLine(
                    "Nope, ValueOne: {0} is NOT larger than ValueTwo: {1}",
                    valueOne, valueTwo);
            }        // end else

        }        // end Main
    }        // end class
}        // end namespace
```
Output:
```
Testing valueOne against valueTwo...
Nope, ValueOne: 10 is NOT larger than ValueTwo: 20
```

Because the test in the if statement fails (valueOne is *not* larger than valueTwo), the body of the if statement is skipped and the body of the else statement is executed. Had the test succeeded, the if statement body would execute and the else statement would be skipped.

Nested if Statements

It is possible, and not uncommon, to nest if statements to handle complex conditions. For example, suppose you need to write a program to evaluate the temperature and specifically to return the following types of information:

- If the temperature is 32 degrees or lower, the program should warn you about ice on the road.
- If the temperature is exactly 32 degrees, the program should tell you that there may be ice patches.
- If the temperature is higher than 32 degrees, the program should assure you that there is no ice.

There are many good ways to write this program. Example 6-6 illustrates one approach, using nested if statements.

Example 6-6. Nested if statements

```
using System;
class Values
{
    static void Main()
    {
        int temp = 32;

        if (temp <= 32)
        {
            Console.WriteLine("Warning! Ice on road!");
            if (temp == 32)
            {
                Console.WriteLine(
                  "Temp exactly freezing, beware of water.");
            }
            else
            {
                Console.WriteLine("Watch for black ice! Temp: {0}", temp);
            }
        }

    }
}
```

The logic of Example 6-6 is that it tests whether the temperature is less than or equal to 32. If so, it prints a warning:

```
if (temp <= 32)
{
    Console.WriteLine("Warning! Ice on road!");
```

The program then checks whether the temp is equal to 32 degrees. If so, it prints one message; if not, the temp must be less than 32 and the program prints the next mes-

---

sage. Notice that this second if statement is nested within the first if, so the logic of the else statement is: "since it has been established that the temp is less than or equal to 32, and it isn't equal to 32, it must be less than 32."

 The less-than-or-equal-to operator is <= and the equals operator is ==. Notice that the equals operator is *two* equal signs. C# considers this a single operator, as described in Chapter 7.

Switch Statements

Nested if statements are hard to read, hard to get right, and hard to debug. When you have a complex set of choices to make, the switch statement is a more powerful alternative. The logic of a switch statement is this: "pick a matching value and act accordingly."

```
switch (expression)
{
    case constant-expression:
        statement
        jump-statement
    [default: statement]
}
```

The expression you are "switching on" is put in parentheses in the head of the switch statement. Each case statement compares a constant value with the expression. The constant expression can be a literal, symbolic, or enumerated constant.

The compiler starts with the first case statement and works its way down the list, looking for a value that matches the expression. If a case is matched, the statement (or block of statements) associated with that case is executed.

The case block must end with a jump statement. Typically, the jump statement is break, which abruptly ends the entire switch statement. When you execute a break in a switch statement, execution continues after the closing brace of the switch statement. (We'll consider the use of the optional default keyword later in this section.)

In the next, somewhat whimsical listing (Example 6-7), the user is asked to choose his political affiliation among Democrat, Republican, or Progressive. To keep the code simple, I'll hardwire the choice to be Republican.

Example 6-7. Using a switch statement

```
using System;

class Values
{
    static void Main()
    {
        const int Democrat = 0;
        const int Republican = 1;
```

Example 6-7. Using a switch statement (continued)

```
        const int Progressive = 2;

        // hard wire to Republican
        int myChoice = Republican;

        // switch on the value of myChoice
        switch (myChoice)
        {
            case Democrat:
                Console.WriteLine("You voted Democratic.");
                break;
            case Republican:
                Console.WriteLine("You voted Republican.");
                break;
            case Progressive:
                Console.WriteLine("You voted Progressive.");
                break;
        }
        Console.WriteLine("Thank you for voting.");
    }
}
```
Output:
```
You voted Republican.
Thank you for voting.
```

Rather than using a complicated if statement, Example 6-7 uses a switch statement. The user's choice is evaluated in the head of the switch statement, and the block of statements that gets executed depends on whatever case matches (in this instance, Republican).

The statements between the case statement and the break are executed in series. You can have more than one statement here without braces; in effect the case statement and the closing break statement act as the braces.

It is possible that the user will not make a choice among Democrat, Republican, and Progressive. You may want to provide a default case that will be executed whenever no valid choice has been made. Do that with the default keyword, as shown in Example 6-8.

Example 6-8. A default statement
```
using System;

class Values
{
    static void Main()
    {
        const int Democrat = 0;
        const int Republican = 1;
        const int Progressive = 2;
```

Example 6-8. A default statement (continued)

```
    // hard wire to Republican
    int myChoice = 5;

    // switch on the value of myChoice
    switch (myChoice)
    {
        case Democrat:
            Console.WriteLine("You voted Democratic.\n");
            break;
        case Republican:
            Console.WriteLine("You voted Republican.\n");
            break;
        case Progressive:
            Console.WriteLine("You voted Progressive.\n");
            break;
        default:
            Console.WriteLine("You did not make a valid choice.");
            break;
    }
    Console.WriteLine("Thank you for voting.");
  }
}
Output
You did not make a valid choice.
Thank you for voting.
```

If the user does not choose one of the values that correspond to a case statement, the default statements will execute. In this case, a message is simply printed telling the user he did not make a valid choice.

Falling Through and Jumping to Cases

If two cases will execute the same code, you can create what's known as a "fall through" case, grouping the case statements together with the same code, as shown here:

```
case CompassionateRepublican:
case Republican:
    Console.WriteLine("You voted Republican.\n");
    Console.WriteLine("Don't you feel compassionate?");
    break;
```

In this example, if the user chooses either CompassionateRepublican or Republican, the same set of statements will be executed.

Note that you can only fall through if the first case executes no code. In this example, the first case, CompassionateRepublican, meets that criteria. Thus, you can fall through to the second case.

If, however, you want to execute a statement with one case and then fall through to the next, you must use the goto keyword to jump to the next case you want to execute.

The goto keyword is an unconditional branch. When the compiler sees this word, it immediately transfers the flow (jumps) to wherever the goto points to. Thus, even within this conditional branching statement, you've inserted an unconditional branch.

For example, if you create a NewLeft party, you might want the NewLeft voting choice to print a message and then fall through to Democrat (that is, continue on with the statements in the Democrat case). You might (incorrectly) try writing the following:

```
case NewLeft:
    Console.WriteLine("The NewLeft members are voting Democratic.");
case Democrat:
    Console.WriteLine("You voted Democratic.\n");
    break;
```

This code will not compile; it will fail with the error:

```
Control cannot fall through from one case label (case '4:') to another
```

This is a very misleading error message. Control *can* fall through from one case label to another, but only if there is no code in the first case label.

Notice that the error displays the name of the case with its numeric value (4) rather than its symbolic value (NewLeft). Remember that NewLeft is just the name of the constant:

```
const int Democrat = 0;
const int CompassionateRepublican = 1;
const int Republican = 2;
const int Progressive = 3;
const int NewLeft = 4;
```

Because the NewLeft case has a statement, the WriteLine() method, you must use a goto statement to fall through:

```
case NewLeft:
    Console.WriteLine("The NewLeft members are voting Democratic.");
    goto case Democrat;
case Democrat:
    Console.WriteLine("You voted Democratic.\n");
    break;
```

This code will compile and execute as you expect.

The goto can jump over labels; you do not need to put NewLeft just above Democrat. In fact, you can put NewLeft last in the list (just before default), and it will continue to work properly.

Switch on string Statements

In the previous example, the switch value was an integral constant. C# also offers the ability to switch on a string. Thus, you can rewrite Example 6-8 to switch on the string "NewLeft," as in Example 6-9.

Example 6-9. Switching on a string

```
using System;

class Values
{
    static void Main()
    {
        String myChoice = "NewLeft";

        // switch on the string value of myChoice
        switch (myChoice)
        {
            case "NewLeft":
                Console.WriteLine(
                    "The NewLeft members are voting Democratic.");
                goto case "Democrat";
            case "Democrat":
                Console.WriteLine("You voted Democratic.\n");
                break;
            case "CompassionateRepublican": // fall through
            case "Republican":
                Console.WriteLine("You voted Republican.\n");
                Console.WriteLine("Don't you feel compassionate?");
                break;
            case "Progressive":
                Console.WriteLine("You voted Progressive.\n");
                break;
            default:
                Console.WriteLine("You did not make a valid choice.");
                break;
        }
        Console.WriteLine("Thank you for voting.");
    }
}
```

Iteration (Looping) Statements

There are many situations in which you will want to do the same thing again and again, perhaps slightly changing a value each time you repeat the action. This is called iteration or looping. Typically, you'll iterate (or loop) over a set of items, taking the same action on each. This is the programming equivalent of an assembly line. On an assembly line, you might take a hundred car bodies and put a windshield on each one as it comes by. In an iterative program, you might work your way through a collection of text boxes on a form, retrieving the value from each in turn and using those values to update a database.

C# provides an extensive suite of iteration statements, including for and while, and also do...while and foreach loops. You can also create a loop by using the goto statement. The remainder of this chapter considers the use of goto, for, while, and do…while. However, you'll have to wait until Chapter 15 to learn more about foreach.

Creating Loops with goto

The goto statement was used previously as an unconditional branch in a switch statement. Its more common usage, however, is to create a loop. In fact, the goto statement is the seed from which all other looping statements have been germinated. Unfortunately, it is a semolina seed, producer of spaghetti code and endless confusion.

Programs that use goto statements outside of switch blocks jump around a great deal. Goto can cause your method to loop back and forth in ways that are difficult to follow.

If you were to try to draw the flow of control in a program that makes extensive use of goto statements, the resulting morass of intersecting and overlapping lines might look like a plate of spaghetti—hence the term "spaghetti code." Spaghetti code is a contemptuous epithet; no one wants to write spaghetti code.

Most experienced programmers properly shun the goto statement, but in the interest of completeness, here's how you use it:

1. Create a label.
2. goto that label.

The label is an identifier followed by a colon. You place the label in your code, and then you use the goto keyword to jump to that label. The goto command is typically tied to an if statement, as illustrated in Example 6-10.

Example 6-10. Using goto

```
using System;
public class Tester
{

    public static void Main()
    {
        int counterVariable = 0;

        repeat:  // the label

        Console.WriteLine(
          "counterVariable: {0}",counterVariable);
```

Example 6-10. Using goto (continued)

```
        // increment the counter
        counterVariable++;

        if (counterVariable < 10)
          goto repeat;  // the dastardly deed
    }
}
```
Output:
```
counterVariable: 0
counterVariable: 1
counterVariable: 2
counterVariable: 3
counterVariable: 4
counterVariable: 5
counterVariable: 6
counterVariable: 7
counterVariable: 8
counterVariable: 9
```

This code is not terribly complex; you've used only a single goto statement. However, with multiple such statements and labels scattered through your code, tracing the flow of execution becomes very difficult.

It was the phenomenon of spaghetti code that led to the creation of alternatives, such as the while loop.

The while Loop

The semantics of the while loop are "while this condition is true, do this work." The syntax is:

```
    while (boolean expression) statement
```

As usual, a Boolean expression is any statement that evaluates to true or false. The statement executed within a while statement can of course be a block of statements within braces. Example 6-11 illustrates the use of the while loop.

Example 6-11. The while loop
```
using System;
public class Tester
{
    public static void Main()
    {
        int counterVariable = 0;

        // while the counter variable is less than 10
        // print out its value
        while (counterVariable < 10)
        {
            Console.WriteLine("counterVariable: {0}",counterVariable);
```

Example 6-11. The while loop (continued)

```
            counterVariable++;
        }
    }
}
```
Output:
```
counterVariable: 0
counterVariable: 1
counterVariable: 2
counterVariable: 3
counterVariable: 4
counterVariable: 5
counterVariable: 6
counterVariable: 7
counterVariable: 8
counterVariable: 9
```

The code in Example 6-11 produces results identical to the code in Example 6-10, but the logic is a bit clearer. The while statement is nicely self-contained, and it reads like an English sentence: "while counterVariable is less than 10, print this message and increment counterVariable."

 The value of counterVariable is incremented (increased by 1) with the increment operator (++).

```
counterVariable++; //increment counterVariable
```
This operator is discussed in detail in Chapter 7.

Notice that the while loop tests the value of counterVariable before entering the loop. This ensures that the loop will not run if the condition tested is false; thus if counterVariable is initialized to 11, the loop will never run.

The do...while Loop

There are times when a while loop might not serve your purpose. In certain situations, you might want to reverse the semantics from "run while this is true" to the subtly different "do this, while this condition remains true." In other words, take the action, and then, after the action is completed, check the condition. Such a loop will *always* run at least once.

To ensure that the action is taken before the condition is tested, use a do...while loop:

```
do statement while (boolean-expression);
```

The syntax is to write the keyword do, followed by your statement (or block), the while keyword, and the condition to test in parentheses. End the statement with a semicolon.

Example 6-12 rewrites Example 6-11 to use a do...while loop.

Example 6-12. The do...while loop

```
using System;
public class Tester
{
    public static void Main()
    {
        int counterVariable = 11;

        // display the message and then test that the value is
        // less than 10
        do
        {
            Console.WriteLine("counterVariable: {0}",counterVariable);
            counterVariable++;
        } while (counterVariable < 10);
    }
}
```

In Example 6-12, counterVariable is initialized to 11 and the while test fails, but only after the body of the loop has run once.

The for Loop

A careful examination of the while loop in Example 6-11 reveals a pattern often seen in iterative statements: initialize a variable (counterVariable=0), test the variable (counterVariable<10), execute a series of statements, and increment the variable (counterVariable++). The for loop allows you to combine all these steps in a single statement. You write a for loop with the keyword for, followed by the for header, using the syntax:

```
for ([initializers]; [expression]; [iterators]) statement
```

The first part of the header is the initializers, in which you initialize a variable. The second part is the Boolean expression to test. The third part is the iterator, in which you update the value of the counter variable. All of this is enclosed in parentheses.

A simple for loop is shown in Example 6-13.

Example 6-13. A for loop

```
using System;
public class Tester
{

    public static void Main()
    {
        for (int counter=0; counter<10; counter++)
        {
            Console.WriteLine(
```

Example 6-13. A for loop (continued)

```
                "counter: {0} ", counter);
        }
    }
}
```

Output:
```
counter: 0
counter: 1
counter: 2
counter: 3
counter: 4
counter: 5
counter: 6
counter: 7
counter: 8
counter: 9
```

The counter variable is initialized to zero in the initializer:

```
for (int counter=0; counter<10; counter++)
```

The value of counter is tested in the expression part of the header:

```
for (int counter=0; counter<10; counter++)
```

Finally, the value of counter is incremented in the iterator part of the header:

```
for (int counter=0; counter<10; counter++)
```

The initialization part runs only once, when the for loop begins. The integer value counter is created and initialized to zero, and the test is then executed. Since counter is less than 10, the body of the for loop runs and the value is displayed.

After the loop completes, the iterator part of the header runs and counter is incremented. The value of the counter is tested, and, if the test evaluates true, the body of the for statement is executed again.

The logic of the for loop is as if you said, "For every value of counter that I initialize to zero, take this action if the test returns true, and after the action, update the value of counter."

Breaking out of a for loop

It is possible to exit from a for loop even before the test condition has been fulfilled. To end a for loop prematurely, use the unconditional branching statement break.

The break statement halts the for loop, and execution resumes after the for loop statement (or closing brace), as in Example 6-14.

Example 6-14. Using break to exit a for loop

```
using System;
public class Tester
{
```

Example 6-14. Using break to exit a for loop (continued)

```csharp
public static void Main()
{
    for (int counter=0; counter<10; counter++)
    {
        Console.WriteLine(
            "counter: {0} ", counter);

        // if condition is met, break out.
        if (counter == 5)                   {
            Console.WriteLine("Breaking out of the loop");
            break;
        }
    }

    Console.WriteLine("For loop ended");
}
}
```

Output:
```
counter: 0
counter: 1
counter: 2
counter: 3
counter: 4
counter: 5
Breaking out of the loop
For loop ended
```

In this for loop you test whether the value counter is equal to 5. If that value is found (and in this case it always will be), you break out of the loop.

The continue statement

Rather than breaking out of a loop, you may at times want the semantics of saying "don't execute any more statements in this loop, but start the loop again from the top of the next iteration." To accomplish this, use the unconditional branching statement continue.

> Break and continue create multiple exit points and make for hard-to-understand, and thus hard-to-maintain, code. Use them with some care.

Example 6-15 illustrates the mechanics of both continue and break. This code, suggested to me by one of my technical reviewers, Donald Xie, is intended to create a traffic signal processing system.

The signals are simulated by entering numerals and uppercase characters from the keyboard, using the Console.ReadLine() method, which reads a line of text from the keyboard. ReadLine() reads a line of text into a string variable. The string ends when you press the Enter key.

The algorithm is simple: receipt of a "0" (zero) means normal conditions, and no further action is required except to log the event. (In this case, the program simply writes a message to the console; a real application might enter a time-stamped record in a database.)

 An algorithm is a well-defined series of steps to accomplish a task.

On receipt of an Abort signal (simulated with an uppercase "A"), the problem is logged and the process is ended. Finally, for any other event, an alarm is raised, perhaps notifying the police. (Note that this sample does not actually notify the police, though it does print out a harrowing message to the console.) If the signal is "X," the alarm is raised but the while loop is also terminated.

Example 6-15. Break and continue

```
using System;
public class Tester
{
    public static int Main()
    {
        string signal = "0";      // initialize to neutral
        while (signal != "X")       // X indicates stop
        {
            Console.Write("Enter a signal. X = stop. A = Abort: ");
            signal = Console.ReadLine();

            // do some work here, no matter what signal you
            // receive
            Console.WriteLine("Received: {0}", signal);

            if (signal == "A")
            {
                // faulty - abort signal processing
                // Log the problem and abort.
                Console.WriteLine("Fault! Abort\n");
                break;
            }

            if (signal == "0")
            {
                // normal traffic condition
                // log and continue on
                Console.WriteLine("All is well.\n");
                continue;
            }

            // Problem. Take action and then log the problem
            // and then continue on
```

Example 6-15. Break and continue (continued)

```
            Console.WriteLine("{0} -- raise alarm!\n",
                signal);
        }
        return 0;
    }
}
```

Output 1:
```
Enter a signal. X = stop. A = Abort: 0
Received: 0
All is well.
Enter a signal. X = stop. A = Abort: 1
Received: 1
1 -- raise alarm!
Enter a signal. X = stop. A = Abort: X
Received: X
X -- raise alarm!
Press any key to continue...
```
Output 2:
```
Enter a signal. X = stop. A = Abort: A
Received: A
Fault! Abort
Press any key to continue...
```

The point of this exercise is that when the A signal is received, the action in the if statement is taken and then the program *breaks* out of the loop, without raising the alarm. When the signal is 0 it is also undesirable to raise the alarm, so the program *continues* from the top of the loop.

 Be sure to use uppercase letters for X and A. To keep the code simple there is no code to check for lowercase letters or other inappropriate input.

Optional for loop header elements

You will remember that the for loop header has three parts—initialization, expression, and iteration—and the syntax is as follows:

```
for ([initializers]; [expression]; [iterators]) statement
```

Each part of the for loop header is optional. You can, for example, initialize the value outside the for loop, as shown in Example 6-16.

Example 6-16. No initialization with for loop
```
using System;
public class Tester
{

    public static void Main()
    {
```

Example 6-16. No initialization with for loop (continued)

```
        int counter = 0;
        // some work here
        counter = 3;
        // more work here

        for ( ; counter<10; counter++)
        {
            Console.WriteLine(
                "counter: {0} ", counter);
        }
    }
}
```
Output:
```
counter: 3
counter: 4
counter: 5
counter: 6
counter: 7
counter: 8
counter: 9
```

In this example, the counter variable was initialized and modified before the for loop began. Notice that a semicolon is used to hold the place of the missing initialization statement.

You can also leave out the iteration step if you have reason to increment the counter variable inside the loop, as shown in Example 6-17.

Example 6-17. Leaving out the iterator step

```
using System;
public class Tester
{

    public static void Main()
    {

        for (int counter = 0; counter<10; ) // no increment
        {
            Console.WriteLine(
                "counter: {0} ", counter);

            // do more work here

            counter++; // increment counter
        }
    }
}
```

You can mix and match which statements you leave out of a for loop. It is even possible to leave *all* the statements out, creating what is known as a *forever* loop:

```
    for ( ;; )
```

You break out of a forever loop with a break statement. A forever loop is shown in Example 6-18.

Example 6-18. A forever loop

```
using System;
public class Tester
{
    public static void Main()
    {
        int counterVariable = 0;  // initialization

        for ( ;; )
        {
            Console.WriteLine(
                "counter: {0} ", counterVariable++); // increment

            if (counterVariable > 10) // test
                break;
        }
    }
}
```
Output:
```
counter: 0
counter: 1
counter: 2
counter: 3
counter: 4
counter: 5
counter: 6
counter: 7
counter: 8
counter: 9
counter: 10
```

Use a forever loop to indicate that the "normal" case is to continue the loop indefinitely. The conditions for breaking out of the loop would then be exceptional and managed inside the body of the loop.

While it is possible to use a forever loop to good effect, Example 6-18 is a degenerate case. The initialization, increment, and test would be done more cleanly in the header of the for loop, and the program would then be easier to understand. It is shown here to illustrate that a forever loop is possible.

The while (true) construct

You can accomplish exactly the same semantics of a forever loop using the while (true) construct, as shown in Example 6-19.

Example 6-19. The while (true) construct

```
using System;
public class Tester
{
    public static void Main()
    {
        int counterVariable = 0;   // initialization

        while (true)
        {
            Console.WriteLine(
                "counter: {0} ", counterVariable++); // increment

            if (counterVariable > 10) // test
                break;
        }
    }
}
```
Output:
```
counter: 0
counter: 1
counter: 2
counter: 3
counter: 4
counter: 5
counter: 6
counter: 7
counter: 8
counter: 9
counter: 10
```

Example 6-19 is identical to Example 6-18 except that the forever construct:

```
for ( ;; )
```

is replaced with a:

```
while (true)
```

statement. Of course, the keyword true always returns the Boolean value true; so like
the forever loop, this while loop runs until the break statement is executed.

CHAPTER 7

Operators

An *operator* is a symbol (e.g., =, +, >, etc.) that causes C# to take an action. That action might be an assignment of a value to a variable, the addition of two values, or a comparison of two values, etc.

In the previous chapters, you've seen a number of operators at work. For example, in Chapter 5 you saw the assignment operator used. The single equal sign (=) is used to assign a value to a variable, in this case the value 15 to the variable myVariable:

```
myVariable = 15;
```

In Chapter 6 you saw more sophisticated operators, such as the greater-than comparison operator (>) used to compare two values:

```
if ( valueOne > valueTwo )
```

The preceding if statement compares valueOne with valueTwo; if the former is larger than the latter, the test evaluates true, and the if statement executes.

This chapter describes many of the operators used in C# in some detail.

The Assignment Operator (=)

The assignment operator causes the operand on the left side of the operator to have its value changed to whatever is on the right side of the operator. The following expression assigns the value 15 to myVariable:

```
myVariable = 15;
```

The assignment operator also allows you to *chain* assignments, assigning the same value to multiple variables as follows:

```
myOtherVariable = myVariable = 15;
```

The previous statement assigns 15 to myVariable, and then also assigns the value (15) to myOtherVariable. This works because the statement:

```
myVariable = 15;
```

is an expression. It evaluates to the value assigned; that is, the expression:

```
myVariable = 15;
```

itself evaluates to 15, and it is this value (15) that is then assigned to myOtherVariable.

 It is important not to confuse the assignment operator (=) with the equality, or equals, operator (==), which has two equal signs and is described in the section "Relational Operators," later in the chapter. The assignment operator does not test for equality; it assigns a value.

Mathematical Operators

C# uses five mathematical operators, four for standard calculations and one to return the remainder when dividing integers. The following sections consider the use of these operators.

Simple Arithmetical Operators (+, −, *, /)

C# offers operators for simple arithmetic: the addition (+), subtraction (-), multiplication (*), and division (/) operators work as you might expect, with the possible exception of integer division.

When you divide two integers, C# divides like a child in the fourth grade: it throws away any fractional remainder. Thus, dividing 17 by 4 returns a value of 4 (17/4 = 4, with C# discarding the remainder of 1).

This limitation is specific to integer division. If you do not want the fractional part thrown away, you can use one of the types that support decimal values, such as float and double. Division between two floats (using the / operator) returns a fractional answer. Integer and fractional division is illustrated in Example 7-1.

Example 7-1. Integer and float division

```
using System;
public class Tester
{
    public static void Main()
    {
        int smallInt = 5;
        int largeInt = 12;
        int intQuotient;
        intQuotient = largeInt / smallInt;
        Console.WriteLine("Dividing integers. {0} / {1} = {2}",
            largeInt, smallInt, intQuotient);

        float smallFloat = 5;
        float largeFloat = 12;
        float FloatQuotient;
```

Example 7-1. Integer and float division (continued)

```
        FloatQuotient = largeFloat / smallFloat;
        Console.WriteLine("Dividing floats. {0} / {1} = {2}",
            largeFloat, smallFloat, FloatQuotient);


    }
}
```
Output:
```
Dividing integers. 12 / 5 = 2
Dividing floats. 12 / 5 = 2.4
```

C# provides a special operator, modulus (%), to retrieve the remainder from integer division.

Using the modulus Operator (%) to Return Remainders

To find the remainder in integer division, use the modulus operator (%). For example, the statement 17%4 returns 1 (the remainder after integer division).

Example 7-2 demonstrates the effect of division on integers, floats, doubles, and decimals.

Writeline Control Characters

Consider this line from Example 7-2:
```
Console.WriteLine("Integer:\t{0}\nfloat:\t\t{1}\n",
    firstInt/secondInt, firstFloat/secondFloat);
```
It begins with a call to Console.Writeline(), passing in this partial string:
```
"Integer:\t{0}\n
```
This will print the characters Integer: followed by a tab (\t), the first parameter ({0}), and a newline character (\n). The next string snippet:
```
float:\t\t{1}\n
```
is very similar. It prints float:, followed by two tabs (to ensure alignment), the contents of the second parameter ({1}), and then another newline. Notice the subsequent line, as well:
```
Console.WriteLine(
    "\nRemainder(modulus) from integer division:\t{0}",
        firstInt%secondInt);
```
This time the string begins with a newline character, which causes a line to be skipped just before the string Modulus: is printed. You can see this effect in the output.

Example 7-2. Modulus and integer division

```
using System;
class Values
{
    static void Main()
    {
        int firstInt, secondInt;
        float firstFloat, secondFloat;
        double firstDouble, secondDouble;
        decimal firstDecimal, secondDecimal;

        firstInt = 17;
        secondInt = 4;
        firstFloat = 17;
        secondFloat = 4;
        firstDouble = 17;
        secondDouble = 4;
        firstDecimal = 17;
        secondDecimal = 4;
        Console.WriteLine("Integer:\t{0}\nfloat:\t\t{1}",
            firstInt/secondInt, firstFloat/secondFloat);
        Console.WriteLine("double:\t\t{0}\ndecimal:\t{1}",
            firstDouble/secondDouble, firstDecimal/secondDecimal);
        Console.WriteLine(
          "\nRemainder(modulus) from integer division:\t{0}",
            firstInt%secondInt);

    }
}
```
Output:
```
Integer:        4
float:          4.25
double:         4.25
decimal:        4.25

Remainder(modulus) from integer division:      1
```

The modulus operator turns out to be more useful than you might at first imagine. When you perform modulus *n* on a number that is a multiple of *n*, the result is zero. Thus 80%10=0 because 80 is an even multiple of 10. This fact allows you to set up loops in which you take an action every *n*th time through the loop, by testing a counter to see if %n is equal to zero, as illustrated in Example 7-3.

Example 7-3. Modulus operator (%)

```
using System;
public class Tester
{

    public static int Main()
    {
        for (int counter=1; counter<=100; counter++)
        {
```

Example 7-3. Modulus operator (%) (continued)

```
        Console.Write("{0} ", counter);

        if ( counter % 10 == 0 )
        {
            Console.WriteLine("\t{0}", counter);
        }
    }
    return 0;
  }
}
```
Output:
```
1 2 3 4 5 6 7 8 9 10      10
11 12 13 14 15 16 17 18 19 20    20
21 22 23 24 25 26 27 28 29 30    30
31 32 33 34 35 36 37 38 39 40    40
41 42 43 44 45 46 47 48 49 50    50
51 52 53 54 55 56 57 58 59 60    60
61 62 63 64 65 66 67 68 69 70    70
71 72 73 74 75 76 77 78 79 80    80
81 82 83 84 85 86 87 88 89 90    90
91 92 93 94 95 96 97 98 99 100   100
```

In Example 7-3, the value of the counter variable is incremented each time through the loop. Within the loop, the value of counter is compared with the result of modulus 10 (counter % 10). When this evaluates to zero, the value of counter is evenly divisible by 10, and the value is printed in the right-hand column.

Increment and Decrement Operators

A common requirement is to add a value to a variable, subtract a value from a variable, or otherwise change the mathematical value, and then to assign that new value back to the original variable.

Calculate and Reassign Operators

Suppose you want to increment the mySalary variable by 5000. You can do this by writing:

```
mySalary = mySalary + 5000;
```

In simple arithmetic, this would make no sense, but in C# this line means "add 5000 to the value in mySalary, and assign the sum back to mySalary." Thus, after this operation completes, mySalary will have been incremented by 5000. You can perform this kind of assignment with any mathematical operator:

```
mySalary = mySalary * 5000;
mySalary = mySalary - 5000;
```

and so forth.

The need to perform this kind of manipulation is so common that C# includes special operators for self-assignment. Among these operators are +=, -=, *=, /=, and %=, which, respectively, combine addition, subtraction, multiplication, division, and modulus, with self-assignment. Thus, you can write the previous examples as:

```
mySalary += 5000;
mySalary *= 5000;
mySalary -= 5000;
```

These three instructions, respectively, increment mySalary by 5000, multiply mySalary by 5000, and subtract 5000 from the mySalary variable.

Increment or Decrement by 1

Because incrementing and decrementing by exactly 1 is a very common need, C# provides two additional special operators for these purposes: increment (++) and decrement (--).

Thus, if you want to increment the variable myAge by 1 you can write:

```
myAge++;
```

The Prefix and Postfix Operators

To complicate matters further, you might want to increment a variable and assign the results to a second variable:

```
resultingValue = originalValue++;
```

The question arises: do you want to assign before you increment the value or after? In other words, if originalValue starts out with the value 10, do you want to end with both resultingValue and originalValue equal to 11, or do you want resultingValue to be equal to 10 (the original value) and originalValue to be equal to 11?

C# offer two specialized ways to use the increment and decrement operators: prefix and postfix. The way you use the ++ operator determines the order in which the increment/decrement and assignment take place. The semantics of the prefix increment operator is "increment the original value, and then assign the incremented value to result" while the semantics of the postfix increment operator is "assign the original value to result, and then increment original."

To use the prefix operator to increment, place the ++ symbol before the variable name; to use the postfix operator to increment, place the ++ symbol after the variable name.

```
result = ++original; // prefix
result = original++; // postfix
```

It is important to understand the different effects of prefix and postfix, as illustrated in Example 7-4. Note the output.

Example 7-4. Prefix and postfix operators

```
using System;
class Values
{
    static void Main()
    {
        int original = 10;
        int result;

        // increment then assign
        result = ++original;
        Console.WriteLine("After prefix: {0}, {1}", original,
            result);

        // assign then increment
        result = original++;
        Console.WriteLine("After postfix: {0}, {1}",
            original, result);
    }
}
After prefix: 11, 11
After postfix: 12, 11
```

The prefix and postfix operators can be applied, with the same logic, to the decrement operators, as shown in Example 7-5. Again, note the output.

Example 7-5. Decrementing prefix and postfix

```
using System;
class Values
{
    static void Main()
    {
        int original = 10;
        int result;

        // increment then assign
        result = --original;
        Console.WriteLine("After prefix: {0}, {1}", original,
            result);

        // assign then increment
        result = original--;
        Console.WriteLine("After postfix: {0}, {1}",
            original, result);
    }
}
```

Output:
```
After prefix: 9, 9
After postfix: 8, 9
```

Relational Operators

Relational operators compare two values and then return a Boolean value (true or false). The greater-than operator (>), for example, returns true if the value on the left of the operator is greater than the value on the right. Thus, 5>2 returns the value true, while 2>5 returns the value false.

The relational operators for C# are shown in Table 7-1. This table assumes two variables: bigValue and smallValue, in which bigValue has been assigned the value 100 and smallValue the value 50.

Table 7-1. C# relational operators (assumes bigValue = 100 and smallValue = 50)

Name	Operator	Given this statement	The expression evaluates to
Equals	==	bigValue == 100	True
		bigValue == 80	False
Not Equals	!=	bigValue != 100	False
		bigValue != 80	True
Greater than	>	bigValue > smallValue	True
Greater than or equal to	>=	bigValue >= smallValue	True
		smallValue >= bigValue	False
Less than	<	bigValue < smallValue	False
Less than or equal to	<=	smallValue <= bigValue	True
		bigValue <= smallValue	False

Each of these relational operators acts as you might expect. Notice that most of these operators are composed of two characters. For example, the greater than or equal to operator (>=) is created with the greater than symbol (>) and the equal sign (=). Notice also that the equals operator is created with two equal signs (==) because the single equal sign alone (=) is reserved for the assignment operator.

 It is not uncommon to confuse the assignment operator (=) with the equals operator (==). Just remember that the latter has two equal signs, the former only one.

The C# equals operator (==) tests for equality between the objects on either side of the operator. This operator evaluates to a Boolean value (true or false). Thus, the statement:

```
myX == 5;
```

evaluates to true if and only if the myX variable has a value of 5.

Use of Logical Operators with Conditionals

If statements (discussed in Chapter 6) test whether a condition is true. Often you will want to test whether two conditions are both true, only one is true, or neither is true. C# provides a set of logical operators for this, shown in Table 7-2. The examples in this table assume two variables, x and y, in which x has the value 5 and y the value 7.

Table 7-2. Logical operators

Name	Operator	Given this statement	The expression evaluates to	Logic
And	&&	(x == 3) && (y == 7)	False	Both must be true
Or	||	(x == 3) || (y == 7)	True	Either or both must be true
Not	!	! (x == 3)	True	Expression must be false

The and operator tests whether two statements are both true. The first line in Table 7-2 includes an example that illustrates the use of the and operator:

    (x == 3) && (y == 7)

The entire expression evaluates false because one side (x == 3) is false. (Remember that x=5 and y=7.)

With the or operator, either or both sides must be true; the expression is false only if both sides are false. So, in the case of the example in Table 7-2:

    (x == 3) || (y == 7)

the entire expression evaluates true because one side (y==7) is true.

With a not operator, the statement is true if the expression is false, and vice versa. So, in the accompanying example:

    ! (x == 3)

the entire expression is true because the tested expression (x==3) is false. (The logic is: "it is true that it is not true that x is equal to 3.")

The Conditional Operator

Although most operators are unary (require one term, e.g., myValue++) or binary (two terms, e.g., a+b), there is one ternary (three terms) operator: the conditional operator (?:).

    cond-expr ? expression1 : expression2

This operator evaluates a *conditional* expression (an expression that returns a value of type bool) and then invokes either *expression1* if the value returned from the conditional expression is true, or *expression2* if the value returned is false. The logic is: "if this is true, do the first; otherwise do the second." Example 7-6 illustrates.

Example 7-6. The ternary operator

```
using System;
class Values
{
    static void Main()
    {
        int valueOne = 10;
        int valueTwo = 20;

        int maxValue = valueOne > valueTwo ?  valueOne : valueTwo;

        Console.WriteLine("ValueOne: {0}, valueTwo: {1}, maxValue: {2}",
            valueOne, valueTwo, maxValue);

    }
}
```
Output:
```
ValueOne: 10,  valueTwo: 20,  maxValue: 20
```

In Example 7-6, the ternary operator is being used to test whether valueOne is greater than valueTwo. If so, the value of valueOne is assigned to the integer variable maxValue; otherwise the value of valueTwo is assigned to maxValue.

Short-Circuit Evaluation

Consider the following code snippet:

```
int x = 8;
if ((x == 8) || (y == 12))
```

The if statement here is a bit complicated. The entire if statement is in parentheses, as are all if statements in C#. Thus, everything within the outer set of parentheses must evaluate true for the if statement to be true.

Within the outer parentheses are two expressions, (x == 8) and (y == 12), which are separated by an or operator (||). Because x is 8, the first term (x == 8) evaluates true. There is no need to evaluate the second term (y == 12). It doesn't matter whether y is 12; the entire expression will be true. Similarly, consider this snippet:

```
int x = 8;
if ((x == 5) && (y == 12))
```

Again, there is no need to evaluate the second term. Because the first term is false, the and must fail. (Remember, for an and statement to evaluate true, both tested expressions must evaluate true.)

In cases such as these, the C# compiler will short-circuit the evaluation; the second test will never be performed.

Operator Precedence

The compiler must know the order in which to evaluate a series of operators. For example, if I write:

```
myVariable = 5 + 7 * 3;
```

there are three operators for the compiler to evaluate (=, +, and *). It could, for example, operate left to right, which would assign the value 5 to myVariable, then add 7 to the 5 (12) and multiply by 3 (36)—but of course then it would throw that 36 away. This is clearly not what is intended.

The rules of precedence tell the compiler which operators to evaluate first. As is the case in algebra, multiplication has higher precedence than addition, so 5+7*3 is equal to 26 rather than 36. Both addition and multiplication have higher precedence than assignment, so the compiler will do the math and then assign the result (26) to myVariable only after the math is completed.

In C#, parentheses are also used to change the order of precedence much as they are in algebra. Thus, you can change the result by writing:

```
myVariable = (5+7) * 3;
```

Grouping the elements of the assignment in this way causes the compiler to add 5+7, multiply the result by 3, and then assign that value (36) to myVariable.

Table 7-3 summarizes operator precedence in C#, using x and y as possible terms to be operated upon.[*]

Table 7-3. Precedence

Category	Operators
Primary	(x) x.y x->y f(x) a[x] x++ x-- new typeof sizeof checked unchecked stackalloc
Unary	+ - ! ~ ++x --x (T)x *x &x
Multiplicative	* / %
Additive	+ -
Shift	<< >>
Relational	< > <= >= is as
Equality	== !=
Logical AND	&
Logical XOR	^
Logical OR	|
Conditional AND	&&

[*] See my more advanced book Programming C#, Second Edition (O'Reilly) for more information on the more obscure operators.

Table 7-3. Precedence (continued)

Category	Operators
Conditional OR	||
Conditional	?:
Assignment	= *= /= %= += -= <<= >>= &= ^= |=

The operators are listed in precedence order according to the category in which they fit. That is, the primary operators (e.g., ++) are evaluated before the unary operators (e.g., !). Multiplication is evaluated before addition.

In some complex equations, you might need to nest parentheses to ensure the proper order of operations. For example, assume I want to know how many seconds my family wastes each morning. The adults spend 20 minutes over coffee each morning and 10 minutes reading the newspaper. The children waste 30 minutes dawdling and 10 minutes arguing.

Here's my algorithm:

```
(((minDrinkingCoffee  + minReadingNewspaper )* numAdults ) +
((minDawdling + minArguing) * numChildren)) * secondsPerMinute.
```

Although this works, it is hard to read and hard to get right. It's much easier to use interim variables:

```
wastedByEachAdult = minDrinkingCoffee  +  minReadingNewspaper;
wastedByAllAdults =  wastedByEachAdult * numAdults;
wastedByEachKid =  minDawdling  + minArguing;
wastedByAllKids =  wastedByEachKid * numChildren;
wastedByFamily = wastedByAllAdults + wastedByAllKids;
totalSeconds =  wastedByFamily * 60;
```

The latter example uses many more interim variables, but it is far easier to read, understand, and (most importantly) debug. As you step through this program in your debugger, you can see the interim values and make sure they are correct. See Chapter 10 for more information.

CHAPTER 8

Classes and Objects

Chapter 5 discusses the intrinsic types, built into the C# language. As you may recall, these simple types allow you to hold and manipulate numeric values and strings. The true power of C#, however, lies in its capacity to let the programmer define new types to suit particular problems. It is this ability to create new types that characterizes an object-oriented language. You specify new types in C# by declaring and defining classes.

Particular instances of a class are called objects. The difference between a class and an object is the same as the difference between the concept of a Dog and the particular dog who is sitting at your feet as you read this. You can't play fetch with the definition of a Dog, only with an instance.

A Dog class describes what dogs are like; they have weight, height, eye color, hair color, disposition, and so forth. They also have actions they can take, such as eat, walk, bark, and sleep. A particular dog (such as my dog Milo) will have a specific weight (62 pounds), height (22 inches), eye color (black), hair color (yellow), disposition (angelic), and so forth. He is capable of all the actions—methods, in programming parlance—of any dog (though if you knew him you might imagine that eating is the only method he implements).

The huge advantage of classes in object-oriented programming is that classes encapsulate the characteristics and capabilities of a type in a single, self-contained unit.

Suppose, for instance, you want to sort the contents of an instance of a Windows listbox control. The listbox control is defined as a class. One of the properties of that class is that it knows how to sort itself. Sorting is encapsulated within the class, and the details of how the listbox sorts itself are not made visible to other classes. If you want a listbox sorted, you just tell the listbox to sort itself, and it takes care of the details.

So, you simply write a method that tells the listbox to sort itself—and that's what happens. How it sorts is of no concern; that it does so is all you need to know.

As noted in Chapter 3, this is called encapsulation, which, along with polymorphism and inheritance, is one of three cardinal principles of object-oriented programming. Chapter 11 discusses polymorphism and inheritance.

An old programming joke asks, how many object-oriented programmers does it take to change a light bulb? Answer: none, you just tell the light bulb to change itself.* This chapter explains the C# language features that are used to specify new classes. The elements of a class—its behaviors and its state—are known collectively as its *class members*.

Class behavior is created by writing methods (sometimes called member functions). A method is a small routine that every object of the class can execute. For example, a Dog class might have a bark method, and a listbox class might have a sort method.

Class state is maintained by fields (sometimes called member variables). Fields may be primitive types (e.g., an int to hold the age of the dog or a set of strings to hold the contents of the listbox), or fields may be objects of other classes (e.g., an Employee class may have a field of type Address).

Finally, classes may also have properties, which act like methods to the creator of the class, but look like fields to clients of the class. A client is any object that interacts with instances of the class.

Defining Classes

When you define a new class, you define the characteristics of all objects of that class, as well as their behaviors. For example, if you create your own windowing operating system, you might want to create screen widgets, (known as a control in Windows). One control of interest might be a listbox, a control that is very useful for presenting a list of choices to the user and enabling the user to select from the list.

Listboxes have a variety of characteristics: height, width, location, and text color, for example. Programmers have also come to expect certain behaviors of listboxes—they can be opened, closed, sorted, and so on.

Object-oriented programming allows you to create a new type, ListBox, which encapsulates these characteristics and capabilities.

To define a new type or class, you first declare it and then define its methods and fields. You declare a class using the class keyword. The complete syntax is as follows:

```
[attributes] [access-modifiers] class identifier [:base-class]
{class-body}
```

---

* Alternative answer: none, Microsoft has changed the standard to darkness.

Attributes are used to provide special metadata about a class (that is, information about the structure or use of the class). You will not need attributes for routine C# programming.

Access modifiers are discussed later in this chapter. (Typically, your classes will use the keyword public as an access modifier.)

The *identifier* is the name of the class that you provide. Typically, C# classes are named with nouns (e.g., Dog, Employee, ListBox). The naming convention (not required, but strongly encouraged) is to use Pascal notation. In Pascal notation, you don't use underbars or hyphens, but if the name has two words (Golden Retriever) you push the two words together, each word beginning with an uppercase letter (GoldenRetriever).

As mentioned earlier, inheritance is one of the pillars of object-oriented programming. The optional *base-class* is explained when inheritance is discussed in Chapter 11.

The member definitions that make up the *class-body* are enclosed by open and closed curly braces ({}).

```
class Dog
{
    int age;  // the dog's age
    int weight;  // the dog's weight
    Bark() { //… }
    Eat() { // … }
}
```

Methods within the class definition of Dog describe all the things a dog can do. The fields (member variables) such as age and weight describe all the dog's attributes or state.

Instantiating Objects

To make an actual instance, or object, of the Dog class, you must declare the object and allocate memory for the object. These two steps combined are necessary to create, or *instantiate*, the object. Here's how you do it.

First, you declare the object by writing the name of the class (Dog) followed by an identifier (name) for the object or instance of that class:

```
Dog milo;  // declare milo to be an instance of Dog
```

This is not unlike the way you create a local variable; you declare the type (in this case Dog) followed by the identifier (milo). Notice also that (as with variables) by convention the identifier for the object uses Camel Notation. Camel Notation is just like Pascal Notation except that the very first letter is lowercase. Thus, a variable or object name might be myDog, designatedDriver, or plantManager.

The declaration alone doesn't actually create an instance, however. To create an instance of a class you must also allocate memory for the object using the keyword new.

```
milo = new Dog();  // allocate memory for milo
```

You can combine the declaration of the Dog type with the memory allocation into a single line:

```
Dog milo = new Dog();
```

This code declares milo to be an object of type Dog and also creates a new instance of Dog. You'll see what the parentheses are for later in this chapter in the discussion of the constructor.

In C#, *everything* happens within a class. No methods can run outside of a class, not even Main(). The Main() method is the entry point for your program; it is called by the operating system, and it is where execution of your program begins. Typically, you'll create a small class to house Main(), because like every method, Main() must live within a class. Some of the examples in this book use of a class named Tester to house Main():

```
public class Tester
{
    public static void Main()
    {
      //...
    }
}
```

Even though Tester was created to house the Main() method, you've not yet instantiated any objects of type Tester. To do so you would write:

```
Tester myTester = new Tester(); // instantiate an object of type Tester
```

As you'll see later in this chapter, creating an instance of the Tester class allows you to call other methods on the object you've created (myTester).

Classes versus objects

One way to understand the difference between a class and an instance (object) is to consider the distinction between the type int and a variable of type int.

You can't assign a value to a type:

```
int = 5;  // error
```

Instead, you assign a value to an object of that type (in this case, a variable of type int):

```
int myInteger;
myInteger = 5; // ok
```

Similarly, you can't assign values to fields in a class; you must assign values to fields in an object. Thus, you can't write:

```
Dog.weight = 5;
```

This is not meaningful. It isn't true that every dog's weight is 5 pounds. You must instead write:

```
milo.weight = 5;
```

This says that a particular dog's weight (milo's weight) is 5 pounds.

Memory Allocation: The Stack Versus the Heap

Objects created within methods are called local variables. They are local to the method, as opposed to belonging to the object, as member variables do. The object is created within the method, used within the method, and then destroyed when the method ends. Local objects are not part of the object's state—they are temporary value holders, useful only within the particular method.

Local variables of intrinsic types such as int are created on a portion of memory known as *the stack*. The stack is allocated and de-allocated as methods are invoked. When you start a method, all the local variables are created on the stack. When the method ends, local variables are destroyed.

These variables are referred to as local because they exist (and are visible) only during the lifetime of the method. They are said to have *local scope*. When the method ends, the variable goes out of scope and is destroyed.

C# divides the world of types into value types and reference types. Value types are created on the stack. All the intrinsic types (int, long, etc.) are value types, and thus are created on the stack.

Classes, on the other hand, are reference types. Reference types are created on an undifferentiated block of memory known as *the heap*. When you declare an instance of a reference type, what you are actually declaring is a reference, which is a variable that refers to another object. The reference acts like an alias for the object.

That is, when you write:

```
Dog milo = new Dog();
```

the new operator creates a Dog object on the heap and returns a reference to it. That reference is assigned to milo. Thus, milo is a reference object that refers to a Dog object on the heap. It is common to say that milo is a reference to a dog, or even that milo is a Dog object, but technically that is incorrect. milo is actually a reference object that refers to an (unnamed) Dog object on the heap.

The reference milo acts as an alias for that unnamed object. For all practical purposes, however, you can treat milo as if it were the Dog object itself.

The implication of using references is that you can have more than one reference to the same object. To see this difference between creating value types and reference types, examine Example 8-1. A complete analysis follows the output.

Example 8-1. Creating value types and reference types

```
using System;

namespace heap
{
    public class Dog
    {
        public int weight;
    }

    class Tester
    {
        public void Run()
        {
            // create an integer
            int firstInt = 5;

            // create a second integer
            int secondInt = firstInt;

            // display the two integers
            Console.WriteLine("firstInt: {0} secondInt: {1}",
                firstInt, secondInt);

            // modify the second integer
            secondInt = 7;

            // display the two integers
            Console.WriteLine("firstInt: {0} secondInt: {1}",
                firstInt, secondInt);

            // create a dog
            Dog milo = new Dog();

            // assign a value to weight
            milo.weight = 5;

            // create a second reference to the dog
            Dog fido = milo;

            // display their values
            Console.WriteLine("Milo: {0}, fido: {1}",
                milo.weight, fido.weight);

            // assign a new weight to the second reference
            fido.weight = 7;

            // display the two values
```

Example 8-1. Creating value types and reference types (continued)

```
        Console.WriteLine("Milo: {0}, fido: {1}",
            milo.weight, fido.weight);
    }

    static void Main()
    {
        Tester t = new Tester();
        t.Run();
    }
  }
}
```
Output:
```
firstInt: 5 secondInt: 5
firstInt: 5 secondInt: 7
Milo: 5, fido: 5
Milo: 7, fido: 7
```

The program begins by creating an integer, firstInt, and initializing it with the value 5. The second integer, secondInt, is then created and initialized with the value in firstInt. Their values are displayed as output:

```
firstInt: 5 secondInt: 5
```

These values are identical. Because int is a value type, a copy of the firstInt value is made and assigned to secondInt; secondInt is an independent second variable, as illustrated in Figure 8-1.

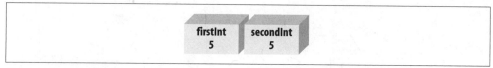

Figure 8-1. secondInt is a copy of firstInt

Then the program assigns a new value to secondInt:

```
secondInt = 7;
```

Because these variables are value types, independent of one another, the first variable is unaffected. Only the copy is changed, as illustrated in Figure 8-2.

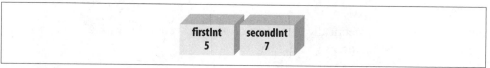

Figure 8-2. Only the copy is changed

When the values are displayed, they are different:

```
firstInt: 5 secondInt: 7
```

Your next step is to create a simple Dog class with only one member variable (field) called weight. Note that this field is given a keyword, public, which specifies that any method of any class can access this field. public is what is known as an *access modifier*. (Generally you will not make member variables public. The weight field was made public to simplify this example.) Access modifiers are covered in detail later in this chapter.

You instantiate a Dog object and save a reference to that dog in the reference milo.

```
Dog milo = new Dog();
```

You assign the value 5 to milo's weight field:

```
milo.weight = 5;
```

You commonly say that you've set milo's weight to 5, but actually you've set the weight of the unnamed object on the heap to which milo refers, as shown in Figure 8-3.

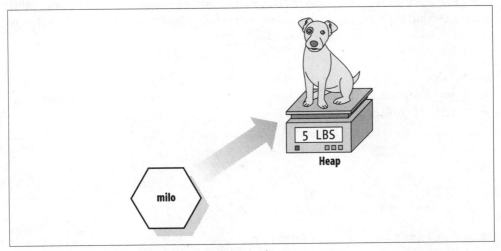

Figure 8-3. milo is a reference to an unnamed Dog object

Next you create a second reference to Dog and initialize it by setting it equal to milo. This creates a new reference to the same object on the heap.

```
Dog fido = milo;
```

Notice that this is syntactically similar to creating a second int variable and initializing it with an existing int, as you did before:

```
int secondInt = firstInt;
Dog fido     = milo;
```

The difference is that Dog is a reference type, so fido is not a copy of milo—it is a second reference to the same object to which milo refers. That is, you now have an object on the heap with two references to it, as illustrated in Figure 8-4.

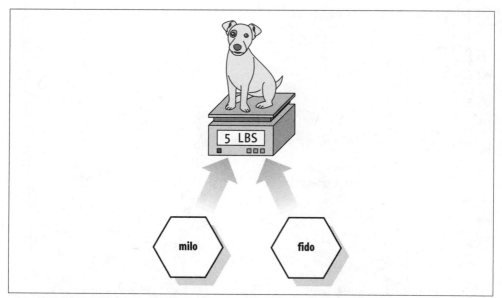

Figure 8-4. fido is a second reference to the Dog object

When you change the weight of that object through the fido reference:

```
fido.weight = 7;
```

you change the weight of the same object to which milo refers. The output reflects this:

```
Milo: 7, fido: 7
```

It isn't that fido is changing milo, it is that by changing the (unnamed) object on the heap to which fido refers, you simultaneously change the value of milo because they refer to the same unnamed object.

Creating a Time Class

Now consider a class to keep track of and display the time of day. The internal state of the class must be able to represent the current year, month, date, hour, minute, and second. You probably would also like the class to display the time in a variety of formats.

You might implement such a class by defining a single method and six variables, as shown in Example 8-2.

Example 8-2. The Time class

```
using System;

public class Time
{
    // private variables
```

Example 8-2. The Time class (continued)

```csharp
    private int year;
    private int month;
    private int date;
    private int hour;
    private int minute;
    private int second;

    // public methods
    public void DisplayCurrentTime()
    {
        Console.WriteLine(
            "stub for DisplayCurrentTime");
    }
}

public class Tester
{
    static void Main()
    {
        Time timeObject = new Time();
        timeObject.DisplayCurrentTime();
    }

}
```

This code creates a new user-defined type: Time. The Time class definition begins with the declaration of a number of member variables: Year, Month, Date, Hour, Minute, and Second.

The keyword private indicates that these values can only be called by methods of this class. The private keyword is an access modifier, explained later in this chapter.

 Many C# programmers prefer to put all of the member fields together, either at the very top or the very bottom of the class declaration, though that is not required by the language.

The only method declared within the Time class is the method DisplayCurrent-Time(). The DisplayCurrentTime() method is defined to return void; that is, it will not return a value to the method that invokes it. For now, the body of this method has been "stubbed out."

Stubbing out a method is a temporary measure you might use when you first write a program to allow you to think about the overall structure without filling in every detail when you create a class. When you stub out a method body you leave out the internal logic and just mark the method, perhaps with a message to the console:

```csharp
    public void DisplayCurrentTime()
    {
        Console.WriteLine(
```

```
             "stub for DisplayCurrentTime");
    }
```

After the closing brace, a second class, Tester, is defined. Tester contains our now familiar Main() method. In Main() an instance of Time is created, named timeObject.

```
Time timeObject = new Time();
```

Technically, an unnamed instance of Time is created on the heap and a reference to that object is returned and used to initialize the Time reference named timeObject. Because that is cumbersome, we'll simply say that a Time instance named timeObject was created.

Because timeObject is an instance of Time, Main() can make use of the DisplayCurrentTime() method available with objects of that type and call it to display the time:

```
timeObject.DisplayCurrentTime();
```

You invoke a method on an object by writing the name of the object (timeObject) followed by the dot operator (.), the method name (DisplayCurrentTime), and the parameter list in parentheses (in this case, empty). You'll see how to pass in values to initialize the member variables in the discussion of constructors, later in this chapter.

Access Modifiers

An access modifier determines which class methods—including methods of other classes—can see and use a member variable or method within a class. Table 8-1 summarizes the C# access modifiers.

Table 8-1. Access modifiers

Access modifier	Restrictions
public	No restrictions. Members that are marked public are visible to any method of any class.
private	The members in class A that are marked private are accessible only to methods of class A.
protected	The members in class A that are marked protected are accessible to methods of class A and also to methods of classes derived from class A. The protected access modifier is used with derived classes, as explained in Chapter 11.
internal	The members in class A that are marked internal are accessible to methods of any class in A's assembly.[a]
protected internal	The members in class A that are marked protected internal are accessible to methods of class A, to methods of classes derived from class A, and also to any class in A's assembly. This is effectively protected or internal; there is no concept of protected and internal.

[a] An assembly is a collection of files that appear to the programmer as a single executable or DLL.

Public methods are part of the class's public interface: they define how this class behaves. Private methods are "helper methods" used by the public methods to accomplish the work of the class. Because the internal workings of the class are private, helper methods need not (and should not) be exposed to other classes.

The Time class and its method DisplayCurrentTime() are both declared public so that any other class can make use of them. If DisplayCurrentTime() had been private, it would not be possible to invoke DisplayCurrentTime from any method of any class other than methods of Time. In Example 8-2, DisplayCurrentTime was invoked from a method of Tester (not Time), and this was legal because both the class (Time) and the method (DisplayCurrentTime) were marked public.

 It is good programming practice to explicitly set the accessibility of all methods and members of your class. Although you can rely on the fact that class members are declared private by default, making their access explicit indicates a conscious decision and is self-documenting.

Method Arguments

The behavior of a class is defined by the methods of that class. To make your methods as flexible as possible, you can define parameters: information passed into the method when the method is invoked. Thus, rather than having to write one method when you want to sort your listbox from A-Z and a second method when you want to sort it from Z-A, you define a more general Sort() method and pass in a parameter specifying the order of the sort.

Methods can take any number of parameters.* The parameter list follows the method name and is enclosed in parentheses. Each parameter's type is identified before the name of the parameter.

For example, the following declaration defines a method named MyMethod() that returns void (that is, it returns no value at all) and takes two parameters (an int and a button):

```
void MyMethod (int firstParam, button secondParam)
{
  // ...
}
```

Within the body of the method, the parameters act as local variables, as if you had declared them in the body of the method and initialized them with the values passed in. Example 8-3 illustrates how you pass values into a method, in this case values of type int and float.

---

* The terms "argument" and "parameter" are often used interchangeably, though some programmers insist on differentiating between the parameter declaration and the arguments passed in when the method is invoked.

Example 8-3. Passing parameters

```
using System;

public class MyClass
{
    public void SomeMethod(int firstParam, float secondParam)
    {
        Console.WriteLine(
            "Here are the parameters received: {0}, {1}",
            firstParam, secondParam);
    }

}

public class Tester
{
    static void Main()
    {
        int howManyPeople = 5;
        float pi = 3.14f;
        MyClass mc = new MyClass();
        mc.SomeMethod(howManyPeople, pi);
    }
}
```
Output:
```
Here are the parameters received: 5, 3.14
```

Note that when you pass in a float with a decimal part (3.14) you must append the letter f (3.14f) to signal to the compiler that the value is a float and not a double.

The method SomeMethod() takes two parameters, firstParam and secondParam, and displays them using Console.WriteLine(). FirstParam is an int, and secondParam is a float. These parameters are treated as local variables within SomeMethod(). You can manipulate these values within the method, but they "go out of scope" and are destroyed when the method ends.

In the calling method (Main), two local variables (howManyPeople and pi) are created and initialized. These variables are passed as the parameters to SomeMethod(). The compiler maps howManyPeople to firstParam and pi to secondParam, based on their relative positions in the parameter list.

Constructors

In Example 8-2, notice that the statement that creates the Time object looks as though it is invoking a Time() method:

```
Time timeObject = new Time();
```

In fact, a member method *is* invoked whenever you instantiate an object. This method is called a *constructor*. Each time you define a class, you are free to define your own constructor, but if you don't, the compiler will provide one for you invisibly and automatically.

The job of a constructor is to create an instance of the object specified by a class and to put it into a valid state. Before the constructor runs, the object is just a blob of memory; after the constructor completes, the memory holds a valid instance of the class.

The Time class of Example 8-3 does not define a constructor. As noted earlier, if you do not declare a constructor the compiler implicitly provides one for you. The constructor provided by the compiler creates the object but takes no other action.

 Any constructor that takes no arguments is called a *default constructor*. The constructor provided by the compiler takes no arguments, and hence is a default constructor. This terminology has caused a great deal of confusion. You can create your own default constructor, and if you do not create a constructor at all, the compiler will create a default constructor for you, by default.

If you do not explicitly initialize your member variables, they are initialized to innocuous values (integers to 0, strings to the empty string, etc.). Table 8-2 lists the default values assigned to various types.

Table 8-2. Primitive types and their default values

Type	Default value
numeric (int, long, etc.)	0
bool	false
char	'\0' (null)
enum	0
reference	null

Typically, you'll want to define your own constructor and provide it with arguments, so that the constructor can set the initial state for your object. In Example 8-4, you want to pass in the current year, month, date, and so forth, so that the object is created with meaningful data.

You declare a constructor like any other member method except:

- The name of the constructor must be the same as the name of the class.
- Constructors have no return type (not even void).

If there are arguments to be passed, you define an argument list just as you would for any other method. Example 8-4 declares a constructor for the Time class that accepts a single argument, an object of type DateTime. DateTime is a type provided by the .NET Framework Class Library.

Example 8-4. Creating a constructor

```
using System;

public class Time
{
    // private member variables
    int year;
    int month;
    int date;
    int hour;
    int minute;
    int second;

    // public method
    public void DisplayCurrentTime()
    {
        System.Console.WriteLine("{0}/{1}/{2} {3}:{4}:{5}",
            month, date, year, hour, minute, second);
    }

    // constructor
    public Time(int theYear, int theMonth, int theDate,
        int theHour, int theMinute, int theSecond)
    {
        year = theYear;
        month = theMonth;
        date = theDate;
        hour = theHour;
        minute = theMinute;
        second = theSecond;
    }
}

public class Tester
{
    static void Main()
    {
        Time timeObject = new Time(2005,3,25,9,35,20);
        timeObject.DisplayCurrentTime();
    }
}
```

Output:
3/25/2005 9:35:20

In this example, the constructor takes a series of integer values and initializes all the member variables based on these parameters.

When the constructor finishes, the Time object exists and the values have been initialized. When DisplayCurrentTime() is called in Main(), the values are displayed.

Try commenting out one of the assignments and running the program again. You'll find that each member variable is initialized by the compiler to 0. Integer member variables are set to 0 if you don't otherwise assign them. Remember that value types (e.g., integers) must be initialized; if you don't tell the constructor what to do, it sets innocuous values.

Initializers

It is possible to initialize the values of member variables in an *initializer*, instead of having to do so in the constructor. You create an initializer by assigning an initial value to a class member:

```
private int Second  = 30;  // initializer
```

Assume that the semantics of the Time object are such that no matter what time is set, the seconds are always initialized to 30. You might rewrite your Time class to use an initializer so that the value of Second is always initialized, as shown in Example 8-5.

Example 8-5. Using an initializer

```
using System;

public class Time
{
    // private member variables
    int year;
    int month;
    int date;
    int hour;
    int minute;
    int second = 30;

    // public method
    public void DisplayCurrentTime()
    {
        System.Console.WriteLine("{0}/{1}/{2} {3}:{4}:{5}",
            month, date, year, hour, minute, second);
    }

    // constructor
    public Time(int theYear, int theMonth, int theDate,
        int theHour, int theMinute)
    {
        year = theYear;
        month = theMonth;
        date = theDate;
        hour = theHour;
```

Example 8-5. Using an initializer (continued)

```
        minute = theMinute;
    }
}

public class Tester
{
    static void Main()
    {
        Time timeObject = new Time(2005,3,25,9,35);
        timeObject.DisplayCurrentTime();
    }
}
```
Output:
3/25/2005 9:35:30

If you do not provide a specific initializer, the constructor initializes each integer member variable to zero (0). In the case shown, however, the Second member is initialized to 30:

```
    private int Second  = 30;  // initializer
```

Later in this chapter you will see that you can have more than one constructor. If you initialize Second to 30 in more than one of these, you can avoid the problem of having to keep all the constructors consistent with one another by initializing the Second member, rather than assigning 30 in each of the constructors.

Copy Constructors

A *copy constructor* creates a new object by copying variables from an existing object of the same type. For example, you might want to pass a Time object to a Time constructor so that the new Time object has the same values as the old one.

C# does not provide a copy constructor, so if you want one you must provide it yourself. Such a constructor copies the elements from the original object into the new one:

```
    public Time(Time existingTimeObject)
    {
        year = existingTimeObject.year;
        month = existingTimeObject.month;
        date = existingTimeObject.date;
        hour = existingTimeObject.hour;
        minute = existingTimeObject.minute;
        second = existingTimeObject.second;
    }
```

A copy constructor is invoked by instantiating an object of type Time and passing it the name of the Time object to be copied:

```
    Time newCopy = new Time(existingTimeObject);
```

Here an existing Time object (existingTimeObject) is passed as a parameter to the copy constructor which will create a new Time object (newCopy).

The this Keyword

The keyword this refers to the current instance of an object. The this reference is a hidden parameter in every nonstatic method of a class (static methods are discussed later in this chapter). There are three ways in which the this reference is typically used. The first way is to qualify instance members that have the same name as parameters, as in the following:

```
public void SomeMethod (int hour)
{
    this.hour = hour;
}
```

In this example, SomeMethod() takes a parameter (hour) with the same name as a member variable of the class. The this reference is used to resolve the ambiguity. While this.hour refers to the member variable, hour refers to the parameter.

You can, for example, use the this pointer to make a copy constructor more explicit:

```
public Time(Time that)
{
    this.Year = that.Year;
    this.Month = that.Month;
    this.Date = that.Date;
    this.Hour = that.Hour;
    this.Minute = that.Minute;
    this.Second = that.Second;
}
```

In this snippet, this refers to the current object (the object whose constructor is running) and that refers to the object passed in.

> The argument in favor of this style is that you pick the right variable name and then use it both for the parameter and for the member variable. The counter-argument is that using the same name for both the parameter and the member variable can be confusing

The second use of the this reference is to pass the current object as a parameter to another method, as in the following code:

```
Class SomeClass
{
  public void FirstMethod(OtherClass otherObject)
  {
    otherObject.SecondMethod(this);
  }
  // …
}
```

This code snippet establishes two classes, SomeClass and OtherClass. SomeClass has a method named FirstMethod(), and OtherClass has a method named Second-Method().

Inside FirstMethod, we'd like to invoke SecondMethod, passing in the current object (an instance of SomeClass) for further processing. To do so, you pass in the this reference, which refers to the current instance of SomeClass.

The third use of this is with indexers, which are covered in Chapter 15.

Static and Instance Members

The fields, properties, and methods of a class can be either *instance members* or *static members*. Instance members are associated with instances of a type, while static members are associated with the class and not with any particular instance. Methods are instance methods unless you explicitly mark them with the keyword static.

The vast majority of methods will be instance methods. The semantics of an instance method are that you are taking an action on a specific object. From time to time, however, it is convenient to be able to invoke a method without having an instance of the class, and for that you will use a static method.

You access a static member through the name of the class in which it is declared. For example, suppose you have a class named Button and have instantiated objects of that class named btnUpdate and btnDelete.

Suppose that the Button class has an instance method Draw() and a static method GetButtonCount(). The job of Draw() is to draw the current button, and the job of GetButtonCount is to return the number of buttons currently visible on the form.

You access an instance method through an instance of the class—that is, through an object:

```
btnUpdate.SomeMethod();
```

You access a static method through the class name, not through an instance:

```
Button.GetButtonCount();
```

Invoking Static Methods

Static methods are said to operate on the class, rather than on an instance of the class. They do not have a this reference, as there is no instance to point to.

Static methods cannot directly access nonstatic members. You will remember that Main() is marked static. For Main() to call a nonstatic method of any class, including its own class, it must instantiate an object.

For the next example, use Visual Studio .NET to create a new console application named StaticTester. VS.NET creates a namespace StaticTester and a class named

Class1. Rename Class1 to Tester. Get rid of all the comments and the attribute [STATThread] that Visual Studio .NET puts above Main(). Delete the args parameter to Main(). When you are done, your source code should look like this:

```
using System;
namespace StaticTester
{
    class Tester
    {
        static void Main()
        {
        }
    }
}
```

That is a good starting point. Until now, you've always done all the work of the program right in the Main() method, but now you'll create an instance method, Run(). The work of the program will now be done in the Run() method, rather than in the Main() method.

Within the class, but not within the Main() method, declare a new instance method named Run(). When you declare a method you write the accessor (public), followed by the return type, the identifier, and then parentheses.

```
public void Run()
```

The parentheses will hold parameters, but Run() won't have any parameters, so you can just leave the parentheses empty. Create braces for the method, and within the braces, just print Hello World to the console.

```
public void Run()
{
    Console.WriteLine("Hello world");
}
```

Run() is an instance method. Main() is a static method and cannot invoke Run() directly. You will therefore create an instance of the Tester class and call Run() on that instance:

```
Tester t = new Tester();
```

When you type the keyword new, IntelliSense tries to help you with the class name. You'll find that Tester is in the list; it is a legitimate class like any other.

On the next line, invoke Run() on your Tester object t. When you type t followed by the dot operator, IntelliSense presents all the public methods of the Tester class, as shown in Figure 8-5.

Notice that the Tester class has a number of methods you did not create (e.g., Equals, Finalize, etc.). Every class in C# is an object, and these methods are part of the Object class. This is covered in Chapter 11.

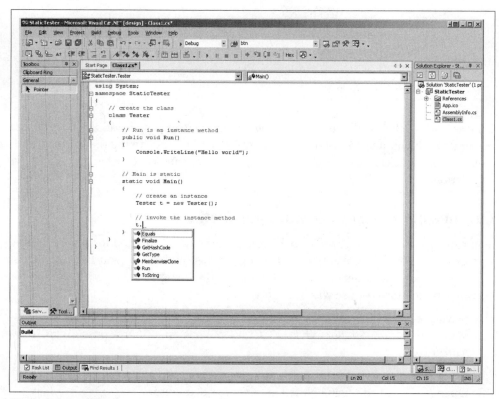

Figure 8-5. IntelliSense

When your program is complete it looks like Example 8-6.

Example 8-6. Instance methods

```
using System;
namespace StaticTester
{
    // create the class
    class Tester
    {
        // Run is an instance method
        public void Run()
        {
            Console.WriteLine("Hello world");
        }

        // Main is static
        static void Main()
        {
            // create an instance
            Tester t = new Tester();

            // invoke the instance method
```

Example 8-6. Instance methods (continued)

```
        t.Run();
    }
  }
}
```
Output:
```
Hello world
```

This is the model you'll use from now on in console applications. The Main() method will be limited to instantiating an object and then invoking the Run method. You can modify Visual Studio .NET to set this up for you, as described in the following section.

Customizing VS.NET to Create a Run Method

You can customize Visual Studio .NET to create the Run() method for you each time you create a console application. Before doing this, make sure you have a current backup of your entire installation. Then follow these steps to create a template for console applications for use with this book:

1. Navigate to the Templates directory. Typically this path is *Program Files\ Microsoft Visual Studio .NET\ VC#\ VC#Wizards\ CSharpConsoleWiz\ Templates\ 1033.*

2. Make a copy of *file1.cs*.

3. Open *file1.cs* to edit using Notepad or similar text editor.

4. Remove whatever comments you no longer want in your console applications.

5. Change the class name from [! output SAFE_CLASS NAME] to Tester.

6. Remove the parameters to Main() and the attribute above it.

7. Add the Run() method.

8. Instantiate Tester and invoke Run from within Main(). When you are done, your *file1.cs* file should look like this:

```
// Customized for Getting Started With C#
// Copyright (c) 2002 Liberty Associates, Inc.

using System;

namespace [!output SAFE_NAMESPACE_NAME]
{
   class Tester
   {
      public void Run()
      {
      }

      static void Main()
      {
```

```
                    Tester t = new Tester();
                    t.Run();
                }
            }
        }
```

9. Save the file and start up Visual Studio .NET. Create a new console application to test that your code worked.

If at any time you decide you'd like to revert to the original template, simply restore the backup copy of *file1.cs* that you made earlier.

Using Static Fields

A common use of static member variables, or fields, is to keep track of the number of instances/objects that currently exist for your class. In the next example, you create a Cat class. The Cat class might be used in a pet-store simulation.

For this example, the Cat class has been stripped to its absolute essentials. The complete listing is shown in Example 8-7. Analysis follows.

Example 8-7. Static fields

```
using System;

namespace Test_Console_App_3
{

    // declare a Cat class
    // stripped down
    public class Cat
    {
        // a private static member to keep
        // track of how many Cat objects have
        // been created
        private static int instances = 0;
        private int weight;
        private String name;

        // cat constructor
        // increments the count of Cats
        public Cat(String name, int weight)
        {
            instances++;
            this.name = name;
            this.weight = weight;
        }

        // Static method to retrieve
        // the current number of Cats
        public static void HowManyCats()
        {
            Console.WriteLine("{0} cats adopted",
                instances);
```

Example 8-7. Static fields (continued)

```
        }
        public void TellWeight()
        {
            Console.WriteLine("{0} is {1} pounds",
                name, weight);
        }
    }

    class Tester
    {
        public void Run()
        {
            Cat.HowManyCats();
            Cat frisky = new Cat("Frisky", 5);
            frisky.TellWeight();
            Cat.HowManyCats();
            Cat whiskers = new Cat("Whisky", 7);
            whiskers.TellWeight();
            Cat.HowManyCats();
        }

        static void Main()
        {
            Tester t = new Tester();
            t.Run();
        }
    }
}
```

Output:

```
0 cats adopted
Frisky is 5 pounds
1 cats adopted
Whisky is 7 pounds
2 cats adopted
```

The Cat class begins by defining a static member variable, instances, that is initialized to zero. This static member field will keep track of the number of Cat objects created. Each time the constructor runs (creating a new object), the instances field is incremented.

The Cat class also defines two instance fields: name and weight. These track the name and weight of each individual Cat object.

The Cat class defines two methods: HowManyCats() and TellWeight(). HowMany-Cats() is static. The number of Cats is not an attribute of any given Cat; it is an attribute of the entire class. TellWeight() is an instance method. The name and weight of each cat is per instance (i.e., each Cat has his own name and weight).

In the Tester class, Main() creates an instance of Tester, which then calls Run(). The Run() method accesses the static HowManyCats() method directly, through the class:

```
Cat.HowManyCats();
```

Run() then creates an instance of Cat and accesses the instance method, Tell-Weight(), through the instance of Cat:

```
Cat frisky = new Cat()
frisky.TellWeight();
```

Each time a new Cat is created, HowManyCats() reports the increase.

Destroying Objects

Unlike many other programming languages (C, C++, Pascal, etc.), C# provides garbage collection. Your objects are automatically destroyed when you are done with them. You do not need to worry about cleaning up after your objects unless you use unmanaged resources. An unmanaged resource is an operating-system feature outside of the .NET Framework, such as a file handle or a database connection.

If you do control an unmanaged resource, you need to explicitly free that resource when you are done with it. Implicit control over this resource is provided with a *destructor*, which is called by the garbage collector when your object is destroyed. Note that this material is fairly advanced; it is included here for completeness.

You declare a C# destructor with a tilde as follows:

```
~MyClass(){}
```

It is not legal to call a destructor explicitly—your destructor will be called by the garbage collector. If you do handle precious unmanaged resources (such as file handles) that you want to close and dispose of as quickly as possible, you ought to implement the IDisposable interface. (You will learn more about interfaces in Chapter 14.)

The IDisposable interface requires you to create a method named Dispose(), which will be called by your clients.

If you provide a Dispose() method, you should stop the garbage collector from calling your object's destructor. To stop the garbage collector, call the static method GC.SuppressFinalize(), passing in the this reference for your object. Your destructor can then call your Dispose() method. Thus, you might write:

```
using System;
class Testing : IDisposable
{
  bool is_disposed = false;
  protected virtual void Dispose(bool disposing)
  {
    if (!is_disposed) // only dispose once!
    {
      if (disposing)
      {
        Console.WriteLine("Not in destructor, OK to reference other objects");
      }
      // perform cleanup for this object
```

```
        Console.WriteLine("Disposing...");
      }
      this.is_disposed = true;
    }

    public void Dispose()
    {
      Dispose(true);
      // tell the GC not to finalize
      GC.SuppressFinalize(this);
    }

    ~Testing()
    {
      Dispose(false);
      Console.WriteLine("In destructor.");
    }
  }
```

For some objects, you'd rather have your clients call the Close() method. (For example, Close makes more sense than Dispose() for file objects.) You can implement this by creating a private Dispose() method and a public Close() method and having your Close() method invoke Dispose().

Because you cannot be certain that your user will call Dispose() reliably, and because finalization is nondeterministic (i.e., you can't control when the GC will run), C# provides a using statement to ensure that Dispose() is called at the earliest possible time. The idiom is to declare which objects you are using and then to create a scope for these objects with curly braces. When the close brace is reached, the Dispose() method will be called on the object automatically, as illustrated here:

```
using System.Drawing;
class Tester
{
    public static void Main()
    {
        using (Font theFont = new Font("Arial", 10.0f))
        {
          // use the font
        }
    }
}
```

The Font object is created within the using statement. When the using statement ends, Dispose() is called on the Font object.

CHAPTER 9

Inside Methods

In Chapter 8 you saw that classes consist of fields and methods. Fields hold the state of the object, and methods define the object's behavior.

In this chapter, you'll explore how methods work in more detail. You've already seen how to create methods, and in this chapter you'll learn about method overloading, a technique that allows you to create more than one method with the same name. This enables your clients to invoke the method with different parameter types.

This chapter also introduces properties. Properties look to clients of your class like member variables, but properties are implemented as methods. This allows you to maintain good data-hiding, while providing your clients with convenient access to the state of your class.

Chapter 8 described the difference between value types (i.e., primitives such as int, long, etc.) and reference types (i.e., classes). This chapter explores the implications of passing value types to methods and shows how you can pass value types *by reference*, allowing the called method to act on the original object in the calling method.

Overloading Methods

Often you'll want to have more than one method with the same name. The most common example of this is to have more than one constructor with the same name, which allows you to create the object with different parameters. For example, if you were creating a Time object, you might have circumstances where you want to create the Time object by passing in the date, hours, minutes, and seconds. Other times, you might want to create a Time object by passing in an existing Time object. Still other times, you might want to pass in just a date, without hours and minutes. Overloading the constructor allows you to provide these various options.

Chapter 8 explained that your constructor is automatically invoked when your object is created. Let's return to the Time class created in that chapter. It is possible to create a Time object by passing in a DateTime object to the constructor.

It would be convenient also to allow the client to create a new Time object by passing in year, month, date, hour, minute, and second values. Some clients might prefer one or the other constructor; you can provide both and the client can decide which better fits the situation.

In order to overload your constructor, you must make sure that each constructor has a unique *signature*. The signature of a method is composed of its name and its parameter list. Two methods differ in their signatures if they have different names or different parameter lists. Parameter lists can differ by having different numbers or types of parameters.

```
void myMethod(int p1);
void myMethod(int p1, int p2);       // different number
void myMethod(int p1, string s1);    // different types
void someMethod(int p1);             // different name
```

The previous four lines of code show how you might distinguish methods by signature.

The first three methods are all overloads of the myMethod() method. The first differs from the second and third in the number of parameters. The second closely resembles the third version, but the second parameter in each is a different type. In the second method, the second parameter (p2) is an integer; in the third method, the second parameter (s1) is a string. These changes to the number or type of parameters are sufficient changes in the signature to allow the compiler to distinguish the methods.

The fourth method differs from the other three methods by having a different name. This is not method overloading, just different methods, but it illustrates that two methods can have the same number and type of parameters if they have different names. Thus, the fourth and first have the same parameter list, but their names are different.

A class can have any number of methods, as long as each one's signature differs from that of all the others. Example 9-1 illustrates a Time class with two constructors: one that takes a DateTime object and one that takes six integers.

Example 9-1. Overloading a method

```
using System;

namespace MethodOverloading
{
    public class Time
    {
        // private member variables
        private int Year;
        private int Month;
        private int Date;
        private int Hour;
```

Example 9-1. Overloading a method (continued)

```
        private int Minute;
        private int Second;

        // public accessor methods
        public void DisplayCurrentTime()
        {
            System.Console.WriteLine("{0}/{1}/{2} {3}:{4}:{5}",
                Month, Date, Year, Hour, Minute, Second);
        }

        // constructors
        public Time(System.DateTime dt)
        {
            Year =      dt.Year;
            Month =     dt.Month;
            Date =      dt.Day;
            Hour =      dt.Hour;
            Minute =    dt.Minute;
            Second =    dt.Second;
        }

        public Time(int Year, int Month, int Date,
            int Hour, int Minute, int Second)
        {
            this.Year =     Year;
            this.Month =    Month;
            this.Date =     Date;
            this.Hour =     Hour;
            this.Minute =   Minute;
            this.Second =   Second;
        }
    }

class Tester
{
    public void Run()
    {
        System.DateTime currentTime = System.DateTime.Now;

        Time time1 = new Time(currentTime);
        time1.DisplayCurrentTime();

        Time time2 = new Time(2000,11,18,11,03,30);
        time2.DisplayCurrentTime();
    }

    static void Main()
    {
        Tester t = new Tester();
        t.Run();
    }
}
```

Example 9-1. Overloading a method (continued)

```
}
```
Output:
```
3/26/2002 16:17:32
11/18/2000 11:3:30
```

If a function's signature consisted only of the function name, the compiler would not know which constructors to call when constructing the new Time objects time1 and time2. However, because the signature includes the parameters and their types, the compiler is able to match the constructor call for time1 with the constructor whose signature requires a DateTime object.

```
System.DateTime currentTime
Time time1 = new Time(currentTime);
public Time(System.DateTime dt)
```

Likewise, the compiler is able to associate the time2 constructor call with the constructor whose signature specifies six integer arguments.

```
Time time2 = new Time(2000,11,18,11,03,30);
public Time(int Year, int Month, int Date,
    int Hour, int Minute, int Second)
```

 When you overload a method, you must change the signature (the name, number, or type of the parameters). You are free, as well, to change the return type, but this is optional. Changing only the return type does not overload the method, and creating two methods with the same signature but differing return types generates a compile error.

Encapsulating Data with Properties

It is generally desirable to designate the member variables of a class as private. This means that only member methods of that class can access their value. You make member variables private to support *data hiding*, which is part of the encapsulation of a class.

Object-oriented programmers are told that member variables should be private. That is fine, but how do you provide access to this data to your clients? The answer for C# programmers is properties. Properties allow clients to access class state as if they were accessing member fields directly, while actually implementing that access through a class method.

This is ideal. The client wants direct access to the state of the object. The class designer, however, wants to hide the internal state of the class in class fields and provide indirect access through a method. The property provides both: the illusion of direct access for the client and the reality of indirect access for the class developer.

By decoupling the class state from the method that accesses that state, the designer is free to change the internal state of the object as needed. When the Time class is first created, the Hour value might be stored as a member variable. When the class is redesigned, the Hour value might be computed or retrieved from a database. If the client had direct access to the original Hour member variable, the change to computing the value would break the client. By decoupling and forcing the client to go through a property, the Time class can change how it manages its internal state without breaking client code.

In short, properties provide the data hiding required by good object-oriented design. Example 9-2 creates a property called Hour, which is then discussed in the paragraphs that follow.

Example 9-2. Properties

```
using System;

namespace Properties
{
    public class Time
    {

        // private member variables
        private int year;
        private int month;
        private int date;
        private int hour;
        private int minute;
        private int second;

        // create a property
        public int Hour
        {
            get
            {
                return hour;
            }

            set
            {
                hour = value;
            }
        }

        // public accessor methods
        public void DisplayCurrentTime()
        {
            System.Console.WriteLine(
                "Time: {0}/{1}/{2} {3}:{4}:{5}",
                month, date, year, hour, minute, second);
        }


        // constructors
```

Example 9-2. Properties (continued)

```
        public Time(System.DateTime dt)
        {
            year =      dt.Year;
            month =     dt.Month;
            date =      dt.Day;
            hour =      dt.Hour;
            minute =    dt.Minute;
            second =    dt.Second;
        }


    }
    class Tester
    {
        public void Run()
        {
            System.DateTime currentTime = System.DateTime.Now;
            Time t = new Time(currentTime);
            t.DisplayCurrentTime();

            // access the hour to a local variable
            int theHour = t.Hour;

            // display it
            System.Console.WriteLine("Retrieved the hour: {0}",
                theHour);

            // increment it
            theHour++;

            // reassign the incremented value back through
            // the property
            t.Hour = theHour;

            // display the property
            System.Console.WriteLine("Updated the hour: {0}", t.Hour);
        }

        [STAThread]
        static void Main()
        {
            Tester t = new Tester();
            t.Run();
        }
    }
}
```

Output:

```
Time    : 3/26/2002 12:7:43
Retrieved the hour: 12
Updated the hour: 13
```

You create a property by writing the property type and name followed by a pair of braces. Within the braces you can declare the get and set accessors. These accessors are very similar to methods, but they are actually part of the property itself.

Neither of these accessors has explicit parameters, though the set accessor has an implicit parameter value.

 By convention, property names are written in Pascal notation (initial uppercase).

In Example 9-2, the declaration of the Hour property creates both get and set accessors:

```
public int Hour
{
    get
    {
        return hour;
    }

    set
    {
        hour = value;
    }
}
```

Each accessor has an *accessor-body*, which does the work of retrieving and setting the property value. The property value might be stored in a database (in which case the accessor would do whatever work is needed to interact with the database), or it might just be stored in a private member variable (in this case, hour):

```
private int hour;
```

The get Accessor

The body of the get accessor is similar to a class method that returns an object of the type of the property. In Example 9-2, the accessor for the Hour property is similar to a method that returns an int. It returns the value of the private member variable hour in which the value of the property has been stored:

```
get
{
    return hour;
}
```

In this example, the value of a private int member variable is returned, but you could just as easily retrieve an integer value from a database or compute it on the fly.

Whenever you reference the property (other than to assign to it), the get accessor is invoked to read the value of the property. For example, in the following code the value of the Time object's Hour property is assigned to a local variable. The get accessor is called, which returns the value of the Hour member variable, and that value is assigned to the local variable named theHour.

```
Time t = new Time(currentTime);
int theHour = t.Hour;
```

The set Accessor

The set accessor sets the value of a property. When you define a set accessor you must use the value keyword to represent the argument whose value is passed to and stored by the property.

```
set
{
    hour = value;
}
```

Here, again, a private member variable is used to store the value of the property, but the set accessor could write to a database or update other member variables as needed.

When you assign a value to the property, the set accessor is automatically invoked, and the implicit parameter value is set to the value you assign:

```
theHour++;
t.Hour = theHour;
```

The advantage of this approach is that the client can interact with the properties directly, without sacrificing the data hiding and encapsulation sacrosanct in good object-oriented design.

 You can create a read-only property by not implementing the set part of the property. Similarly, you can create a write-only property by not implementing the get part.

Returning Multiple Values

Methods can return only a single value. But this isn't always convenient. Let's return to the Time class. It would be great to create a GetTime() method to return the hour, minutes, and seconds. You can't return all three of these as return values, but perhaps you can pass in three parameters, let the GetTime() method modify the parameters, and then examine the result in the calling method, in this case Run(). Example 9-3 is a first attempt.

Example 9-3. Retrieving multiple values, first attempt

```
using System;

namespace PassByRef
{
```

Example 9-3. Retrieving multiple values, first attempt (continued)

```csharp
public class Time
{
    // private member variables
    private int Year;
    private int Month;
    private int Date;
    private int Hour;
    private int Minute;
    private int Second;

    // Property (read only)
    public int GetHour()
    {
        return Hour;
    }

    // public accessor methods
    public void DisplayCurrentTime()
    {
        System.Console.WriteLine("{0}/{1}/{2} {3}:{4}:{5}",
            Month, Date, Year, Hour, Minute, Second);
    }

    public void GetTime(int h, int m, int s)
    {
        h = Hour;
        m = Minute;
        s = Second;
    }

    // constructor
    public Time(System.DateTime dt)
    {

        Year = dt.Year;
        Month = dt.Month;
        Date = dt.Day;
        Hour = dt.Hour;
        Minute = dt.Minute;
        Second = dt.Second;
    }


}

class Tester
{
    public void Run()
    {
        System.DateTime currentTime = System.DateTime.Now;
        Time t = new Time(currentTime);
        t.DisplayCurrentTime();
```

Example 9-3. Retrieving multiple values, first attempt (continued)

```
            int theHour = 0;
            int theMinute = 0;
            int theSecond = 0;
            t.GetTime(theHour, theMinute, theSecond);
            System.Console.WriteLine("Current time: {0}:{1}:{2}",
                theHour, theMinute, theSecond);

        }

        static void Main()
        {
            Tester t = new Tester();
            t.Run();
        }
    }
}
```
Output:
```
3/26/2002 12:22:19
Current time: 0:0:0
```

Notice that the "Current time" in the output is 0:0:0. Clearly, this first attempt did not work. The problem is with the parameters. We pass in three integer parameters to GetTime(), and we modify the parameters in GetTime(), but when the values are accessed back in Run(), they are unchanged. This is because integers are value types.

Passing by Value and by Reference

C# divides the world of types into value types and reference types. All intrinsic types (such as int and long) are value types. Classes are reference types.

When you pass a value type (such as an int) into a method, a copy is made. When you make changes to the parameter, you make changes to the copy. Back in the Run() method, the original integer variables, theHour, theMinute, and theSecond are unaffected by the changes made in GetTime().

What you need is a way to pass in the integer parameters by reference. When you pass an object by reference, no copy is made. A reference to the original variable is passed in. Thus when you make changes in GetTime(), the changes are also made to the original variables in Run().

This requires two small modifications to the code in Example 9-3. First, change the parameters of the GetTime() method to indicate that the parameters are ref (reference) parameters:

```
    public void GetTime(ref int h, ref int m, ref int s)
    {
        h = Hour;
        m = Minute;
        s = Second;
    }
```

Second, modify the call to GetTime() to pass the arguments as references:

```
t.GetTime(ref theHour, ref theMinute, ref theSecond);
```

 If you leave out the second step of marking the arguments with the keyword ref, the compiler will complain that the argument cannot be converted from an int to a ref int.

These changes are shown in Example 9-4.

Example 9-4. Passing by reference

```
using System;

namespace PassByRef
{

    public class Time
    {
        // private member variables
        private int Year;
        private int Month;
        private int Date;
        private int Hour;
        private int Minute;
        private int Second;

        // Property (read only)
        public int GetHour()
        {
            return Hour;
        }

        // public accessor methods
        public void DisplayCurrentTime()
        {
            System.Console.WriteLine("{0}/{1}/{2} {3}:{4}:{5}",
                Month, Date, Year, Hour, Minute, Second);
        }

        // takes references to ints
        public void GetTime(ref int h, ref int m, ref int s)
        {
            h = Hour;
            m = Minute;
            s = Second;
        }

        // constructor
        public Time(System.DateTime dt)
        {

            Year = dt.Year;
            Month = dt.Month;
```

Example 9-4. Passing by reference (continued)

```
            Date = dt.Day;
            Hour = dt.Hour;
            Minute = dt.Minute;
            Second = dt.Second;
        }


    }

    class Tester
    {
        public void Run()
        {
            System.DateTime currentTime = System.DateTime.Now;
            Time t = new Time(currentTime);
            t.DisplayCurrentTime();

            int theHour = 0;
            int theMinute = 0;
            int theSecond = 0;

            // pass the ints by reference
            t.GetTime(ref theHour, ref theMinute, ref theSecond);

            System.Console.WriteLine("Current time: {0}:{1}:{2}",
                theHour, theMinute, theSecond);

        }

        static void Main()
        {
            Tester t = new Tester();
            t.Run();
        }
    }
}
```
Output:
```
3/26/2002 12:25:41
Current time: 12:25:41
```

The results now show the correct time.

By declaring these parameters to be ref parameters, you instruct the compiler to pass them by reference. Instead of a copy being made, the parameters in GetTime() are references to the corresponding variables (theHour, theMinute, theSecond) that were created in Run(). When you change these values in GetTime(), the change is reflected in Run().

Keep in mind that ref parameters are references to the actual original value—it is as if you said "here, work on this one." Conversely, value parameters are copies— it is as if you said "here, work on one *just like* this."

Out Parameters and Definite Assignment

As noted in Chapter 5, C# imposes *definite assignment*, which requires that all variables be assigned a value before they are used. In Example 9-4, if you don't initialize theHour, theMinute, and theSecond before you pass them as parameters to Get-Time(), the compiler will complain. Yet the initialization that is done merely sets their values to 0 before they are passed to the method:

```
int theHour = 0;
int theMinute = 0;
int theSecond = 0;
t.GetTime( ref theHour, ref theMinute, ref theSecond);
```

It seems silly to initialize these values because you immediately pass them by reference into GetTime where they'll be changed, but if you don't, the following compiler errors are reported:

```
Use of unassigned local variable 'theHour'
Use of unassigned local variable 'theMinute'
Use of unassigned local variable 'theSecond'
```

C# provides the out modifier for situations like this, in which initializing a parameter is only a formality. The out modifier removes the requirement that a reference parameter be initialized. The parameters to GetTime(), for example, provide no information to the method; they are simply a mechanism for getting information out of it. Thus, by marking all three as out parameters using the out keyword, you eliminate the need to initialize them outside the method.

Within the called method, the out parameters must be assigned a value before the method returns. Here are the altered parameter declarations for GetTime():

```
public void GetTime(out int h, out int m, out int s)
{
    h = Hour;
    m = Minute;
    s = Second;
}
```

and here is the new invocation of the method in Main():

```
t.GetTime( out theHour, out theMinute, out theSecond);
```

To summarize, value types are passed into methods by value. Ref parameters are used to pass value types into a method by reference. This allows you to retrieve their modified value in the calling method. Out parameters are used only to return information from a method.

CHAPTER 10

Basic Debugging

The debugger is your friend. There is simply no more powerful tool than a debugger for learning C# and for writing quality C# programs. The debugger helps you understand what is really going on when your program is running. It is the x-ray of software development, allowing you to see inside programs and diagnose potential problems.

Without a debugger you are guessing; with a debugger you are seeing. It is as simple as that. Whatever time you invest in learning to use your debugger is time well spent.

The debugger is also a powerful tool for understanding code written by others. By putting someone else's code into the debugger and stepping through it, you can see exactly how the methods work and what data they manipulate.

This book assumes you are working with Visual Studio .NET. The debugger we'll investigate is the powerful symbolic debugger integrated within Visual Studio .NET.

The VS.NET debugger provides a number of windows for watching and interacting with your program while it executes. Getting comfortable with the debugger can make the difference between quickly finding bugs and struggling for hours or days.

Setting a Breakpoint

To get started with the debugger, return to Example 9-1. Put a *breakpoint* on the first line of Main() to see how this code actually works. A breakpoint is an instruction to the debugger to stop running. You set a breakpoint and then run the program and the debugger runs the program up until the breakpoint. Then you have the opportunity to examine the value of your variables at this point in the execution. Examining your program as it runs can help you untangle otherwise impenetrable problems. It is common to set multiple breakpoints, which allows you to zip through your program, examining the state of your object at selected locations.

You can set a breakpoint in many different ways. The easiest is to click in the far-left margin. This causes a red dot to appear in the margin next to the relevant line of code, which is also highlighted in red, as shown in Figure 10-1. Notice that as you hover over the breakpoint it tells you the line on which the breakpoint appears.

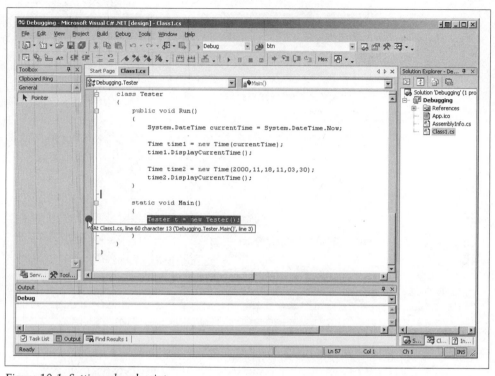

Figure 10-1. Setting a breakpoint

You are now ready to run the program to the breakpoint. Again, there are a number of ways to do so. You can click on the Start button (see Figure 4-6), or you can choose the Start item from the Debug menu (or use the keyboard shortcut for the menu item, the F5 key). In any case, the program starts and runs to the breakpoint, as shown in Figure 10-2.

The next statement to be executed is highlighted (in this case, the instantiation of the Tester object). There are a number of other helpful windows open as well, which will be examined in detail.

To step into the code, press the F11 function key twice. With the first keypress, the Tester is created. The second keypress moves you to the next line in the code, which calls the Run() method. Press the key once more to step inside the code for the Run() method and assign the value of System.DateTime.Now to the currentTime variable.

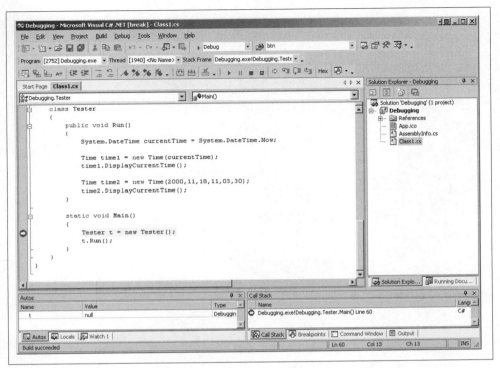

```
Debugging - Microsoft Visual C# .NET [break] - Class1.cs

File   Edit   View   Project   Build   Debug   Tools   Window   Help

Program [2752] Debugging.exe   Thread [1940] <No Name>   Stack Frame Debugging.exe!Debugging.Teste

Start Page   Class1.cs

Debugging.Tester                                    Main()

        class Tester
        {
            public void Run()
            {
                System.DateTime currentTime = System.DateTime.Now;

                Time time1 = new Time(currentTime);
                time1.DisplayCurrentTime();

                Time time2 = new Time(2000,11,18,11,03,30);
                time2.DisplayCurrentTime();
            }

            static void Main()
            {
                Tester t = new Tester();
                t.Run();
            }
        }


Solution Explorer - Debugging

Solution 'Debugging' (1 project)
 Debugging
    References
    App.ico
    AssemblyInfo.cs
    Class1.cs


Autos                                               Call Stack

Name        Value                    Type           Name                                          Langu
t           null                     Debuggin       Debugging.exe!Debugging.Tester.Main() Line 60   C#

Autos   Locals   Watch 1             Call Stack   Breakpoints   Command Window   Output

Build succeeded                                    Ln 60       Col 13       Ch 13       INS
```

Figure 10-2. At the breakpoint

F11 and F10 are the step commands. The difference between them is that F10 steps over method calls, while F11 steps into them.

The methods are executed with F10, but you don't see each step in the debugger; the highlighting jumps to the next statement past the method call.

If you use F11 to step into a method you meant to step over, Shift-F11 will step you out. The method you stepped into will run to completion, and you'll break on the first line back in the calling method.

In the code shown in Figure 10-2, there is no functional difference between using F10 and using F11 because all the work is done in a single method.

Using the Debug Menu to Set Your Breakpoint

Rather than clicking in the margin to set your breakpoint, you can use the New Breakpoint item on the Debug menu (or use the keyboard shortcut for the menu item, Control-B). This brings up the New Breakpoint dialog box, as shown in Figure 10-3.

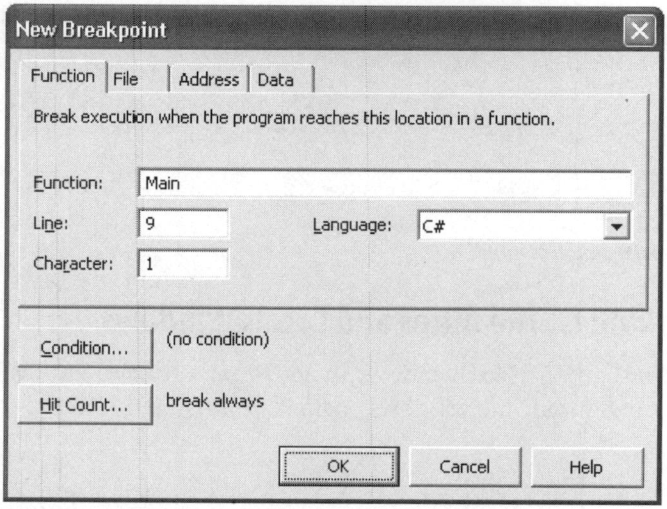

Figure 10-3. The New Breakpoint dialog

The New Breakpoint dialog gives you far greater control over your breakpoint. For example, you can set it to break only when a specific condition is hit (e.g., when counter > 10).

You can also set the *hit count* to designate that you only want the debugger to break in when the line has been hit a specified number of times (or a multiple of a specific number, etc.), as shown in Figure 10-4.

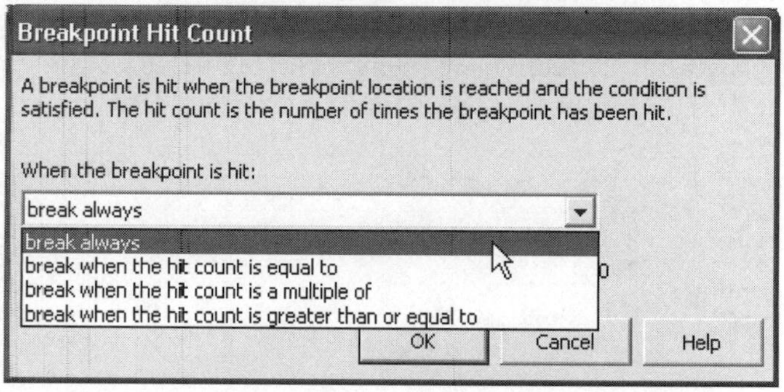

Figure 10-4. Breakpoint hit count

This can be very useful when you are in a loop (as described in Chapter 6). Rather than breaking each time through a loop of 100 iterations, you can choose the conditions under which to break.

You can also examine and manipulate all the breakpoints together in the breakpoint window, as shown in Figure 10-5.

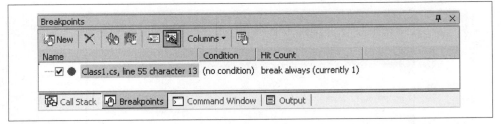

Figure 10-5. The Breakpoints window

Examining Values: The Autos and Locals Windows

Look at the bottom left-hand windows, where your variables are displayed. These variables are organized in windows named Autos and Locals, as shown in Figure 10-6.

 The debugger stacks the Autos and Locals windows together with tabs as shown in Figure 10-6. You are free to separate these windows or to move them to be tabbed with other windows. You can simply drag and drop the windows where you want them. When you drop one window on another, the two windows are tabbed together.

You can use the Autos and Locals windows to display the current value of each variable (and parameter) in your program. The Autos window shows variables used in the current statement and the previous statement. (The current statement is the statement at the current execution location, which is highlighted *automatically* in the debugger—thus the window's name.) The Locals window displays all the variables in the current method, including parameters. In Figure 10-6, the Autos window shows you that the current time has been set to the current date.

Autos		
Name	Value	Type
⊞ System.DateTime.Now	{3/26/2002}	System.D
⊞ currentTime	{3/26/2002}	System.D
⊞ this	{Debugging.Tester}	Debuggin
time1	null	Debuggin

Figure 10-6. The Autos window

Since the value of currentTime has just been set it is shown in red. Notice the plus sign (+) next to the currentTime variable. This variable is of type System.DateTime, which is a type with many members. Expanding the plus sign reveals the state of this object, as shown in Figure 10-7.

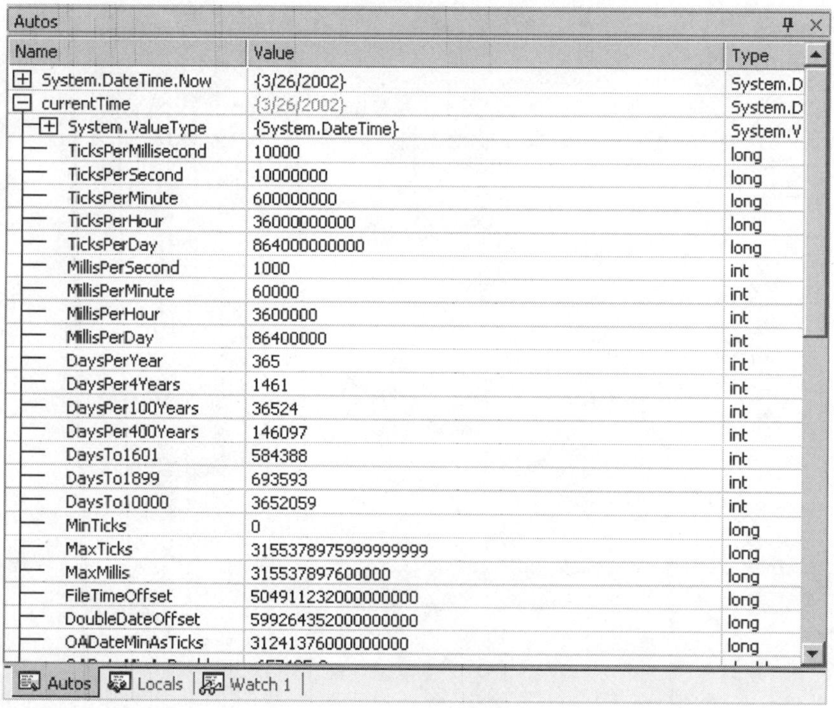

Autos		⃞ ×
Name	Value	Type
⊞ System.DateTime.Now	{3/26/2002}	System.D
⊟ currentTime	{3/26/2002}	System.D
⊞ System.ValueType	{System.DateTime}	System.V
TicksPerMillisecond	10000	long
TicksPerSecond	10000000	long
TicksPerMinute	600000000	long
TicksPerHour	36000000000	long
TicksPerDay	864000000000	long
MillisPerSecond	1000	int
MillisPerMinute	60000	int
MillisPerHour	3600000	int
MillisPerDay	86400000	int
DaysPerYear	365	int
DaysPer4Years	1461	int
DaysPer100Years	36524	int
DaysPer400Years	146097	int
DaysTo1601	584388	int
DaysTo1899	693593	int
DaysTo10000	3652059	int
MinTicks	0	long
MaxTicks	3155378975999999999	long
MaxMillis	315537897600000	long
FileTimeOffset	504911232000000000	long
DoubleDateOffset	599264352000000000	long
OADateMinAsTicks	31241376000000000	long

🖳 Autos | 🖳 Locals | 🖳 Watch 1

Figure 10-7. Expanding the variable

Press F11 again to step into the Time class constructor. When you step into the Time constructor, the Autos window changes to show you the new values, appropriate to the current line of code.

The debugger also provides a way for you to look at all the variables in the current method simultaneously: the Locals window. In this series of examples, clicking on the Locals window reveals the local variables dt (the parameter) and this (the current object). Expand the this variable and you'll see the Time object, with its controls uninitialized. Press F11 to progress through the assignment of values to the member variables of the Time class. As you hit the F11 key, the update is reflected in the Locals window, as shown in Figure 10-8.

Explore the Locals and Autos windows as you step through the program. When you want to stop, choose the Stop debugging item from the Debug menu to stop processing and return to the editor.

Set Your Watch

In a program with many local variables, it can be difficult to keep track of the particular variables you want to keep an eye on. You can track variables and objects in the

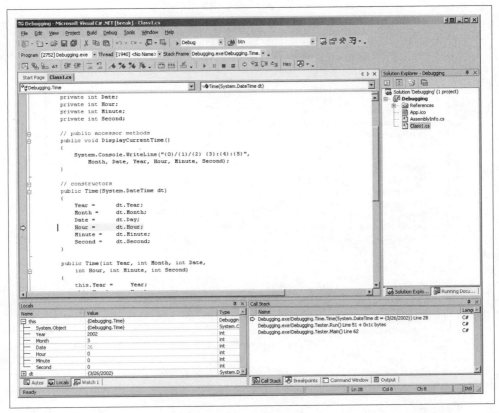

Figure 10-8. Watching assignment

Watch window. You can have up to four Watch windows at a time. Watch windows are like by-invitation versions of the Locals window; they list the objects you ask the debugger to keep an eye on, and you can see their values change as you step through the program, as illustrated in Figure 10-9.

Name	Value	Type
⊟ currentTime	{3/26/2002}	System.DateTime
⊞ System.ValueType	{System.DateTime}	System.ValueType
TicksPerMillisecond	10000	long
TicksPerSecond	10000000	long
TicksPerMinute	600000000	long
TicksPerHour	36000000000	long
TicksPerDay	864000000000	long
MillisPerSecond	1000	int
MillisPerMinute	60000	int

Figure 10-9. A Watch window

The Watch windows are usually tabbed with the Locals window. You can create more than one Watch window to organize the variables you keep an eye on.

You can add a watch by right-clicking on a variable and choosing Add Watch. You might instead choose Add QuickWatch, which opens a dialog box with watch information about a single object, as shown in Figure 10-10.

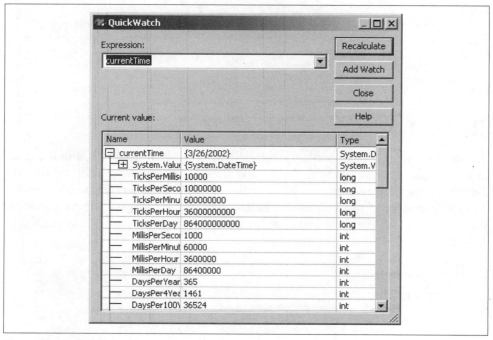

Figure 10-10. QuickWatch

You can enter any expression and evaluate it from within the QuickWatch window. For example, suppose you had integer variables named varOne and varTwo:

```
int varOne = 5;
int varTwo = 7;
```

If you want to know the impact of multiplying them, enter:

```
varOne * varTwo
```

into the Expression window and click Recalculate. The value is shown in the Current value window, as in Figure 10-11.

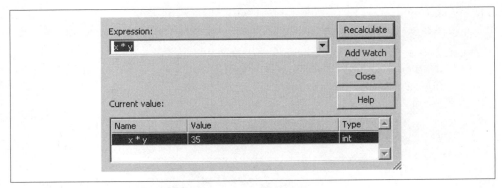

Figure 10-11. QuickWatch recalculation

The Call Stack

As you step in and out of methods, the Call Stack window keeps track of the order and hierarchy of method calls. If you look back at Figure 10-2, you'll see the Call Stack window in the lower right-hand corner of the application. Figure 10-12 shows a close-up picture of the Call Stack window. You can see that the Time constructor was called by the Run() method, while the Run() method was in turn called by Main().

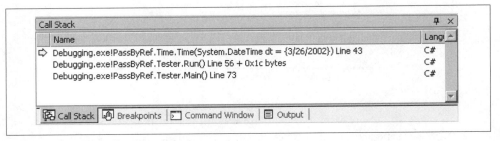

Figure 10-12. The Call Stack window

In this case, if you double-click on the second line in the Call Stack window, the debugger shows you the line in Run() that called the Time constructor, as shown in Figure 10-13.

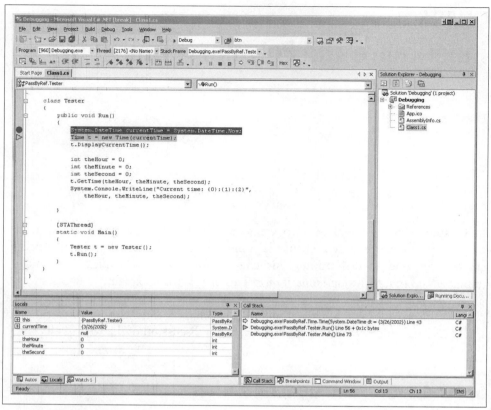

Figure 10-13. Tracing the call stack

CHAPTER 11

Inheritance and Polymorphism

In Chapter 8 you learned how to create new types by declaring classes, and in Chapter 3 you saw a discussion of the principle object relationships of association, aggregation, and specialization. This chapter focuses on *specialization*, which is implemented in C# through *inheritance*. This chapter also explains how instances of more specialized classes can be treated as if they were instances of more general classes, a process known as *polymorphism*. This chapter ends with a consideration of *sealed classes*, which cannot be specialized, and a discussion of the root of all classes, the Object class.

Specialization and Generalization

Classes and their instances (objects) do not exist in a vacuum but rather in a network of interdependencies and relationships, just as we, as social animals, live in a world of relationships and categories.

One of the most important relationships among objects in the real world is specialization, which can be described as an *is-a* relationship. When we say that a Dog *is a* mammal, we mean that the Dog is a specialized kind of Mammal. It has all the characteristics of any Mammal (it bears live young, nurses with milk, has hair), but it specializes these characteristics to the familiar characteristics of *canine domesticus*. A Cat is also a mammal. As such we expect it to share certain characteristics with the Dog that are generalized in Mammal, but to differ in those characteristics that are specialized in Cat.

The specialization and generalization relationships are both reciprocal and hierarchical. They are reciprocal because specialization is the obverse side of the generalization coin. Thus, Dog and Cat specialize Mammal, and Mammal generalizes from Dog and Cat.

These relationships are hierarchical because they create a relationship tree, with specialized types branching off from more generalized types. As you move up the hierarchy you achieve greater generalization. You move up toward Mammal to generalize that Dogs and Cats and Horses all bear live young. As you move down the hierarchy you specialize. Thus, the Cat specializes Mammal in having claws (a characteristic) and purring (a behavior).

Similarly, when you say that ListBox and Button *are* Windows, you indicate that there are characteristics and behaviors of Windows that you expect to find in both of these types. In other words, Window generalizes the shared characteristics of both ListBox and Button, while each specializes its own particular characteristics and behaviors.

The Unified Modeling Language (UML) is a standardized language for describing an object-oriented system. In the UML, classes are represented as boxes. The name of the class appears at the top of the box, and (optionally) methods and members can be listed in the sections within the box.

In the UML, you model specialization relationships as shown in Figure 11-1. Note that the arrow points from the more specialized class up to the more general class. In the figure, the more specialized Button and ListBox classes point up to the more general Window class.

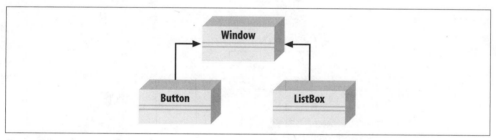

Figure 11-1. An is-a relationship

It is not uncommon for two classes to share functionality. When this occurs, you can *factor out* these commonalities into a shared base class, which is more general than the more specialized classes. This provides you with greater reuse of common code and gives you code that is easier to maintain.

For example, suppose you started out creating a series of objects as illustrated in Figure 11-2. After working with RadioButtons, CheckBoxes, and Command buttons for a while, you realize that they share certain characteristics and behaviors that are more specialized than Window but more general than any of the three. You might factor these common traits and behaviors into a common base class, Button, and rearrange your inheritance hierarchy as shown in Figure 11-3. This is an example of how generalization is used in object-oriented development.

The UML diagram in Figure 11-3 depicts the relationship among the factored classes and shows that both ListBox and Button derive from Window and that Button is specialized into CheckBox and Command. Finally, RadioButton derives from CheckBox.

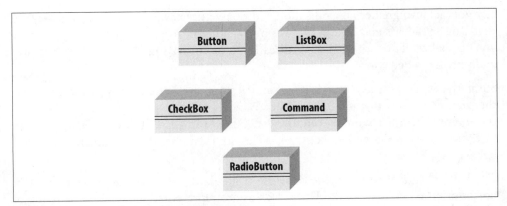

Figure 11-2. Objects deriving from Window

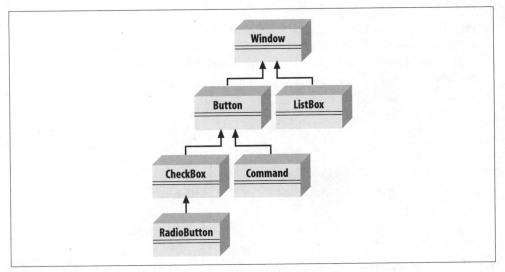

Figure 11-3. Factoring a Button class

You can thus say that RadioButton is a CheckBox, which in turn is a Button, and that Buttons are Windows.

This is not the only, or even necessarily the best, organization for these objects, but it is a reasonable starting point for understanding how these types (classes) relate to one another.

 Actually, although this might reflect how some widget hierarchies are organized, I am very skeptical of any system in which the model does not reflect how I perceive reality, and when I find myself saying that a RadioButton is a CheckBox, I have to think long and hard about whether that makes sense. I suppose a RadioButton *is* a kind of check-box. It is a checkbox that supports the idiom of mutually exclusive choices. That said, it is a bit of a stretch and might be a sign of a shaky design.

Inheritance

In C#, the specialization relationship is implemented using a principle called inheritance. This is not the only way to implement specialization, but it is the most common and most natural way to implement this relationship.

Saying that ListBox inherits from (or derives from) Window indicates that it specializes Window. Window is referred to as the *base* class, and ListBox is referred to as the *derived* class. That is, ListBox derives its characteristics and behaviors from Window and then specializes to its own particular needs.

Implementing Inheritance

In C#, you create a derived class by adding a colon after the name of the derived class, followed by the name of the base class:

```
public class ListBox : Window
```

This code declares a new class, ListBox, that derives from Window. You can read the colon as "derives from."

The derived class inherits all the members of the base class (both member variables and methods). These members can be treated just as if they were created in the derived class.

The derived class is free to implement its own version of a base class method. This is called *hiding* the base class method and is accomplished by marking the method with the keyword new.

 This is a different use of the keyword new than you've seen earlier in this book. In Chapter 8, new was used to create an object on the heap; here new is used to replace the base class method. Programmers say the keyword new is overloaded, which means that the word has more than one meaning or use.

The new keyword indicates that the derived class has intentionally hidden and replaced the base class method, as shown in the Example 11-1. (The new keyword is also discussed in the section "Versioning with new and override," later in this chapter.)

Example 11-1. Deriving a new class

```
using System;

public class Window
{
    // constructor takes two integers to
    // fix location on the console
    public Window(int top, int left)
    {
```

Example 11-1. Deriving a new class (continued)

```
            this.top = top;
            this.left = left;
    }

    // simulates drawing the window
    public void DrawWindow()
    {
        Console.WriteLine("Drawing Window at {0}, {1}",
            top, left);
    }

    // these members are private and thus invisible
    // to derived class methods; we'll examine this
    // later in the chapter
    private int top;
    private int left;
}

// ListBox derives from Window
public class ListBox : Window
{
    // constructor adds a parameter
    public ListBox(
        int top,
        int left,
        string theContents):
        base(top, left)  // call base constructor
    {
        mListBoxContents = theContents;
    }

    // a new version (note keyword) because in the
    // derived method we change the behavior
    public new void DrawWindow()
    {
        base.DrawWindow();  // invoke the base method
        Console.WriteLine ("Writing string to the listbox: {0}",
            mListBoxContents);
    }
    private string mListBoxContents;  // new member variable
}

public class Tester
{
    public static void Main()
    {
        // create a base instance
        Window w = new Window(5,10);
        w.DrawWindow();

        // create a derived instance
        ListBox lb = new ListBox(20,30,"Hello world");
```

Example 11-1. Deriving a new class (continued)

```
        lb.DrawWindow();
    }
}
```
Output:
```
Drawing Window at 5, 10
Drawing Window at 20, 30
Writing string to the listbox: Hello world
```

Example 11-1 starts with the declaration of the base class Window. This class implements a constructor and a simple DrawWindow() method. There are two private member variables, top and left. The program is analyzed in detail in the following sections.

Calling Base Class Constructors

In Example 11-1, the new class ListBox derives from Window and has its own constructor, which takes three parameters. The ListBox constructor invokes the constructor of its parent by placing a colon (:) after the parameter list and then invoking the base class constructor with the keyword base:

```
public ListBox(
    int theTop,
    int theLeft,
    string theContents):
    base(theTop, theLeft)  // call base constructor
```

Because classes cannot inherit constructors, a derived class must implement its own constructor and can only make use of the constructor of its base class by calling it explicitly.

If the base class has an accessible default constructor, the derived constructor is not required to invoke the base constructor explicitly; instead, the default constructor is called implicitly. However, if the base class does not have a default constructor, every derived constructor *must* explicitly invoke one of the base class constructors using the base keyword. The keyword base identifies the base class for the current object.

 As discussed in Chapter 8, if you do not declare a constructor of any kind, the compiler creates a default constructor for you. Whether you write it yourself or you use the one provided by default by the compiler, a default constructor is one that takes no parameters. Note, however, that once you do create a constructor of any kind (with or without parameters) the compiler does *not* create a default constructor for you.

Overriding Base Methods

Notice in Example 11-1 that ListBox implements a new version of DrawWindow():

```
public new void DrawWindow()
```

The keyword new indicates that the programmer is intentionally creating a new version of this method in the derived class.

In Example 11-1, the DrawWindow() method of ListBox hides and replaces the base class method. When you call DrawWindow() on an object of type ListBox, it is ListBox.DrawWindow() that is invoked, not Window.DrawWindow(). Note, however, that ListBox.DrawWindow() can invoke the DrawWindow() method of its base class with the code:

```
base.DrawWindow();  // invoke the base method
```

Controlling Access

You can restrict the visibility of a class and its members through the use of access modifiers, such as public, private, and protected. (See Chapter 8 for a discussion of access modifiers.)

As you've seen, public allows a member to be accessed by the member methods of other classes, while private indicates that the member is visible only to member methods of its own class. The protected keyword extends visibility to methods of derived classes.

Classes as well as their members can be designated with any of these accessibility levels. If a class member has a different access designation than the class, the more restricted access applies. Thus, if you define a class, myClass, as follows:

```
public class myClass
{
   // ...
   protected int myValue;
}
```

the accessibility for myValue is protected even though the class itself is public. A public class is one that is visible to any other class that wishes to interact with it.

Polymorphism

There are two powerful aspects to inheritance. One is code reuse. When you create a ListBox class, you're able to reuse some of the logic in the base (Window) class.

What is arguably more powerful, however, is the second aspect of inheritance: polymorphism. *Poly* means many and *morph* means form. Thus, polymorphism refers to being able to use many forms of a type without regard to the details.

When the phone company sends your phone a ring signal, it does not know what type of phone is on the other end of the line. You might have an old-fashioned Western Electric phone that energizes a motor to ring a bell, or you might have an electronic phone that plays digital music.

As far as the phone company is concerned, it knows only about the "base type" phone and expects that any "instance" of this type knows how to ring. When the phone company tells your phone to ring, it simply expects the phone to "do the right thing." Thus, the phone company treats your phone polymorphically.

Creating Polymorphic Types

Because a ListBox *is a* Window and a Button *is a* Window, you expect to be able to use either of these types in situations that call for a Window. For example, a form might want to keep a collection of all the instances of Window it manages so that when the form is opened, it can tell each of its Windows to draw itself. For this operation, the form does not want to know which elements are ListBoxes and which are Buttons; it just wants to tick through its collection and tell each to "draw." In short, the form wants to treat all its Window objects polymorphically. You implement this polymorphism with polymorphic methods.

Creating polymorphic methods

To create a method that supports polymorphism, you need only mark it as virtual in its base class. For example, to indicate that the method DrawWindow() of class Window in Example 11-1 is polymorphic, simply add the keyword virtual to its declaration, as follows:

```
public virtual void DrawWindow()
```

Now each derived class is free to implement its own version of DrawWindow(), and the method will be invoked polymorphically. To do so, simply override the base class virtual method by using the keyword override in the derived class method definition, and then add the new code for that overridden method.

In the following excerpt from Example 11-2 (which appears later in this section), ListBox derives from Window and implements its own version of DrawWindow():

```
public override void DrawWindow()
{
    base.DrawWindow();  // invoke the base method
    Console.WriteLine ("Writing string to the listbox: {0}",
        listBoxContents);
}
```

The keyword override tells the compiler that this class has intentionally overridden how DrawWindow() works. Similarly, you'll override this method in another class, Button, also derived from Window.

In the body of Example 11-2, you'll create three objects: a Window, a ListBox, and a Button. You'll then call DrawWindow() on each:

```
Window win = new Window(1,2);
ListBox lb = new ListBox(3,4,"Stand alone list box");
Button b = new Button(5,6);
```

```
win.DrawWindow();
lb.DrawWindow();
b.DrawWindow();
```

This works much as you might expect. The correct DrawWindow() method is called for each. So far, nothing polymorphic has been done. The real magic starts when you create an array of Window objects.

 Example 11-2 uses an array, which is a collection of objects that are all the same type. You create an array by indicating the type of objects to hold and then allocating space for a given number of those objects. For example, the following code declares winArray to be an array of three Window objects:

```
Window[] winArray = new Window[3];
```

You access the members of the array with square brackets. The first element is accessed with winArray[0], the second with winArray[1], and so forth. Arrays are explained in detail in Chapter 15.

Because a ListBox is a Window, you are free to place a ListBox into an array of Windows. You can also place a Button into an array of Window objects because a Button is also a Window:

```
Window[] winArray = new Window[3];
winArray[0] = new Window(1,2);
winArray[1] = new ListBox(3,4,"List box in array");
winArray[2] = new Button(5,6);
```

The first line of code declares an array named winArray that will hold three Window objects. The next three lines add new Window objects to the array. The first adds a Window. The second adds a ListBox (which is a Window because ListBox derives from Window), and the third adds a Button (Button also derives from Window).

What happens when you call DrawWindow() on each of these objects?

```
for (int i = 0;i < 3; i++)
{
    winArray[i].DrawWindow();
}
```

This code uses i as a counter variable. It calls DrawWindow() on each element in the array in turn. The value i is evaluated each time through the loop, and that value is used as an index into the array.

All the compiler knows is that it has three Window objects and that you've called DrawWindow() on each. If you had not marked DrawWindow() as virtual, Window's original DrawWindow() method would be called three times.

However, because you did mark DrawWindow() as virtual, and because the derived classes override that method, when you call DrawWindow() on the array, the right thing happens for each object in the array. Specifically, the compiler determines the runtime type of the actual objects (a Window, a ListBox, and a Button) and calls the right method on each. This is the essence of polymorphism.

 The runtime type of an object is the actual (derived) type. At compile time you do not have to decide what kind of objects will be added to your collection, so long as they all derive from the declared type (in this case Window). At runtime the actual type is discovered and the right method is called. This allows you to pick the actual type of objects to add to the collection while the program is running.

The complete code for this example is shown in Example 11-2.

Example 11-2. Virtual methods

```
using System;

public class Window
{
    // constructor takes two integers to
    // fix location on the console
    public Window(int top, int left)
    {
        this.top = top;
        this.left = left;
    }

    // simulates drawing the window
    public virtual void DrawWindow()
    {
        Console.WriteLine("Window: drawing Window at {0}, {1}",
            top, left);
    }

    // these members are protected and thus visible
    // to derived class methods. We'll examine this
    // later in the chapter
    protected int top;
    protected int left;

}

// ListBox derives from Window
public class ListBox : Window
{
    // constructor adds a parameter
    public ListBox(
        int top,
        int left,
        string contents):
        base(top, left)  // call base constructor
    {
```

Example 11-2. Virtual methods (continued)

```
        listBoxContents = contents;
    }

    // an overridden version (note keyword) because in the
    // derived method we change the behavior
    public override void DrawWindow()
    {
        base.DrawWindow();  // invoke the base method
        Console.WriteLine ("Writing string to the listbox: {0}",
            listBoxContents);
    }

    private string listBoxContents;  // new member variable
}

public class Button : Window
{
    public Button(
        int top,
        int left):
        base(top, left)
    {
    }

    // an overridden version (note keyword) because in the
    // derived method we change the behavior
    public override void DrawWindow()
    {
        Console.WriteLine("Drawing a button at {0}, {1}\n",
            top, left);
    }
}

public class Tester
{
    static void Main()
    {
        Window win = new Window(1,2);
        ListBox lb = new ListBox(3,4,"Stand alone list box");
        Button b = new Button(5,6);
        win.DrawWindow();
        lb.DrawWindow();
        b.DrawWindow();

        Window[] winArray = new Window[3];
        winArray[0] = new Window(1,2);
        winArray[1] = new ListBox(3,4,"List box in array");
        winArray[2] = new Button(5,6);

        for (int i = 0;i < 3; i++)
        {
            winArray[i].DrawWindow();
```

Example 11-2. Virtual methods (continued)

```
        }
    }
}
```
Output:
```
Window: drawing Window at 1, 2
Window: drawing Window at 3, 4
Writing string to the listbox: Stand alone list box
Drawing a button at 5, 6

Window: drawing Window at 1, 2
Window: drawing Window at 3, 4
Writing string to the listbox: List box in array
Drawing a button at 5, 6
```

Note that throughout this example, the overridden methods are marked with the keyword override:

```
    public override void DrawWindow()
```

The compiler now knows to use the overridden method when treating these objects polymorphically. The compiler is responsible for tracking the real type of the object and for handling the late binding so that ListBox.DrawWindow() is called when the Window reference really points to a ListBox object.

Versioning with new and override

In C#, the programmer's decision to override a virtual method is made explicit with the override keyword. This helps you release new versions of your code; changes to the base class will not break existing code in the derived classes. The requirement to use the override keyword helps prevent that problem.

Here's how: assume for a moment that Company A wrote the Window base class of the previous example. Suppose also that the ListBox and RadioButton classes were written by programmers from Company B using a purchased copy of the Company A Window class as a base. The programmers in Company B have little or no control over the design of the Window class, including future changes that Company A might choose to make.

Now suppose that one of the programmers for Company B decides to add a Sort() method to ListBox:

```
    public class ListBox : Window
    {
        public virtual void Sort() {...}
    }
```

This presents no problems until Company A, the author of Window, releases Version 2 of its Window class, and the programmers in Company A also add a Sort() method to their public class Window:

```
public class Window
{
    // ...
    public virtual void Sort() {...}
}
```

In other object-oriented languages (such as C++), the new virtual Sort() method in Window would now act as a base method for the virtual Sort() method in ListBox. The compiler would call the Sort() method in ListBox when you intend to call the Sort() in Window. In Java, if the Sort() in Window had a different return type, the class loader would consider the Sort() in ListBox to be an invalid override and would fail to load.

C# prevents this confusion. In C#, a virtual function is always considered to be the root of virtual dispatch; that is, once C# finds a virtual method, it looks no further up the inheritance hierarchy. If a new virtual Sort() function is introduced into Window, the runtime behavior of ListBox is unchanged.

When ListBox is compiled again, however, the compiler generates a warning:

```
...\class1.cs(54,24): warning CS0114: 'ListBox.Sort()' hides
inherited member 'Window.Sort()'.
To make the current member override that implementation,
add the override keyword. Otherwise add the new keyword.
```

To remove the warning, the programmer must indicate what she intends. She can mark the ListBox Sort() method new to indicate that it is *not* an override of the virtual method in Window:

```
public class ListBox : Window
{
    public new virtual void Sort() {...}
```

This action removes the warning. If, on the other hand, the programmer does want to override the method in Window, she need only use the override keyword to make that intention explicit:

```
public class ListBox : Window
{
    public override void Sort() {...}
```

 To avoid this warning, it might be tempting to add the new keyword to all your virtual methods. This is a bad idea. When new appears in the code, it ought to document the versioning of code. It points a potential client to the base class to see what it is that you are not overriding. Using new scattershot undermines this documentation. The warning exists to help identify a real issue.

Abstract Classes

Each type of Window has a different shape and appearance. Drop-down listboxes look very different from buttons. Clearly, every subclass of Window *should* implement its own DrawWindow() method—but so far, nothing in the Window class enforces that they must do so. To require subclasses to implement a method of their base, you need to designate that method as *abstract*.

An abstract method has no implementation. It creates a method name and signature that must be implemented in all derived classes. Furthermore, making at least one method of any class abstract has the side effect of making the class abstract.

Abstract classes establish a base for derived classes, but it is not legal to instantiate an object of an abstract class. Once you declare a method to be abstract, you prohibit the creation of any instances of that class.

The Idea Behind Abstraction

Abstract classes should not just be an implementation trick; they should represent the idea of an abstraction that establishes a "contract" for all derived classes. In other words, abstract classes mandate the public methods of the classes that will implement the abstraction.

The idea of an abstract Window class ought to lay out the common characteristics and behaviors of all windows, even though you never intend to instantiate the abstraction Window itself.

The idea of an abstract class is implied in the word "abstract." It serves to implement the abstraction "Window" that will be manifest in the various concrete instances of Window, such as browser window, frame, button, listbox, drop-down, and so forth. The abstract class establishes what a Window is, even though we never intend to create a "Window" per se. An alternative to using abstract is to define an interface, as described in Chapter 14.

Thus, if you were to designate DrawWindow() as an abstract method in the Window class, the Window class would become abstract. Then you could derive from Window, but you could not create any Window instances. If the Window class is an abstraction, there is no such thing as a simple Window object, only objects derived from Window.

Making Window.DrawWindow() abstract means that each class derived from Window would have to implement its own DrawWindow() method. If the derived class failed to implement the abstract method, that derived class would also be abstract, and again no instances would be possible.

Designating a method as abstract is accomplished by placing the abstract keyword at the beginning of the method definition, as follows:

```
abstract public void DrawWindow();
```

(Because the method can have no implementation, there are no braces, only a semicolon.)

If one or more methods are abstract, the class definition must also be marked abstract, as in the following:

```
abstract public class Window
```

Example 11-3 illustrates the creation of an abstract Window class and an abstract DrawWindow() method.

Example 11-3. Abstract methods

```
using System;

abstract public class Window
{
    // constructor takes two integers to
    // fix location on the console
    public Window(int top, int left)
    {
        this.top = top;
        this.left = left;
    }

    // simulates drawing the window
    // notice: no implementation
    abstract public void DrawWindow();

    protected int top;
    protected int left;

}

// ListBox derives from Window
public class ListBox : Window
{
    // constructor adds a parameter
    public ListBox(
        int top,
        int left,
        string contents):
        base(top, left)  // call base constructor
    {

        listBoxContents = contents;
    }

    // an overridden version implementing the
```

Example 11-3. Abstract methods (continued)

```
    // abstract method
    public override void DrawWindow()
    {

        Console.WriteLine ("Writing string to the listbox: {0}",
            listBoxContents);
    }

    private string listBoxContents;  // new member variable
}

public class Button : Window
{
    public Button(
        int top,
        int left):
        base(top, left)
    {
    }

    // implement the abstract method
    public override void DrawWindow()
    {
        Console.WriteLine("Drawing a button at {0}, {1}\n",
            top, left);
    }

}

public class Tester
{
    static void Main()
    {
        Window[] winArray = new Window[3];
        winArray[0] = new ListBox(1,2,"First List Box");
        winArray[1] = new ListBox(3,4,"Second List Box");
        winArray[2] = new Button(5,6);

        for (int i = 0;i < 3; i++)
        {
            winArray[i].DrawWindow();
        }
    }
}
Writing string to the listbox: First List Box
Writing string to the listbox: Second List Box
Drawing a button at 5, 6
```

In Example 11-3, the Window class has been declared abstract and therefore cannot be instantiated. If you replace the first array member:

```
    winArray[0] = new ListBox(1,2,"First List Box");
```

with this code:

```
winArray[0] = new Window(1,2);
```

the program generates the following error:

```
Cannot create an instance of the abstract class or interface 'Window'
```

You can instantiate the ListBox and Button objects because these classes override the abstract method, thus making the classes *concrete* (i.e., not abstract).

Sealed Classes

The opposite side of the design coin from abstract is *sealed*. In contrast to an abstract class, which is intended to be derived from and to provide a template for its subclasses to follow, a sealed class does not allow classes to derive from it at all. The sealed keyword placed before the class declaration precludes derivation. Classes are most often marked sealed to prevent accidental inheritance.

If the declaration of Window in Example 11-3 is changed from abstract to sealed (eliminating the abstract keyword from the DrawWindow() declaration as well), the program fails to compile. If you try to build this project, the compiler returns the following error message:

```
'ListBox' cannot inherit from sealed class 'Window'
```

among many other complaints (such as that you cannot create a new protected member in a sealed class).

Microsoft recommends using sealed "when it will not be necessary to create derived classes"* and also when your class consists of nothing but static methods and properties.

The Root of All Classes: Object

All C# classes, of any type, are treated as if they ultimately derive from a single class: Object. Object is the base class for all other classes.

A base class is the immediate "parent" of a derived class. A derived class can be the base to further derived classes, creating an inheritance "tree" or hierarchy. A root class is the topmost class in an inheritance hierarchy. In C#, the root class is Object. The nomenclature is a bit confusing until you imagine an upside-down tree, with the root on top and the derived classes below. Thus, the base class is considered to be "above" the derived class.

---

* Visual Studio .NET Combined Collection: Base Class Usage Guidelines.

Object provides a number of methods that subclasses can and do override. These include Equals(), which determines if two objects are the same, GetType(), which returns the type of the object, and ToString(), which returns a string to represent the current object. Specifically, ToString() returns a string with the name of the class to which the object belongs. Table 11-1 summarizes the methods of Object.

Table 11-1. The Object class

Method	What it does
Equals()	Evaluates whether two objects are equivalent
GetHashCode()	Allows objects to provide their own hash function for use in collections (see Chapter 16)
GetType()	Provides access to the type object
ToString()	Provides a string representation of the object
Finalize()	Cleans up nonmemory resources; implemented by a destructor
MemberwiseClone()	Creates copies of the object; should never be implemented by your type
ReferenceEquals()	Evaluates whether two objects refer to the same instance

In Example 11-4, the Dog class overrides the ToString() method inherited from Object, to return the weight of the Dog. This example also takes advantage of the startling fact that intrinsic types (int, long, etc.) can also be treated as if they derive from Object, and thus you can call ToString() on an int variable! Calling ToString() on an intrinsic type returns a string representation of the variable's value.

Example 11-4. Overriding ToString

```
using System;

public class Dog
{
    private int weight;

    // constructor
    public Dog(int weight)
    {
        this.weight = weight;
    }

    // override Object.ToString
    public override string ToString()
    {
        return weight.ToString();
    }
}


public class Tester
{
    static void Main()
    {
```

Example 11-4. Overriding ToString (continued)

```
    int i = 5;
    Console.WriteLine("The value of i is: {0}", i.ToString());

    Dog milo = new Dog(62);
    Console.WriteLine("My dog Milo weighs {0} pounds", milo.ToString());
  }
}
```
Output:
```
The value of i is: 5
My dog Milo weighs 62 pounds
```

The documentation for Object.ToString() reveals its signature:

```
public virtual string ToString();
```

It is a public virtual method that returns a string and takes no parameters. All the built-in types, such as int, derive from Object and so can invoke Object's methods.

> The Console class' Write() and WriteLine() methods call ToString() for you on objects that you pass in for display.

If you comment out the overridden function, the base method will be invoked. The base class default behavior is to return a string with the name of the class itself. Thus, the output would be changed to the meaningless:

```
My dog Milo weighs Dog pounds
```

> Classes do not need to declare explicitly that they derive from Object; the inheritance is implicit.

Boxing and Unboxing Types

Boxing and *unboxing* are the processes that enable value types (e.g., integers) to be treated as reference types (objects). The value is "boxed" inside an Object and subsequently "unboxed" back to a value type. It is this process that allowed us to call the ToString() method on the integer in Example 11-4. (You will see additional uses for boxing and unboxing in Chapter 16.)

Boxing Is Implicit

Boxing is an implicit conversion of a value type to the type Object. Boxing a value allocates an instance of Object and copies the value into the new object instance, as shown in Figure 11-4.

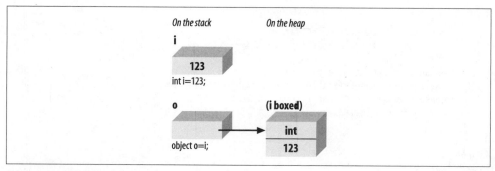

On the stack

i

123

int i=123;

On the heap

o

object o=i;

(i boxed)

int

123

Figure 11-4. Boxing value types

Boxing is implicit when you provide a value type where a reference is expected. The compiler notices that you've provided a value type and silently boxes it within an object. You can, of course, first cast the value type to a reference type, as in the following:

```
int myIntegerValue = 5;
object myObject = myIntegerValue;  // cast to an object
myObject.toString();
```

This is not necessary, however, as the compiler boxes the value for you silently and with no action on your part:

```
int myIntegerValue = 5;
myIntegerValue.toString();  // myIntegerValue is boxed
```

Unboxing Must Be Explicit

To return the boxed object back to a value type, you must explicitly unbox it. For the unboxing to succeed, the object being unboxed must really be of the type you indicate when you unbox it.

You should accomplish unboxing in two steps:

1. Make sure the object instance is a boxed value of the given value type.
2. Copy the value from the instance to the value-type variable.

Example 11-5 illustrates boxing and unboxing.

Example 11-5. Boxing and unboxing

```
using System;
public class UnboxingTest
{
    public static void Main()
    {
        int myIntegerVariable = 123;

        //Boxing
        object myObjectVariable = myIntegerVariable;
```

Example 11-5. Boxing and unboxing (continued)

```
        Console.WriteLine("myObjectVariable: {0}",
            myObjectVariable.ToString());

        // unboxing (must be explicit)
        int anotherIntegerVaraible = (int) myObjectVariable;
        Console.WriteLine("anotherIntegerVariable: {0}",
            anotherIntegerVariable);
    }
}
```
Output:
```
myObjectVariable: 123
anotherIntegerVariable: 123
```

Figure 11-5 illustrates unboxing.

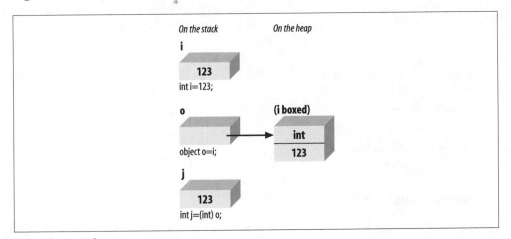

Figure 11-5. Unboxing

Example 11-5 creates an integer myIntegerVariable and implicitly boxes it when it is assigned to the object myObjectVariable; then, to exercise the newly boxed object, its value is displayed by calling toString().

The object is then explicitly unboxed and assigned to a new integer variable, anotherIntegerVariable, whose value is displayed to show that the value has been preserved.

> Typically, you will wrap an unbox operation in a try block, as explained in Chapter 18. If the object being unboxed is null or is a reference to an object of a different type, an InvalidCastException error occurs.

CHAPTER 12

Operator Overloading

One of the goals of C# is to allow you to create new classes that have all the functionality of built-in types such as integer (int) and Boolean (bool). (See Chapter 5 for a discussion of these intrinsic types.) For example, suppose you define a type (Fraction) to represent fractional numbers. The following constructors establish two Fraction objects, the first representing ½ and the second representing ¾:

```
Fraction firstFraction = new Fraction(1,2); // create 1/2
Fraction secondFraction = new Fraction(3,4); // create 3/4
```

The assumption here, of course, is that the first parameter will represent the numerator, and the second parameter will represent the denominator.

Ensuring that the Fraction class has all the functionality of the built-in types means that you must be able to perform arithmetic on instances of your fractions (e.g., add two fractions, multiply, etc.) and to convert fractions to and from built-in types such as int.

Hypothetically, you could implement methods for each of these operations. For example, for your Fraction type you might create an Add() method and invoke it by writing a statement such as:

```
// add 1/2 and 3/4
Fraction theSum = firstFraction.Add(secondFraction);
```

Although this will work, it is ugly and not how the built-in types are used. It would be much better to be able to write:

```
// add 1/2 and 3/4 using + operator
Fraction theSum = firstFraction + secondFraction;
```

Statements that use operators (in this case the plus sign) are intuitive and easy to use. Equally important, this use of operators is consistent with how built-in types are added, multiplied, and so forth.

In this chapter, you will learn techniques for adding standard operators to be used with your user-defined types. When you create an operator for a class, you say you have "overloaded" that operator, much as you might overload a member method (discussed in Chapter 9). The C# syntax for overloading an operator is to write the keyword operator followed by the operator to overload. The next section demonstrates how you might do this for the Fraction class.

The chapter also discusses the special case of overloading the equals operator, which is used to test whether two objects are equal. Overriding this operator also requires you to override the class's Equals() method.

Later in the chapter, you will learn how to add conversion operators to your user-defined types so that they can be implicitly and explicitly converted to other types.

Using the operator Keyword

In C#, operators are static methods. The return value of an operator represents the result of an operation. The operator's parameters are the operands.

Thus, to create an addition operator for a Fraction class, you use the C# syntax of combining the operator keyword with the plus sign (+) operator to create a static method, operator+. In this example, the overloaded addition operator (the operator+ method) takes two Fraction objects (the fractions you want to add) as parameters and returns another Fraction object representing the sum of the two parameters. Here is its signature:

```
public static Fraction operator+(Fraction lhs, Fraction rhs)
```

And here's what you can do with it. Assume, for instance, you've defined two fractions representing the portion of a pie you've eaten for breakfast and lunch, respectively. (You love pie.)

```
Fraction pieIAteForBreakfast = new Fraction(1,2);  // 1/2 of a pie
Fraction pieIAteForLunch = new Fraction(1,3);  // 1/3 of a pie
```

The overloaded operator+ allows you to figure out how much pie you've eaten in total. You can write:

```
Fraction totalPigOut = pieIAteForBreakfast + pieIAteForLunch;
```

The compiler takes the first operand (pieIAteForBreakfast) and passes it to operator+ as the parameter lhs; it passes the second operand (pieIAteForLunch) as rhs. These two Fractions are then added, and the result is returned and assigned to the Fraction object named totalPigOut.

 It is my convention to name the parameters to a binary operator lhs and rhs. A binary operator is an operator that takes two operands. The parameter name lhs stands for "left-hand side" and reminds me that the first parameter represents the left-hand side of the operation. Similarly, rhs stands for "right-hand side."

To see how this works, you'll create a Fraction class, as described previously. The complete listing is shown in Example 12-1, followed by a detailed analysis.

Example 12-1. Implementing operator+ for Fraction

```
using System;

public class Fraction
{
    private int numerator;
    private int denominator;

    // create a fraction by passing in the numerator
    // and denominator
    public Fraction(int numerator, int denominator)
    {
        this.numerator=numerator;
        this.denominator=denominator;
    }

    // overloaded operator + takes two fractions
    // and returns their sum
    public static Fraction operator+(Fraction lhs, Fraction rhs)
    {
        // like fractions (shared denominator) can be added
        // by adding their numerators
        if (lhs.denominator == rhs.denominator)
        {
            return new Fraction(lhs.numerator+rhs.numerator,
                lhs.denominator);
        }

        // simplistic solution for unlike fractions
        // 1/2 + 3/4 == (1*4) + (3*2) / (2*4) == 10/8
        // this method does not reduce.
        int firstProduct = lhs.numerator * rhs.denominator;
        int secondProduct = rhs.numerator * lhs.denominator;
        return new Fraction(
            firstProduct + secondProduct,
            lhs.denominator * rhs.denominator
            );
    }

    // return a string representation of the fraction
    public override string ToString()
    {
        String s = numerator.ToString() + "/" +
            denominator.ToString();
        return s;
    }
}


public class Tester
{
    public void Run()
    {
```

Example 12-1. Implementing operator+ for Fraction (continued)

```
    Fraction f1 = new Fraction(3,4);
    Console.WriteLine("f1: {0}", f1.ToString());

    Fraction f2 = new Fraction(2,4);
    Console.WriteLine("f2: {0}", f2.ToString());

    Fraction f3 = f1 + f2;
    Console.WriteLine("f1 + f2 = f3: {0}", f3.ToString());

}
static void Main()
{
    Tester t = new Tester();
    t.Run();
}
}
```

Output:
```
f1: 3/4
f2: 2/4
f1 + f2 = f3: 5/4
```

In Example 12-1, you start by creating a Fraction class. The private member data is the numerator and denominator, stored as integers:

```
public class Fraction
{
    private int numerator;
    private int denominator;
```

The constructor just initializes these values. The overloaded addition operator takes two Fraction objects:

```
public static Fraction operator+(Fraction lhs, Fraction rhs)
{
```

If the denominators for the fractions are the same, you add the numerators and return a new Fraction object created by passing in the sum of the numerators as the new numerator and the shared denominator as the new denominator:

```
if (lhs.denominator == rhs.denominator)
{
    return new Fraction(lhs.numerator+rhs.numerator,
        lhs.denominator);
}
```

The Fraction objects f1 and f2 are passed in to the overloaded addition operator as lhs and rhs, respectively. The new Fraction is created on the heap and returned to the calling method, Run(), where it is assigned to f3.

```
Fraction f3 = f1 + f2;
Console.WriteLine("f1 + f2 = f3: {0}", f3.ToString());
```

Back in the implementation of the operator, if the denominators are different, you cross multiply before adding. This allows you to add like Fractions.

```
int firstProduct = lhs.numerator * rhs.denominator;
int secondProduct = rhs.numerator * lhs.denominator;
return new Fraction(
    firstProduct + secondProduct,
    lhs.denominator * rhs.denominator
    );
```

The two local variables, firstProduct and secondProduct, are temporary; they are destroyed when the method returns. The new Fraction created, however, is not temporary; it is created on the heap, and a reference is returned as previously.

 A good Fraction class would, no doubt, implement all the arithmetic operators (addition, subtraction, multiplication, division). To overload the multiplication operator (*) you would write operator*; to overload the division operator you would write operator/.

The Fraction class overrides the ToString() method (inherited from Object) to allow you to display the fractions by passing them to Console.WriteLine(). (For more information about overloading methods, see Chapter 9.)

Supporting Other .NET Languages

Operator overloading is a feature of C#; it is not supported by every .NET language. It is important to ensure that your class supports other ways to achieve the same results so that your C# program can work with objects created in languages that do not support operator overloading.

Thus, if you overload the addition operator (+), you might also want to provide an Add() method that does the same work. This unattractive solution is required to ensure compatibility with other .NET languages that do not support operator overloading (e.g., Visual Basic .NET). For this reason, operator overloading ought to be seen as a syntactic shortcut and not as the only path for your objects to accomplish a given task.

Creating Useful Operators

Operator overloading can make your code more intuitive and enable it to act more like the built-in types. However, if you break the common idiom for the use of operators, operator overloading can make your code unmanageably complex and obtuse. Therefore you should always resist the temptation to use operators in new and idiosyncratic ways.

For example, although it might be tempting to overload the increment operator (++) on an employee class to invoke a method incrementing the employee's pay level, this can create tremendous confusion for clients of your class. The increment operator normally means "increase this scalar value by one." Giving it the new meaning of "increase this employee's pay level" will be obvious to the person implementing the operator, but may be very confusing to future clients of the class. It is best to use operator overloading sparingly and only when its meaning is clear and consistent with how the built-in classes operate.

Logical Pairs

It is quite common to overload the equals operator (==) to test whether two objects are equal. C# insists that if you overload the equals operator, you must also over- load the not-equals operator (!=). Similarly, the less than (<) and greater than (>) operators must be paired, as must the less than or equals (<=) and greater than or equals (>=) operators.

The Equals Operator

The Object class (which is the root of every class in C#) offers a virtual method called Equals(). (Virtual methods are discussed in Chapter 11.) If you overload the equals operator (==), it is recommended that you also *override* the Equals() method.

Overriding the Equals() method allows your class to be polymorphic and provides compatibility with other .NET languages that do not overload operators (but do sup- port method overloading).

 The classes in the .NET Framework Class Library do not use the over- loaded operators but do expect your classes to implement the underly- ing methods, such as Equals().

The Object class implements the Equals() method with this signature:

```
public virtual bool Equals(object o)
```

From this signature you can see that your override of this method will take an object as a parameter and return a bool (true if the two objects are equal).

By overriding this method, you allow your Fraction class to act polymorphically with all other objects. That is, anywhere you can call Equals() on two Objects, you can call Equals() on two Fractions.

Inside the body of Equals(), you need to ensure that you are comparing one Fraction object with another Fraction object. If the other object is not a fraction, they cannot be equal, and you'll return false.

```
public override bool Equals(object o)
```

```
    {
        if (! (o is Fraction) )
        {
            return false;
        }
        return this == (Fraction) o;
    }
```

The is operator is used to check whether the runtime type of an object is compatible with the operand (in this case, Fraction). Thus o is Fraction evaluates true if o is in fact a Fraction or a type derived from Fraction.

If you are comparing two Fractions, you can delegate the decision as to their equality to the overloaded operator (operator==) that you've already written. This allows you to avoid duplicate code.

```
    public override bool Equals(object o)
    {
        if (! (o is Fraction) )
        {
            return false;
        }
        return this == (Fraction) o;
    }
```

In this way, the Equals() method determines only that you do in fact have two fractions. If so, it delegates deciding if the two fractions are truly equal to the already implemented operator equals, as described earlier.

The complete modification of the Fraction class is shown in Example 12-2, followed by the analysis.

Example 12-2. Implementing equality operators

```
using System;

public class Fraction
{
    private int numerator;
    private int denominator;

    // create a fraction by passing in the numerator
    // and denominator
    public Fraction(int numerator, int denominator)
    {
        this.numerator=numerator;
        this.denominator=denominator;
    }

    // overloaded operator+ takes two fractions
    // and returns their sum
    public static Fraction operator+(Fraction lhs, Fraction rhs)
    {
        // like fractions (shared denominator) can be added
```

Example 12-2. Implementing equality operators (continued)

```
        // by adding thier numerators
        if (lhs.denominator == rhs.denominator)
        {
            return new Fraction(lhs.numerator+rhs.numerator,
                lhs.denominator);
        }

        // simplistic solution for unlike fractions
        // 1/2 + 3/4 == (1*4) + (3*2) / (2*4) == 10/8
        // this method does not reduce.
        int firstProduct = lhs.numerator * rhs.denominator;
        int secondProduct = rhs.numerator * lhs.denominator;
        return new Fraction(
            firstProduct + secondProduct,
            lhs.denominator * rhs.denominator
            );
    }

    // test whether two Fractions are equal
    public static bool operator==(Fraction lhs, Fraction rhs)
    {
        if (lhs.denominator == rhs.denominator &&
            lhs.numerator == rhs.numerator)
        {
            return true;
        }
        // code here to handle unlike fractions
        return false;
    }

    // delegates to operator ==
    public static bool operator !=(Fraction lhs, Fraction rhs)
    {
        return !(lhs==rhs);
    }

    // tests for same types, then delegates
    public override bool Equals(object o)
    {
        if (! (o is Fraction) )
        {
            return false;
        }
        return this == (Fraction) o;
    }

    // return a string representation of the fraction
    public override string ToString()
    {
        String s = numerator.ToString() + "/" +
            denominator.ToString();
        return s;
```

Example 12-2. Implementing equality operators (continued)

```
    }
}


public class Tester
{
    public void Run()
    {
        Fraction f1 = new Fraction(3,4);
        Console.WriteLine("f1: {0}", f1.ToString());

        Fraction f2 = new Fraction(2,4);
        Console.WriteLine("f2: {0}", f2.ToString());

        Fraction f3 = f1 + f2;
        Console.WriteLine("f1 + f2 = f3: {0}", f3.ToString());

        Fraction f4 = new Fraction(5,4);
        if (f4 == f3)
        {
            Console.WriteLine("f4: {0} == F3: {1}",
                f4.ToString(),
                f3.ToString());
        }

        if (f4 != f2)
        {
            Console.WriteLine("f4: {0} != F2: {1}",
                f4.ToString(),
                f2.ToString());
        }


        if (f4.Equals(f3))
        {
            Console.WriteLine("{0}.Equals({1})",
                f4.ToString(),
                f3.ToString());
        }


    }
    static void Main()
    {
        Tester t = new Tester();
        t.Run();
    }
}
```
Output:
```
f1: 3/4
f2: 2/4
f1 + f2 = f3: 5/4
```

Example 12-2. Implementing equality operators (continued)

```
f4: 5/4 == F3: 5/4
f4: 5/4 != F2: 2/4
5/4.Equals(5/4)
```

Example 12-2 starts by implementing the overloaded equals operator, `operator==`. If the fractions have the same denominator, you test whether the numerators are equal. If they are, you return true, otherwise you return false.

```
public static bool operator==(Fraction lhs, Fraction rhs)
{
    if (lhs.denominator == rhs.denominator &&
        lhs.numerator == rhs.numerator)
    {
        return true;
    }
    // code here to handle unlike fractions
    return false;
}
```

This method is invoked in the Run() method when you write:

```
if (f4 == f3)
```

The `if` statement expects a Boolean value, which is what `operator==` returns.

 The test for unlike fractions (i.e., fractions with different denominators) is left as an exercise for the reader.

As noted previously, if you implement the equality operator (`==`) you must also implement the inequality operator (`!=`). They are a matched pair. It is good programming practice to have the inequality operator delegate its work to the equality operator, so that if you change the definition of equality you are assured that the inequality operator will use the new definition.

```
public static bool operator !=(Fraction lhs, Fraction rhs)
{
    return !(lhs==rhs);
}
```

This operator is invoked in Run() when you write:

```
if (f4 != f2)
```

Put a breakpoint on this line of code and run to this line in Visual Studio .NET, as shown in Figure 12-1. (For more about VS.NET, see Chapter 4.)

Press F11 to step into the method call—you'll step into the `!=` operator at the return statement. Press F11 again and step into the `==` operator. Whatever value is returned by the `==` operator is negated when it is returned by the `!=` operator. If false is returned by `==`, then true is returned by `!=`.

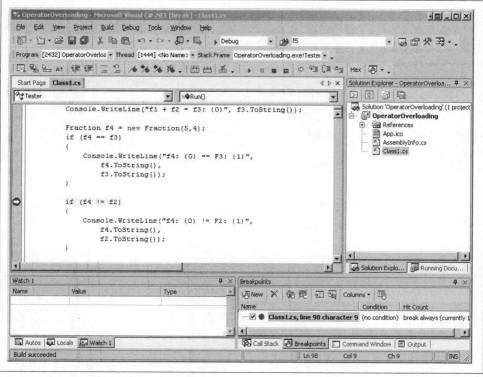

Figure 12-1. Running to the breakpoint

You can make the reversal of equality explicit by adding a temporary Boolean variable named "equality." Rewrite the != operator as follows:

```
public static bool operator !=(Fraction lhs, Fraction rhs)
{
    bool equality = lhs==rhs;
    return !(equality);
}
```

You can now put a breakpoint on the second line of this method and examine the value returned by operator==, as shown in Figure 12-2.

You can see in the Autos window that the value of equality (shown circled and highlighted) is false. The fractions have been expanded to show their values (5/4 and 2/4), and they are not equal. The value returned by the != operator is the opposite of false, that is, true.

In addition to implementing the == and != operator, you implement the Equals() method, for the reasons explained previously.

```
public override bool Equals(object o)
{
    if (! (o is Fraction) )
```

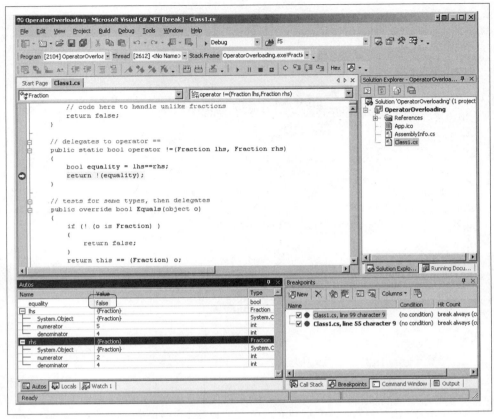

Figure 12-2. Examining the interim value

```
    {
        return false;
    }
    return this == (Fraction) o;
}
```

If the two objects are not both Fractions, you return false; otherwise you delegate to the == operator, casting o to a Fraction type. Put a breakpoint on the return line, and you'll find that you step back into operator==. The value returned by operator== is the value returned by the Equals() method if both objects are fractions.

The Meaning of Equality

It is up to you, as the class designer, to decide what it means for two instances of your class to be equal. Two employees might be equal if they have the same name, or you might decide they are only equal if they have the same Employee ID.

Conversion Operators

C# will convert (for example) an int to a long implicitly and will allow you to convert a long to an int explicitly. The conversion from int to long is implicit because you know that any int will fit into the memory representation of a long. The reverse operation, from long to int, must be explicit (using a cast) because it is possible to lose information in the conversion:

```
int myInt = 5;
long myLong;
myLong = myInt;      // implicit
myInt = (int) myLong; // explicit
```

You want to be able to convert your Fraction objects to intrinsic types (e.g., int) and back. Given an int, you can support an implicit conversion to a fraction because any whole value is equal to that value over 1 (e.g., 15==15/1).

Given a fraction, you might want to provide an explicit conversion back to an integer, understanding that some value might be lost. Thus, you might convert 9/4 to the integer value 2 (truncating to the nearest whole number).

> A more sophisticated Fraction class might not truncate, but rather round to the nearest whole number. This idea is left, as they say, as an exercise for the reader.

You use the keyword implicit when the conversion is guaranteed to succeed and no information will be lost; otherwise you use explicit. Implicit and explicit are actually operators, often called cast or casting operators because their job is to cast from one type to another (e.g., int to Fraction or Fraction to int).

Example 12-3 illustrates how you might implement implicit and explicit conversions; detailed analysis follows.

Example 12-3. Conversion operators

```
using System;

public class Fraction
{
    private int numerator;
    private int denominator;

    // create a fraction by passing in the numerator
    // and denominator
    public Fraction(int numerator, int denominator)
    {
        this.numerator=numerator;
        this.denominator=denominator;
    }
```

Example 12-3. Conversion operators (continued)

```
// overload the constructor to create a
// fraction from a whole number
public Fraction(int wholeNumber)
{
    Console.WriteLine("In constructor taking a whole number");
    numerator = wholeNumber;
    denominator = 1;
}

// convert ints to Fractions implicitly
public static implicit operator Fraction(int theInt)
{
    Console.WriteLine("Implicitly converting int to Fraction");
    return new Fraction(theInt);
}

// convert Fractions to ints explicitly
public static explicit operator int(Fraction theFraction)
{
    Console.WriteLine("Explicitly converting Fraction to int");
    return theFraction.numerator /
        theFraction.denominator;
}


// overloaded operator + takes two fractions
// and returns their sum
public static Fraction operator+(Fraction lhs, Fraction rhs)
{
    // like fractions (shared denominator) can be added
    // by adding thier numerators
    if (lhs.denominator == rhs.denominator)
    {
        return new Fraction(lhs.numerator+rhs.numerator,
            lhs.denominator);
    }

    // simplistic solution for unlike fractions
    // 1/2 + 3/4 == (1*4) + (3*2) / (2*4) == 10/8
    // this method does not reduce.
    int firstProduct = lhs.numerator * rhs.denominator;
    int secondProduct = rhs.numerator * lhs.denominator;
    return new Fraction(
        firstProduct + secondProduct,
        lhs.denominator * rhs.denominator
        );
}

// test whether two Fractions are equal
public static bool operator==(Fraction lhs, Fraction rhs)
{
```

Example 12-3. Conversion operators (continued)

```
            if (lhs.denominator == rhs.denominator &&
                lhs.numerator == rhs.numerator)
            {
                return true;
            }
            // code here to handle unlike fractions
            return false;
        }

        // delegates to operator ==
        public static bool operator !=(Fraction lhs, Fraction rhs)
        {
            bool equality = lhs==rhs;
            return !(equality);
        }

        // tests for same types, then delegates
        public override bool Equals(object o)
        {
            if (! (o is Fraction) )
            {
                return false;
            }
            return this == (Fraction) o;
        }

        // return a string representation of the fraction
        public override string ToString()
        {
            String s = numerator.ToString() + "/" +
                denominator.ToString();
            return s;
        }
    }


}


public class Tester
{
    public void Run()
    {
        Fraction f1 = new Fraction(3,4);
        Fraction f2 = new Fraction(2,4);
        Fraction f3 = f1 + f2;

        Console.WriteLine("adding f3 + 5...");
        Fraction f4 = f3 + 5;
        Console.WriteLine("f3 + 5 = f4: {0}", f4.ToString());

        Console.WriteLine("\nAssigning f4 to an int...");
        int truncated = (int) f4;
```

Example 12-3. Conversion operators (continued)

```
        Console.WriteLine("When you truncate f4 you get {0}",
            truncated);
    }
    static void Main()
    {
        Tester t = new Tester();
        t.Run();
    }
}
```

Output:
```
adding f3 + 5...
Implicitly converting int to Fraction
In constructor taking a whole number
f3 + 5 = f4: 25/4

Assigning f4 to an int...
Explicitly converting Fraction to int
When you truncate f4 you get 6
```

In Example 12-3, you add a second constructor that takes a whole number and creates a Fraction:

```
public Fraction(int wholeNumber)
{
    Console.WriteLine("In constructor taking a whole number");
    numerator = wholeNumber;
    denominator = 1;
}
```

 Notice that in this and the following code samples you add Write-Line() statements to indicate when you've entered the method. This is an alternative to stepping through in a debugger. While using the debugger is usually more effective, this kind of output can help you trace the execution of your program for review at a later time.

You want to be able to convert Fractions to and from ints. To do so, create the conversion operators. As discussed previously, converting from a Fraction to an int requires truncating the value, and so must be explicit:

```
public static explicit operator int(Fraction theFraction)
{
    Console.WriteLine("Explicitly converting Fraction to int");
    return theFraction.numerator /
        theFraction.denominator;
}
```

Note the use of the explicit keyword, indicating that this requires an explicit cast from a Fraction to an int. You see the cast in the Run() method:

```
int truncated = (int) f4;
```

The cast from an int to a Fraction, on the other hand, is perfectly safe, so it can be implicit:

```
Fraction f4 = f3 + 5;
```

Notice that there is no explicit cast (in parentheses). When you add the int to the Fraction, the int is implicitly cast to a Fraction. The implementation of this is to create a new Fraction object and to return it:

```
public static implicit operator Fraction(int theInt)
{
    Console.WriteLine("Implicitly converting int to Fraction");
    return new Fraction(theInt);
}
```

Calling the implicit cast operator causes the constructor to be invoked:

```
public Fraction(int wholeNumber)
{
    Console.WriteLine("In constructor taking a whole number");
    numerator = wholeNumber;
    denominator = 1;
}
```

You see this sequence of events represented in the output.

```
Implicitly converting int to Fraction
In constructor taking a whole number
```

CHAPTER 13
Structs

So far, the only user-defined type you've seen is the class. The class, as you know, defines a new type. Instances of a class are called objects. Classes are reference types; when you create a new instance of a class you get back a reference to the newly created object on the heap. (Creating classes is discussed in Chapter 8.)

A second type of user-defined type is a *struct* (or structure). Structs are designed to be lightweight alternatives to classes. In this case, the term lightweight means that structs use fewer resources (i.e., less memory) than classes, but they offer less functionality.

Structs are similar to classes in that they can contain constructors, properties, methods, fields, operators, nested types, and indexers. (See Chapter 15 for more on indexers.) There are, however, significant differences between classes and structs.

For example, structs don't support inheritance or destructors. More importantly, while a class is a reference type, a struct is a value type.

The consensus view is that you ought to use structs only for types that are small, simple, and similar in their behavior and characteristics to built-in types. For example, if you were creating a class to represent a point on the screen (x,y coordinates), you might consider using a struct rather than a class.

In this chapter, you will learn how to define and work with structs and how to use constructors to initialize their values.

 It is entirely possible to create robust commercial applications without structs. You can skip this chapter and come back to it when you actually need structs.

Defining a Struct

The syntax for declaring a struct is almost identical to that for a class:

```
[attributes] [access-modifiers] struct identifier [:interface-list]
{ struct-members }
```

Attributes are not discussed in this book. [Refer to *Programming C#*, Second Edition (O'Reilly), for more information about attributes.] Access modifiers (public, private, etc.) work just as they do with classes. (See Chapter 8 for a discussion of access modifiers.) The keyword struct is followed by an identifier (the name of the struct). The optional interface list is explained in Chapter 14. Within the braces is the body of the struct (fields and methods, also called the struct members).

Example 13-1 defines a struct named Location to hold the x,y coordinates of an object displayed on the screen and demonstrates that structs are value objects. When you pass a struct to a method, you pass it by value.

To create this application, open a console application in Visual Studio .NET and name it StructDemonstration.

Example 13-1. Creating a struct for x,y coordinate location

```
using System;

namespace StructDemonstration
{
    // declare a struct named Location
    public struct Location
    {
        // the struct has private data
        private int xVal;
        private int yVal;

        // constructor
        public Location(int xCoordinate, int yCoordinate)
        {
            xVal = xCoordinate;
            yVal = yCoordinate;
        }

        // property
        public int XVal
        {
            get { return xVal; }
            set { xVal = value;}
        }

        public int YVal
        {
            get { return yVal; }
            set { yVal = value; }
        }

        // Display the Struct as a String
        public override string ToString()
        {
            return (String.Format("{0}, {1}", xVal,yVal));
        }
    }       // end struct
```

Example 13-1. Creating a struct for x,y coordinate location (continued)

```
public class Tester
{
    public void Run()
    {
        // create an instance of the struct
        Location loc1 = new Location(200,300);

        // display the values in the struct
        Console.WriteLine("Loc1 location: {0}", loc1);

        // invoke the default constructor
        Location loc2 = new Location();
        Console.WriteLine("Loc2 location: {0}", loc2);

        // pass the struct to a method
        myFunc(loc1);

        // redisplay the values in the struct
        Console.WriteLine("Loc1 location: {0}", loc1);
    }

    // method takes a struct as a parameter
    public void myFunc(Location loc)
    {
        // modify the values through the properties
        loc.XVal = 50;
        loc.YVal = 100;
        Console.WriteLine("Loc1 location: {0}", loc);
    }

    static void Main()
    {
        Tester t = new Tester();
        t.Run();
    }
}
}
```

Output:
```
Loc1 location: 200, 300
Loc2 location: 0, 0
Loc1 location: 50, 100
Loc1 location: 200, 300
```

The Location structure is defined as public, much as you might define a class:

```
public struct Location
{
```

As with a class, you can define a constructor and properties for the struct. For example, you might create private int member fields xVal and yVal and then provide public properties for them named XVal and YVal (see Chapter 9):

```
// constructor
public Location(int xCoordinate, int yCoordinate)
{
    xVal = xCoordinate;
    yVal = yCoordinate;
}

// property
public int XVal
{
    get { return xVal; }
    set { xVal = value;}
}

public int YVal
{
    get { return yVal; }
    set { yVal = value; }
}
```

Note that there is one significant difference in the way you create constructors and properties for structs and the way you do it for classes: in a struct, you are not permitted to create a custom default constructor. That is, you cannot write a constructor with no parameters. Thus the following code would not compile:

```
// won't compile - no custom default
// constructors for structs
public Location()
{
    xVal = 5;
    yVal = 10;
}
```

Instead, the compiler creates a default constructor for you (whether or not you create other constructors) and that default constructor initializes all the member values to their default values (e.g., ints are initialized to zero).

The Run() method creates an instance of the Location struct named loc1, passing in the initial x,y coordinates of 200,300.

```
Location loc1 = new Location(200,300);
```

The value is then displayed, passing loc1 to WriteLine().

```
Console.WriteLine("Loc1 location: {0}", loc1);
```

As always, when you pass an object to Console.WriteLine() (in this case loc1), WriteLine() automatically invokes the virtual method ToString() on the object. Thus, Location.ToString() is invoked, which displays the x,y coordinates of the loc1 object.

```
Loc1 location: 200, 300
```

Before modifying the values in loc1, the example creates a second instance of the Location struct, named loc2. The creation of loc2 invokes the default constructor (note that there are no parameters passed in).

```
Location loc2 = new Location();
```

The output shows that the compiler-provided default constructor initialized the member variables to default values.

```
Loc2 location: 0, 0
```

Notice that you have not provided a default constructor; instead one has been provided for you by the compiler.

Next pass your first struct, loc1 (whose values are 200,300), to a method, myFunc(). In that method, the parameter is a Location object named loc. Within the myFunc() method, the XVal property is used to set the x coordinate to 50, and the YVal property is used to set the y coordinate to 100; then the new value is displayed using WriteLine():

```
public void myFunc(Location loc)
{
    // modify the values through the properties
    loc.XVal = 50;  // set XVal property
    loc.YVal = 100; // set YVal property
    Console.WriteLine("Loc1 location: {0}", loc);
}
```

As expected, the results show the modification:

```
Loc1 location: 50, 100
```

When you return to the calling method (Run()), the values of loc1 are displayed, and they are unchanged from before the call to myFunc():

```
Loc1 location: 200, 300
```

When you passed loc1 to myFunc(), the struct was passed by value (structs, like the intrinsic types, are value types). A copy was made, and it was on that copy that you changed the values to 50 and 100. The original Location structure (loc1) was unaffected by the changes made within myFunc().

No Inheritance

Unlike classes, structs do not support inheritance. Structs implicitly derive from Object (as do all types in C#, including the built-in types) but cannot inherit from any other class or struct. Structs are also implicitly *sealed* (that is, no class or struct can derive from a struct). See Chapter 11 for a discussion of inheritance and sealed classes.

No Initialization

You cannot initialize fields in a struct. Thus, it is illegal to write:

```
private int xVal = 50;
private int yVal = 100;
```

though this kind of initialization is perfectly legal in a class. You must instead set the value of your member fields in the body of the constructor. As noted earlier, the default constructor (provided by the compiler) sets all the member variables to their default value.

Public Member Data?

Structs are designed to be simple and lightweight. While private member data promotes data hiding and encapsulation, some programmers feel it is overkill for structs. They make the member data public, thus simplifying the implementation of the struct. Other programmers feel that properties provide a clean and simple interface, and that good programming practice demands data hiding even with simple lightweight objects. Which you choose is a matter of design philosophy; the language will support either approach.

CHAPTER 14

Interfaces

There are times when a designer does not want to create a new type. Rather, the designer wants to describe a set of behaviors that any number of types might implement. For example, a designer might want to describe what it means to be storable (i.e., capable of being written to disk) or printable.

Such a description is called an *interface*. An interface is a contract; the designer of the interface says "if you want to provide this capability, you must implement these methods." The *implementer* of the interface agrees to the contract and implements the required methods.

When a class implements an interface, it tells any potential client "I guarantee I'll support the methods, properties, events, and indexers of the named interface." The interface details the return type from each method and the parameters to the methods.

 See Chapter 9 for information about methods and properties; see Chapter 19 for information about events; and see Chapter 15 for coverage of indexers.

When specifying interfaces, it is easy to get confused about who is responsible for what. There are three concepts to keep clear:

The interface
> This is the contract. By convention, interface names begin with a capital I, so your interface might have a name such as IPrintable. The IPrintable interface might describe a Print() method.

The implementing class
> This is the class that agrees to the contract described by the interface. For example, Document might be a class that implements Printable and thus implements the Print() method.

The client class

This is a class that calls methods from the implementing class. For example, you might have an Editor class that calls the Document class's Print() method.

Interfaces Versus Abstract Base Classes

Programmers learning C# often ask about the difference between an interface and an abstract base class. The key difference is subtle: an abstract base class serves as the base class for a family of derived classes, while an interface is meant to be mixed in with other inheritance trees.

Inheriting from an abstract class implements the *is-a* relationship, introduced in Chapter 3. Implementing an interface defines a different relationship, one we've not seen until now: the *implements* relationship. These two relationships are subtly different. A car *is a* vehicle, but it might *implement* the CanBeBoughtWithABigLoan capability (as can a house, for example).

Interfaces are a critical addition to any framework, and they are used extensively throughout .NET. For example, the collection classes (stacks, queues, hashtables) are defined, in large measure, by the interfaces they implement. (The collection classes are explained in detail in Chapter 16.)

In this chapter, you will learn how to create, implement, and use interfaces. You'll learn how one class can implement multiple interfaces, and you will also learn how to make new interfaces by combining existing interfaces or by extending (deriving from) an existing interface. Finally, you will learn how to test whether a class has implemented an interface.

Implementing an Interface

The syntax for defining an interface is very similar to the syntax for defining a class or a struct:

```
[attributes] [access-modifier] interface interface-name [:base-list] {interface-body}
```

The optional attributes are not discussed in this book. Access modifiers (public, private, etc.) work just as they do with classes. (See Chapter 8 for more about access modifiers.) The interface keyword is followed by an identifier (the interface name). It is common (but not required) to begin the name of your interface with a capital I (IStorable, ICloneable, IGetNoKickFromChampagne, etc.). The optional base list is discussed in the section titled "Extending Interfaces," later in this chapter.

The body of the interface is defined within braces, just as the body of a class would be.

Suppose you want to create an interface to define the contract for data being stored to a database or file. Your interface will define the methods and properties a class will need to implement in order to be stored to a database or file. You decide to call this interface IStorable.

In this interface, you might specify two methods, Read() and Write(), which appear in the interface body:

```
interface IStorable
{
   void Read();
   void Write(object);
}
```

Now suppose you are the author of a document class, which specifies that Document objects can be stored in a database. You decide to have Document implement the IStorable interface. It isn't required that you do so, but by implementing the IStorable interface you signal to potential clients that the Document class can be used just like any other IStorable object. This will, for example, allow your clients to add your Document objects to a collection of IStorable objects, and to otherwise interact with your Document in this very general and well-understood way.

To implement the IStorable interface, use the same syntax as if the new Document class were inheriting from IStorable—a colon (:), followed by the interface name:

```
public class Document : IStorable
```

You can read this as "define a public class named Document that implements the IStorable interface." The compiler distinguishes whether the colon indicates inheritance or implementation of an interface by checking to see if there is an interface or base class named IStorable already defined.

Your definition of the Document class might look like this:

```
public class Document : IStorable
{
   public void Read() {...}
   public void Write(object obj) {...}
   // ...
}
```

It is now your responsibility, as the author of the Document class, to provide a meaningful implementation of the IStorable methods. Having designated Document as implementing IStorable, you must implement all the IStorable methods, or you will generate an error when you compile. Example 14-1 illustrates defining and implementing the IStorable interface.

Example 14-1. Document class implementing IStorable

```
using System;

namespace InterfaceDemo
{
```

Example 14-1. Document class implementing IStorable (continued)

```csharp
// define the interface
interface IStorable
{
    void Read();
    void Write(object obj);
    int Status { get; set; }

}

// create a Document class that implements the IStorable interface
public class Document : IStorable
{
    public Document(string s)
    {
        Console.WriteLine("Creating document with: {0}", s);
    }

    // implement the Read method
    public void Read()
    {
        Console.WriteLine(
            "Implementing the Read Method for IStorable");
    }

    // implement the Write method
    public void Write(object o)
    {
        Console.WriteLine(
            "Implementing the Write Method for IStorable");
    }
    // implement the property
    public int Status
    {
        get{ return status; }
        set{ status = value; }
    }

    // store the value for the property
    private int status = 0;
}

class Tester
{
    public void Run()
    {
        Document doc = new Document("Test Document");
        doc.Status = -1;
        doc.Read();
        Console.WriteLine("Document Status: {0}", doc.Status);
    }

    [STAThread]
```

Example 14-1. Document class implementing IStorable (continued)

```
    static void Main()
    {
        Tester t = new Tester();
        t.Run();
    }
  }
}
Output:
Creating document with: Test Document
Implementing the Read Method for IStorable
Document Status: -1
```

Example 14-1 defines a simple interface, IStorable, with two methods (Read() and Write()) and a property (Status) of type integer:

```
// define the interface
    interface IStorable
    {
        void Read();
        void Write(object obj);
        int Status { get; set; }


    }
```

Notice that the IStorable method declarations for Read() and Write() do not include access modifiers (e.g., public, protected, internal, private). In fact, providing an access modifier generates a compile error. Interface methods are implicitly public because an interface is a contract meant to be used by other classes.

The methods are otherwise defined just like methods in a class: the return type (void), followed by the identifier (Write), followed by the parameter list (object obj), and ended with a semicolon.

An interface can define that the implementing class will provide a property (see Chapter 9 for a discussion of properties). Notice that the declaration of the Status property does not provide an implementation for get() and set(), but simply designates that there *is* a get() and a set():

```
    int Status { get; set; }
```

Once again, it is up to the implementing class to provide the actual implementation of the get and set accessors, just as the implementing class must provide the implementation of the methods.

Once you've defined the IStorable interface, you can define classes that implement the interface. Keep in mind that you cannot create an instance of an interface; instead you instantiate a class that implements the interface.

The class implementing the interface must fulfill the contract exactly and completely. Thus, your Document class must provide both a Read() and a Write() method and the Status property.

```
// create a Document class that implements the IStorable interface
public class Document : IStorable
{

    // implement the Read method
    public void Read()
    {
        Console.WriteLine(
            "Implementing the Read Method for IStorable");
    }

    // implement the Write method
    public void Write(object o)
    {
        Console.WriteLine(
            "Implementing the Write Method for IStorable");
    }
    // implement the property
    public int Status
    {
        get{ return status; }
        set{ status = value; }
    }
}
```

How your Document class fulfills the requirements of the interface, however, is entirely up to you. Although IStorable dictates that Document must have a Status property, it does not know or care whether Document stores the actual status as a member variable or looks it up in a database. Example 14-1 implements the Status property by returning (or setting) the value of a private member variable, status.

Implementing More Than One Interface

Classes can derive from only one class (and if you don't explicitly derive from a class, then you implicitly derive from Object). Classes can implement any number of interfaces. When you design your class, you can choose not to implement any interfaces, you can implement a single interface, or you can implement two or more interfaces. For example, in addition to IStorable, you might have a second interface, ICompressible, for files that can be compressed to save disk space. If your Document class can be stored and compressed, you might choose to have Document implement both the IStorable and ICompressible interfaces.

 Both IStorable and ICompressible are interfaces created for this book and are not part of the standard .NET Framework.

Example 14-2 shows the complete listing of the new ICompressible interface and demonstrates how you modify the Document class to implement the two interfaces.

Example 14-2. IStorable and ICompressible, implemented by Document

```
using System;

namespace InterfaceDemo
{
    interface IStorable
    {
        void Read();
        void Write(object obj);
        int Status { get; set; }

    }

    // here's the new interface
    interface ICompressible
    {
        void Compress();
        void Decompress();
    }


    // Document implements both interfaces
    public class Document : IStorable, ICompressible
    {
        // the document constructor
        public Document(string s)
        {
            Console.WriteLine("Creating document with: {0}", s);

        }

        // implement IStorable
        public void Read()
        {
            Console.WriteLine(
                "Implementing the Read Method for IStorable");
        }

        public void Write(object o)
        {
            Console.WriteLine(
                "Implementing the Write Method for IStorable");
        }

        public int Status
        {
            get { return status; }
            set { status = value; }
        }

        // implement ICompressible
        public void Compress()
        {
```

```
            Console.WriteLine("Implementing Compress");
        }

        public void Decompress()
        {
            Console.WriteLine("Implementing Decompress");
        }


        // hold the data for IStorable's Status property
        private int status = 0;
    }


    class Tester
    {
        public void Run()
        {
            Document doc = new Document("Test Document");
            doc.Status = -1;
            doc.Read();
            doc.Compress();
            Console.WriteLine("Document Status: {0}", doc.Status);
        }

        [STAThread]
        static void Main()
        {
            Tester t = new Tester();
            t.Run();
        }
    }
}
```

```
Output:
Creating document with: Test Document
Implementing the Read Method for IStorable
Implementing Compress
Document Status: -1
```

As Example 14-2 shows, you declare the fact that your Document class will implement two interfaces by adding the second interface to the declaration (in the base list), separating the two interfaces with commas:

```
    public class Document : IStorable, ICompressible
```

Once you've done this, the Document class must also implement the methods specified by the ICompressible interface. ICompressible has only two methods, Compress() and Uncompress(), which are specified as:

```
    interface ICompressible
        {
```

```
    void Compress();
    void Decompress();
}
```

In this simplified example, Document implements these two methods as follows, printing notification messages to the console:

```
public void Compress()
{
    Console.WriteLine("Implementing the Compress Method");
}

public void Decompress()
{
    Console.WriteLine("Implementing the Decompress Method");
}
```

Casting to an Interface

You can access the members (i.e., methods and properties) of an interface through the object of any class that implements the interface. Thus, you can access the methods and properties of IStorable, through the Document object:

```
Document doc = new Document("Test Document");
doc.status = -1;
doc.Read();
```

In Chapter 16, you'll learn that at times you won't know that you have a Document object; rather you'll know only that you have objects that implement IStorable. You can create a variable of type IStorable and cast your Document to that type. You can then access the IStorable methods through the IStorable variable.

When you cast you say to the compiler, "trust me, I know this object is really of this type." In this case you are saying "trust me, I know this document really implements IStorable, so you can treat it as an IStorable."

Casting is safe to do because the Document object implements IStorable and thus is safely treated as an IStorable object. You cast by placing the type you are casting to in parentheses. The following line declares a variable of type IStorable and assigns to that variable the Document object, cast to type IStorable:

```
IStorable isDoc = (IStorable) doc;
```

You can read this line as "cast doc to IStorable and assign the resulting IStorable object to the variable isDoc, which is declared to be of type IStorable." Note that the variable isDoc is now a reference to the same document, but that reference is of type IStorable and so has the methods and properties of IStorable.

You are now free to use this IStorable variable to access the IStorable methods and properties of the document.

```
isDoc.status = 0;
isDoc.Read();
```

In these two lines of code you set the status property of the document to zero, and you call the Read() method of the document. You can do so because Status and Read() are members of the IStorable interface implemented by the document.

You cannot instantiate an interface directly; that is, you cannot write:

```
IStorable isDoc = new IStorable();
```

You can, however, create an instance of the implementing class and then create an instance of the interface by casting the implementing object to the interface type:

```
IStorable isDoc = (IStorable) doc;
```

isDoc is a reference to an IStorable object to which you've assigned the document cast to IStorable.

Note that you can combine these steps by writing:

```
IStorable isDoc =
    (IStorable) new Document("Test Document");
```

In general, it is a better design decision to access the interface methods through an interface reference rather than through an object of a class that implements the interface. Thus, it was better to use isDoc. Read() than doc.Read() in the previous example.

Access through an interface allows you to treat the interface polymorphically. In other words, you can have two or more classes implement the interface, and then by accessing these classes only through the interface, you can ignore their real runtime type and treat them simply as instances of the interface. You'll see the power of this technique in Chapter 16.

Thus far, you have cast the Document object (doc) to IStorable and assigned the result to the reference to an IStorable: isDoc. You knew this was safe to do because you defined the Document class to implement IStorable.

However, there may be instances in which you do not know in advance (at compile time) that an object supports a particular interface. For instance, given a collection of objects, you might not know whether each object in the collection implements IStorable, ICompressible, or both.

You can find out what interfaces are implemented by a particular object by casting blindly and then catching the exceptions that arise when you've tried to cast the object to an interface it hasn't implemented. The code to cast Document to ICompressible might be:

```
Document doc = new Document("Test Document");
ICompressible icDoc = (ICompressible) doc;
icDoc.Compress();
```

If Document implements only the IStorable interface but not the ICompressible interface:

```
public class Document : IStorable
```

the cast to ICompressible would still compile because ICompressible is a valid inter-face. However, because of the illegal cast, an exception will be thrown when the pro-gram is run:

```
An exception of type System.InvalidCastException was thrown.
```

 Exceptions are used to report errors and are covered in detail in Chapter 18.

You could then catch the exception and take corrective action, but this approach is ugly and evil and you should not do things this way. This is like testing whether a gun is loaded by firing it; it's dangerous and it annoys the neighbors.

Rather than firing blindly, you would like to be able to ask the object if it imple-ments an interface, in order to then invoke the appropriate methods. C# provides two operators to help you ask the object if it implements an interface: the is opera-tor and the as operator. The distinction between them is subtle but important.

The is Operator

The is operator lets you query whether an object implements an interface. The form of the is operator is:

expression **is** *type*

The is operator evaluates true if the *expression* (which must be a reference type such as an instance of a class) can be safely cast to *type* (e.g., an Interface) without throw-ing an exception.

Example 14-3 illustrates the use of the is operator to test whether a Document object implements the IStorable and ICompressible interfaces.

Example 14-3. The is operator

```
using System;

namespace InterfaceDemo
{
    interface IStorable
    {
        void Read();
        void Write(object obj);
        int Status { get; set; }

    }

    // here's the new interface
    interface ICompressible
    {
```

Example 14-3. The is operator (continued)

```
        void Compress();
        void Decompress();
    }


    // Document implements both interfaces
    public class Document : IStorable
    {
        // the document constructor
        public Document(string s)
        {
            Console.WriteLine("Creating document with: {0}", s);

        }

        // implement IStorable
        public void Read()
        {
            Console.WriteLine(
                "Implementing the Read Method for IStorable");
        }

        public void Write(object o)
        {
            Console.WriteLine(
                "Implementing the Write Method for IStorable");
        }

        public int Status
        {
            get { return status; }
            set { status = value; }
        }

        // hold the data for IStorable's Status property
        private int status = 0;
    }


class Tester
{
    public void Run()
    {
        Document doc = new Document("Test Document");

        // only cast if it is safe
        if (doc is IStorable)
        {
            IStorable isDoc = (IStorable) doc;
            isDoc.Read();
        }
        else
```

Example 14-3. The is operator (continued)

```
        {
            Console.WriteLine("Could not cast to IStorable");
        }

        // this test will fail
        if (doc is ICompressible)
        {
            ICompressible icDoc = (ICompressible) doc;
            icDoc.Compress();
        }
        else
        {
            Console.WriteLine("Could not cast to ICompressible");
        }

    }

    [STAThread]
    static void Main()
    {
        Tester t = new Tester();
        t.Run();
    }
}
}
Output:
Creating document with: Test Document
Implementing the Read Method for IStorable
Could not cast to ICompressible
```

In Example 14-3, the Document class implements only IStorable:

```
    public class Document : IStorable
```

In the Run() method of the Tester class, you create an instance of Document:

```
    Document doc = new Document("Test Document");
```

and test whether that instance is an IStorable (that is, does it implement the IStorable interface?):

```
    if (doc is IStorable)
```

If so, you cast Document to an IStorable, and you are now free to use the interface to call the methods of that interface.

```
    if (doc is IStorable)
    {
        IStorable isDoc = (IStorable) doc;
        isDoc.Read();
    }
```

Then repeat the test with ICompressible, and if the test fails, print an error message:

```
    if (doc is ICompressible)
    {
```

```
        ICompressible icDoc = (ICompressible) doc;
        icDoc.Compress();
    }
    else
    {
        Console.WriteLine("Could not cast to ICompressible");
    }
```

The output shows that the first test (is IStorable) succeeds (as expected) and the second test (is ICompressible) fails (also as expected).

```
Implementing the Read Method for IStorable
Could not cast to ICompressible
```

The compiler issues a warning when you compile Example 14-3:

```
c:...\class1.cs(64,15): warning CS0183: The given expression is
always of the provided ('InterfaceDemo.IStorable') type
```

The example is contrived, and the compiler recognizes that at compile time you can know for certain that the IStorable test will always succeed. In later chapters you'll see how to add objects to a collection, and when you test objects from the collection it will not be possible to know at compile time whether the test will succeed or not.

The as Operator

The is operator works, but it is not terribly efficient. There is a test done to evaluate the is operator, and another test done when you make the cast. That isn't a big deal if you are just casting a single object, but if you have a large collection of objects, it would be better to use a more efficient mechanism.

The as operator combines the is evaluation and cast operations by testing first to see whether a cast is valid (i.e., whether an is test would return true) and then completing the cast if it is. If the cast is not valid (i.e., if an is test would return false), the as operator returns null.

The keyword null represents a null reference, which does not refer to any object.

Using the as operator eliminates the need to handle cast exceptions, and you avoid the overhead of checking the cast twice. For these reasons, it is optimal to cast interfaces using as rather than is.

The form of the as operator is:

```
type instance = expression as type
```

The *expression* is typically an object of a class that might implement the interface, and the *type* is typically an Interface. What is returned is either a reference to the type or null.

For example, if the Document class (of which doc is an instance) does in fact implement ICompressible, then icDoc will be an ICompressible reference to the doc object. If the Document class does not implement ICompressible, icDoc will be null.

```
ICompressible icDoc = doc as ICompressible
```

The code in Example 14-4 replaces the Run() method in Example 14-3 and uses the as operator rather than the is operator. The rest of the example is unchanged and so is not reproduced here.

Example 14-4. The as operator

```
public void Run()
{
    Document doc = new Document("Test Document");

    // cast using as, then test for null
    IStorable isDoc = doc as IStorable;
    if (isDoc != null)
    {
        isDoc.Read();
    }
    else
    {
        Console.WriteLine("Could not cast to IStorable");
    }


    // cast using as, then test for null
    ICompressible icDoc = doc as ICompressible;
    if (icDoc != null)
    {
        icDoc.Compress();
    }
    else
    {
        Console.WriteLine("Could not cast to ICompressible");
    }
}
```

Extending Interfaces

It is possible to extend an existing interface to add new methods or members, or to modify how existing members work. For example, you might extend ICompressible with a new interface, ILoggedCompressible, which extends the original interface with methods to keep track of the bytes saved. One such method might be called LogSavedBytes(). The following code creates a new interface named ILoggedCompressible that is identical to ICompressible except that it adds the method LogSaved-Bytes.

```
interface ILoggedCompressible : ICompressible
{
    void LogSavedBytes();
}
```

Classes are now free to implement either ICompressible or ILoggedCompressible, depending on whether they need the additional functionality. If a class does implement ILoggedCompressible, it must implement all the methods of both ILogged-Compressible and also ICompressible. Objects of that type can be cast either to ILoggedCompressible or to ICompressible.

Example 14-5 extends ICompressible to create ILoggedCompressible, and then casts the Document first to be of type IStorable, then to be of type ILoggedCompressible. Finally, the example casts the Document object to ICompressible. This last cast is safe because any object that implements ILoggedCompressible must also have implemented ICompressible (the former is a superset of the latter). This is the same logic that says you can cast any object of a derived type to an object of a base type (that is, if Student derives from Human, then all Students are Human, even though not all Humans are Students).

Example 14-5. Extending interfaces

```
using System;

namespace InterfaceDemo
{
    interface IStorable
    {
        void Read();
        void Write(object obj);
        int Status { get; set; }

    }

    // the Compressible interface is now the
    // base for ILoggedCompressible
```

Example 14-5. Extending interfaces (continued)

```
interface ICompressible
{
    void Compress();
    void Decompress();
}

// extend ICompressible to log the bytes saved
interface ILoggedCompressible : ICompressible
{
    void LogSavedBytes();
}


// Document implements both interfaces
public class Document : IStorable, ILoggedCompressible
{
    // the document constructor
    public Document(string s)
    {
        Console.WriteLine("Creating document with: {0}", s);

    }

    // implement IStorable
    public void Read()
    {
        Console.WriteLine(
            "Implementing the Read Method for IStorable");
    }

    public void Write(object o)
    {
        Console.WriteLine(
            "Implementing the Write Method for IStorable");
    }

    public int Status
    {
        get { return status; }
        set { status = value; }
    }

    // implement ICompressible
    public void Compress()
    {
        Console.WriteLine("Implementing Compress");
    }

    public void Decompress()
    {
        Console.WriteLine("Implementing Decompress");
    }
```

Example 14-5. Extending interfaces (continued)

```
        // implement ILoggedCompressible
        public void LogSavedBytes()
        {
            Console.WriteLine("Implementing LogSavedBytes");
        }

        // hold the data for IStorable's Status property
        private int status = 0;
    }


    class Tester
    {
        public void Run()
        {
            Document doc = new Document("Test Document");

            // cast using as, then test for null
            IStorable isDoc = doc as IStorable;
            if (isDoc != null)
            {
                isDoc.Read();
            }
            else
            {
                Console.WriteLine("Could not cast to IStorable");
            }


            ILoggedCompressible ilDoc = doc as ILoggedCompressible;
            if (ilDoc != null)
            {
                Console.Write("\nCalling both ICompressible and ");
                Console.WriteLine("ILoggedCompressible methods...");
                ilDoc.Compress();
                ilDoc.LogSavedBytes();
            }
            else
            {
                Console.WriteLine("Could not cast to ILoggedCompressible");
            }

            // cast using as, then test for null
            ICompressible icDoc = doc as ICompressible;
            if (icDoc != null)
            {
                Console.WriteLine(
                    "\nTreating the object as Compressible... ");
                icDoc.Compress();
            }
            else
```

Example 14-5. Extending interfaces (continued)

```
        {
                Console.WriteLine("Could not cast to ICompressible");
        }
    }

    [STAThread]
    static void Main()
    {
        Tester t = new Tester();
        t.Run();
    }
 }
}
Output:
Creating document with: Test Document
Implementing the Read Method for IStorable

Calling both ICompressible and ILoggedCompressible methods...
Implementing Compress
Implementing LogSavedBytes

Treating the object as Compressible...
Implementing Compress
```

Example 14-5 starts by creating the ILoggedCompressible interface:

```
// extend ICompressible to log the bytes saved
interface ILoggedCompressible : ICompressible
{
void LogSavedBytes();
}
```

Notice that the syntax for extending an interface is the same as that for deriving from a class. This extended interface explicitly defines only one method (LogSaved-Bytes()), but of course any class implementing this interface must also implement the base interface (ICompressible) and all its members.

Define the Document class to implement both IStorable and ILoggedCompressible:

```
public class Document : IStorable, ILoggedCompressible
```

You are now free to cast the Document object to IStorable, ILoggedCompressible, or to ICompressible:

```
IStorable isDoc = doc as IStorable;
ILoggedCompressible ilDoc = doc as ILoggedCompressible;
ICompressible icDoc = doc as ICompressible;
```

If you look back at the output, you'll see that all three of these casts succeed.

Combining Interfaces

You can also create new interfaces by combining existing interfaces and optionally adding new methods or properties. For example, you might decide to combine the definitions of IStorable and ICompressible into a new interface called IStorableCompressible. This interface would combine the methods of each of the other two interfaces, but would also add a new method, LogOriginalSize(), to store the original size of the pre-compressed item:

```
interface IStorableCompressible : IStorable, ILoggedCompressible
{
    void LogOriginalSize();
}
```

Having created this interface, you can now modify Document to implement IStorableCompressible:

```
public class Document : IStorableCompressible
```

You now can cast the Document object to any of the four interfaces you've created so far:

```
IStorable isDoc = doc as IStorable;
ILoggedCompressible ilDoc = doc as ILoggedCompressible;
ICompressible icDoc = doc as ICompressible;
IStorableCompressible iscDoc = doc as IStorableCompressible;
```

When you cast to the new combined interface, you can invoke any of the methods of any of the interfaces it extends or combines. The following code invokes four methods on iscDoc (the IStorableCompressible object). Only one of these methods is defined in IStorableCompressible, but all four are methods defined by interfaces that IStorableCompressible extends or combines.

```
if (iscDoc != null)
{
    iscDoc.Read();                // Read() from IStorable
    iscDoc.Compress();            // Compress() from ICompressible
    iscDoc.LogSavedBytes();       // LogSavedBytes() from
                                  // ILoggedCompressible
    iscDoc.LogOriginalSize();     // LogOriginalSize() from
                                  // IStorableCompressible
}
```

Overriding Interface Implementations

An implementing class is free to mark any or all of the methods from the interface as virtual. Derived classes can then override or provide new implementations, just as they might with any other virtual instance method.

For example, a Document class might implement the IStorable interface and mark its Read() and Write() methods as virtual. The developer might later derive new types

from Document, such as a Note type. While the Document class implements Read()
and Write to save to a File, the Note class might implement Read() and Write() to
read from and write to a database.

Example 14-6 strips down the complexity of the previous examples and illustrates
overriding an interface implementation. In this example, you'll derive a new class
named Note from the Document class.

Document implements the IStorable-required Read() method as a virtual method,
and Note overrides that implementation.

 Notice that Document does not mark Write() as virtual. You'll see the
implications of this decision in the analysis section that follows
Example 14-6.

The complete listing is shown in Example 14-6.

Example 14-6. Overriding an interface implementation

```
using System;

namespace OverridingInterfaces
{
    interface IStorable
    {
        void Read();
        void Write();
    }

    // Simplify Document to implement only IStorable
    public class Document : IStorable
    {
        // the document constructor
        public Document(string s)
        {
            Console.WriteLine(
                "Creating document with: {0}", s);
        }

        // Make read virtual
        public virtual void Read()
        {
            Console.WriteLine(
                "Document Read Method for IStorable");
        }

        // NB: Not virtual!
        public void Write()
        {
            Console.WriteLine(
                "Document Write Method for IStorable");
```

Example 14-6. Overriding an interface implementation (continued)

```csharp
        }
}

// Derive from Document
public class Note : Document
{
    public Note(string s):
        base(s)
    {
        Console.WriteLine(
            "Creating note with: {0}", s);
    }

    // override the Read method
    public override void Read()
    {
        Console.WriteLine(
            "Overriding the Read method for Note!");
    }

    // implement my own Write method
    public new void Write()
    {
        Console.WriteLine(
            "Implementing the Write method for Note!");
    }
}

class Tester
{
    public void Run()
    {
        // Create a Document object
        Document theNote = new Note("Test Note");

        // direct call to the methods
        theNote.Read();
        theNote.Write();

        Console.WriteLine("\n");

        // cast the Document to IStorable
        IStorable isNote = theNote as IStorable;
        if (isNote != null)
        {
            isNote.Read();
            isNote.Write();
        }
        Console.WriteLine("\n");

        // create a note object
        Note note2 = new Note("Second Test");
```

Example 14-6. Overriding an interface implementation (continued)

```
            // directly call the methods
            note2.Read();
            note2.Write();
            Console.WriteLine("\n");

            // Cast the note to IStorable
            IStorable isNote2 = note2 as IStorable;
            if (isNote != null)
            {
                isNote2.Read();
                isNote2.Write();
            }


        }

        static void Main()
        {
            Tester t = new Tester();
            t.Run();
        }
    }
}
```

Output:

```
Creating document with: Test Note
Creating note with: Test Note
Overriding the Read method for Note!
Document Write Method for IStorable

Overriding the Read method for Note!
Document Write Method for IStorable

Creating document with: Second Test
Creating note with: Second Test
Overriding the Read method for Note!
Implementing the Write method for Note!

Overriding the Read method for Note!
Document Write Method for IStorable
```

In Example 14-6, the IStorable interface is simplified for clarity's sake:

```
interface IStorable
{
    void Read();
    void Write();
}
```

The Document class implements the IStorable interface:

```
public class Document : IStorable
```

The designer of Document has opted to make the Read() method virtual but not to make the Write() method virtual:

```
public virtual void Read()
public        void Write()
```

 In a real-world application, you would almost certainly mark both as virtual, but I've differentiated them to demonstrate that the developer is free to pick and choose which methods are made virtual.

The new class, Note, derives from Document:

```
public class Note : Document
```

It is not necessary for Note to override Read(), but it is free to do so and has done so here:

```
public override void Read()
```

To illustrate the implications of marking an implementing method as virtual, the Run() method calls the Read() and Write() methods in four ways:

- Through the base class reference to a derived object
- Through an interface created from the base class reference to the derived object
- Through a derived object
- Through an interface created from the derived object

As you have seen previously, virtual methods are implemented polymorphically, and nonvirtual methods are not. It turns out that the interfaces created from these references work just like the references themselves. That is, virtual implementations of the interface methods are polymorphic, while nonvirtual implementations are not.

The one surprising aspect is this: when you call the nonpolymorphic Write() method on the IStorable interface cast from the derived Note, you actually get the Document's Write method because Write() is implemented in the base class and is nonvirtual.

To illustrate calling the methods through a base class reference to a derived object, instantiate a Document (base class) reference and assign to it the address of a new derived object (of type Note) that is created on the heap:

```
Document theNote = new Note("Test Note");
```

Then invoke the Read and Write methods through that reference:

```
theNote.Read();
theNote.Write();
```

The output reveals that the Read() method is responded to polymorphically and the Write() method is not, just as we would expect:

```
Overriding the Read method for Note!
Document Write Method for IStorable
```

The overridden method of Read() is called because you've created a new Note object.

```
Document theNote = new Note("Test Note");
```

The nonvirtual Write method of Document is called because you've assigned theNote to a reference to a Document.

```
Document theNote = new Note("Test Note");
```

To illustrate calling the methods through an interface that is created from the base class reference to the derived object, create an interface reference named isNote. Use the as operator to cast the Document (theNote) to the IStorable reference:

```
IStorable isNote = theNote as IStorable;
```

Then invoke the Read() and Write() methods for theNote through that interface.

```
if (isNote != null)
{
    isNote.Read();
    isNote.Write();
}
```

The output is the same: once again the virtual Read method is polymorphic, and the nonvirtual Write() method is not:

```
Overriding the Read method for Note
Document Write Method for IStorable
```

Next create a second Note object, this time assigning its address to a reference to a Note, rather than a reference to a Document. This will be used to illustrate the final cases (i.e., a call through a derived object and a call through an interface created from the derived object):

```
Note note2 = new Note("Second Test");
```

Call the methods on the derived object:

```
note2.Read();
note2.Write();
```

Again, the virtual Read() method is polymorphic, and the nonvirtual Write() method is not, but this time you get the Write() method for Note because you are calling the method on a Note object.

```
Overriding the Read method for Note!
Implementing the Write method for Note!
```

Finally, cast the Note object to an IStorable reference and call Read() and Write():

```
IStorable isNote2 = note2 as IStorable;
if (isNote != null)
{
    isNote2.Read();
    isNote2.Write();
}
```

The Read() method is called polymorphically, but the Write() method for Document is called because Document implements IStorable, and Write() is not polymorphic.

```
Overriding the Read method for Note!
Document Write Method for IStorable
```

Explicit Interface Implementation

In the implementation shown so far, the implementing class (Document) creates a member method with the same signature and return type as the method detailed in the interface. It is not necessary to explicitly state that this is an implementation of an interface; this is understood by the compiler implicitly.

What happens, however, if the class implements two interfaces, each of which has a method with the same signature? This might happen if the class implements interfaces defined by two different organizations or even two different programmers. The next example creates two interfaces: IStorable and ITalk. The latter implements a Read() method that reads a book aloud. Unfortunately, this conflicts with the Read() method in IStorable.

Because both IStorable and ITalk have a Read() method, the implementing Document class must use *explicit implementation* for at least one of the methods. With explicit implementation, the implementing class (Document) explicitly identifies the interface for the method:

```
void ITalk.Read()
```

Marking the Read() method as a member of the ITalk interface resolves the conflict between the identical Read() methods. There are some additional aspects you should keep in mind.

First, the explicit implementation method cannot have an access modifier:

```
void ITalk.Read()
```

This method is implicitly public. In fact, a method declared through explicit implementation cannot be declared with the abstract, virtual, override, or new keywords.

Most importantly, you cannot access the explicitly implemented method through the object itself. When you write:

```
theDoc.Read();
```

the compiler assumes you mean the implicitly implemented interface for IStorable. The only way to access an explicitly implemented interface is through a cast to the interface:

```
ITalk itDoc = theDoc as ITalk;
if (itDoc != null)
{
    itDoc.Read();
}
```

Explicit implementation is demonstrated in Example 14-7.

Note that there is no need to use explicit implementation with the other method of ITalk:

```
public void Talk()
```

Because there is no conflict, this can be declared as usual.

Example 14-7. Explicit implementation

```
using System;

namespace OverridingInterfaces
{
    interface IStorable
    {
        void Read();
        void Write();
    }

    interface ITalk
    {
        void Talk();
        void Read();
    }


    // Modify Document to also implement ITalk
    public class Document : IStorable, ITalk
    {
        // the document constructor
        public Document(string s)
        {
            Console.WriteLine(
                "Creating document with: {0}", s);
        }

        // Implicit implementation
        public virtual void Read()
        {
            Console.WriteLine(
                "Document Read Method for IStorable");
        }

        public void Write()
        {
            Console.WriteLine(
                "Document Write Method for IStorable");
        }

        // Explicit implementation
        void ITalk.Read()
        {
```

Example 14-7. Explicit implementation (continued)

```
            Console.WriteLine("Implementing ITalk.Read");
        }

        public void Talk()
        {
            Console.WriteLine("Implementing ITalk.Talk");
        }
    }

    class Tester
    {
        public void Run()
        {
            // Create a Document object
            Document theDoc = new Document("Test Document");
            IStorable isDoc = theDoc as IStorable;
            if (isDoc != null)
            {
                isDoc.Read();
            }

            // Cast to an ITalk interface
            ITalk itDoc = theDoc as ITalk;
            if (itDoc != null)
            {
                itDoc.Read();
            }

            theDoc.Read();
            theDoc.Talk();
        }

        [STAThread]
        static void Main()
        {
            Tester t = new Tester();
            t.Run();
        }
    }
}
Output:
Creating document with: Test Document
Document Read Method for IStorable
Implementing ITalk.Read
Document Read Method for IStorable
Implementing ITalk.Talk
```

CHAPTER 15

Arrays

Most of the examples in previous chapters have dealt with one object at a time. In many applications, however, you want to work with a *collection* of objects all at the same time. The simplest collection in C# is the *array*, the only collection type for which C# provides built-in support. The other collection types, such as stack and queue, are not part of the language; they are part of the Framework Class Library. The collection classes are covered in detail in the next chapter. In this chapter, you will learn to work with three types of arrays: one-dimensional arrays, multidimensional rectangular arrays, and multidimensional jagged arrays.

To picture a one-dimensional array, imagine a series of mailboxes, all lined up one after the other. Each mailbox can hold exactly one object (letter, box, etc.). All the mailboxes must hold the same kind of object; you declare the type of object the mailboxes will hold when you declare the array.

A multidimensional array allows you to create rows of mailboxes, one above the other. If all the rows are the same length, you have a rectangular array. If each row of mailboxes is a different length, you have a jagged array.

You can think of a multidimensional array as being like a grid of rows and columns in which each slot (mailbox) contains information. For example, each column might contain information pertinent to an employee. Each row would contain all the information for a single employee.

Most often you will deal with a two-dimensional array, but larger multidimensional arrays (3-D, 4-D, etc.) are also possible.

A jagged array is a type of multi-dimensional array in which each row can have a different number of columns. A jagged array is less of a grid and more of an array of arrays—that is, an array in which the elements are arrays. This allows you to group a few arrays of varying sizes into a single array. For example, you might have an array of ten buttons, a second array of five listboxes, and a third array of seven checkboxes. You can group all three into a jagged array of controls.

This chapter also introduces the concept of indexers, a feature of C# that makes it possible to create your own classes that can be treated like arrays.

Arrays

An array is an indexed collection of objects, all of the same type (e.g., all ints, all strings, etc.). C# provides a native syntax for the declaration of Array objects:

```
int[] myArray;
```

When you declare an array, you actually create an instance of the Array class in the System namespace (System.Array). Arrays in C# thus provide you with the best of both worlds: easy-to-use syntax built into the language, underpinned with an actual class definition so that instances of an array have access to the methods and properties of System.Array. The System.Array class is discussed in detail later in this chapter.

Declaring Arrays

You declare a C# array with the following syntax:

```
type[] array-name;
```

The square brackets ([]) tell the C# compiler that you are declaring an array. (Note that the square brackets are also called the index operator.) The *type* specifies the type of the elements the array will contain. For example, the following declaration specifies an array called myIntArray that will contain objects of type int (integer):

```
int[] myIntArray;
```

Once you declare an array, you must also instantiate it using the new keyword. For example, the following declaration sets aside memory for an array holding five integers:

```
myIntArray = new int[5];
```

It is important to distinguish between the array itself (which is a collection of elements) and the elements within the array. myIntArray is the array; its elements are the five integers it holds.

> While C# arrays are reference types, created on the heap, the elements of an array are allocated based on their type. Thus, myIntArray is a reference type allocated on the heap and the integer elements in myIntArray are value types allocated on the stack. (While you can *box* a value type so that it can be treated like a reference type, as explained in Chapter 11, it is not necessary or desirable to box the integers in an array.) By contrast, an array that contains reference types, such as Employee or Button, will contain nothing but references to the elements, which are themselves created on the heap.

Understanding Default Values

When you create an array of value types, each element initially contains the default value for the type stored in the array. (See Table 5-1 in Chapter 5.) The following declaration creates an array of five integers, each of whose value is initialized to 0, the default value for integer types:

```
myIntArray = new int[5];
```

With an array of reference types, the elements are *not* initialized to their default values. Instead, they are initialized to null. If you attempt to access any of the elements in an array of reference types before you specifically initialize them, you will generate an exception (exceptions are covered in Chapter 18).

Assume you have created a Button class. Declare an array of Button objects (thus reference types) with the following statement:

```
Button[] myButtonArray;
```

and instantiate the actual array, to hold three Buttons, like this:

```
myButtonArray = new Button[3];
```

Note that you can combine the two steps and write:

```
Button myButtonArray = new Button[3];
```

In either case, unlike with the earlier integer example, this statement does *not* create an array with references to three Button objects. Since Button objects are reference types, this creates the array myButtonArray with three null references. To use this array, you must first construct and assign a Button object for each reference in the array. This is called *populating* the array. You can construct the objects in a loop that adds them one by one to the array. Example 15-1 illustrates creating an array of value types (integers) and reference types (Employee objects).

Example 15-1. Creating an array

```
using System;

namespace ArrayDemo
{
    // a simple class to store in the array
    public class Employee
    {
        private int empID;

        // constructor
        public Employee(int empID)
        {
            this.empID = empID;
        }
    }
```

Example 15-1. Creating an array (continued)

```
class Tester
{
    public void Run()
    {
        int[] intArray;
        Employee[] empArray;
        intArray = new int[5];
        empArray = new Employee[3];

        // populate the array
        for (int i = 0;i<empArray.Length;i++)
        {
            empArray[i] = new Employee(i+5);
        }

    }

    [STAThread]
    static void Main()
    {
        Tester t = new Tester();
        t.Run();
    }
}
}
```

Example 15-1 begins by creating a simple Employee class to add to the array. When Run() begins, two arrays are declared, one of type int and the other of type Employee:

```
int[] intArray;
Employee[] empArray;
```

The int array is populated with ints set to zero. The empArray is initialized with null references.

> The array does not have Employee objects whose member fields are set to null; it does not have Employee objects at all. What is in the cubby holes of the array is just nulls. Nothing. Nada. When you create the Employee objects, you can then store them in the array.

You must populate the Employee array before you can refer to its elements:

```
for (int i = 0;i<empArray.Length;i++)
{
    empArray[i] = new Employee(i+5);
}
```

The exercise has no output. You've added the elements to the array, but how do you use them? How do you refer to them?

Accessing Array Elements

Arrays are zero-based, which means that the index of the first element is always zero—in this case, myArray[0]. The second element is element 1. The numeric value is called the index, or the offset. Index 3 indicates the element offset from the beginning of the array by 3 elements, that is, the fourth element in the array. You access element 3 using the index operator [ ]. Thus, the fourth element is returned by writing:

```
myArray[3]; // return the 4th element (at offset 3)
```

Because arrays are objects, they have properties. One of the more useful properties of the Array class is Length, which tells you how many objects are in an array. Array objects can be indexed from 0 to Length-1. That is, if there are five elements in an array, their indices are 0,1,2,3,4.

In Example 15-1, you created an array of Employees and an array of integers. In Example 15-2, you return to that array and access the elements. You'll override ToString() in the Employee class so that Employee objects can display their value.

Example 15-2. Accessing two simple arrays

```
using System;

namespace ArrayDemo
{

    // a simple class to store in the array
    public class Employee
    {
        private int empID;

        // constructor
        public Employee(int empID)
        {
            this.empID = empID;
        }
        public override string ToString()
        {
            return empID.ToString();
        }
    }

    class Tester
    {
        public void Run()
        {
            int[] intArray;
            Employee[] empArray;
            intArray = new int[5];
            empArray = new Employee[3];
```

Example 15-2. Accessing two simple arrays (continued)

```
            // populate the array
            for (int i = 0;i<empArray.Length;i++)
            {
                empArray[i] = new Employee(i+5);
            }

            Console.WriteLine("The int array...");
            for (int i = 0;i<intArray.Length;i++)
            {
                Console.WriteLine(intArray[i].ToString());
            }

            Console.WriteLine("\nThe employee array...");
            for (int i = 0;i<empArray.Length;i++)
            {
                Console.WriteLine(empArray[i].ToString());
            }
        }

        [STAThread]
        static void Main()
        {
            Tester t = new Tester();
            t.Run();
        }
    }
}
```

Output:
```
The int array...
0
0
0
0
0

The employee array...
5
6
7
```

In this version of the example, the contents of the arrays are printed to ensure that they are filled as intended. Notice that you refer to the individual members of the array using the index operator.

The five integers print their value first, followed by the three Employee objects.

 If you comment out the code in which the Employee objects are created, you'll generate an exception when you try to display the contents of the Employee array. This demonstrates that arrays of reference types are initialized with null references.

The foreach Statement

The foreach looping statement allows you to iterate through all the items in an array (or other collection), examining each item in turn. The syntax for the foreach statement is:

```
foreach (type identifier in expression) statement
```

The foreach statement creates a new object that holds a reference to each of the objects in the collection, in turn, as you loop through the collection. For example, you might write:

```
foreach ( int theInt in intArray )
```

Each time through the loop, the next member of intArray is assigned to the integer variable theInt. You can then use that object to display the value, as in:

```
Console.WriteLine(theInt.ToString());
```

Similarly, you might iterate through the Employee array:

```
foreach ( Employee e in empArray )
```

In the case shown here, e is an object of type Employee. For each turn through the loop, e refers to the next Employee in the array:

```
Console.WriteLine(e.ToString());
```

Example 15-3 rewrites the Run() method of Example 15-2 to use a foreach loop rather than a for loop, but is otherwise unchanged.

Example 15-3. Using a foreach loop

```
public void Run()
{
    int[] intArray;
    Employee[] empArray;
    intArray = new int[5];
    empArray = new Employee[3];

    // populate the array
    for (int i = 0;i<empArray.Length;i++)
    {
        empArray[i] = new Employee(i+5);
    }

    Console.WriteLine("The int array...");
    foreach( int theInt in intArray )
    {
        Console.WriteLine(theInt.ToString());
    }

    Console.WriteLine("\nThe employee array...");
    foreach ( Employee e in empArray )
    {
        Console.WriteLine(e.ToString());
```

Example 15-3. Using a foreach loop (continued)

```
    }
}
```

Output:
```
The int array...
0
0
0
0
0

The employee array...
5
6
7
```

The output for Example 15-3 is identical to Example 15-2. However, rather than creating a for statement that measures the size of the array and uses a temporary counting variable as an index into the array, as in Example 15-2:

```
for (int i = 0; i < empArray.Length; i++)
{
    Console.WriteLine(empArray[i].ToString());
}
```

Example 15-3 iterates over the array with the foreach loop, which automatically extracts the next item from within the array and assigns it to a temporary object. In the following case, the temporary object is of type Employee (it is a reference to an Employee object) and is named e.

```
foreach (Employee e in empArray)
{
    Console.WriteLine(e.ToString());
}
```

Since e is a reference to an Employee, you can call any public method of Employee. In the case shown, you call the ToString() method of Employee, which Employee inherits from Object and overrides to display meaningful information about the Employee object.

Initializing Array Elements

Rather than assigning elements to the array as you have done so far, it is possible to initialize the contents of an array at the time it is instantiated by providing a list of values delimited by curly braces ({}). C# provides two different syntaxes to accomplish the same task:

```
int[] myIntArray = new int[5] { 2, 4, 6, 8, 10 };
int[] myIntArray = { 2, 4, 6, 8, 10 };
```

There is no practical difference between these two statements, and most programmers will use the shorter syntax because we are, by nature, lazy. We are so lazy, we'll work all day to save a few minutes doing a task—which isn't so crazy if we're going to do that task hundreds of times! Example 15-4 again rewrites the Run() method of Example 15-1, this time demonstrating initialization of both arrays.

Example 15-4. Initializing array elements

```
public void Run()
{
    int[] intArray = { 2, 4, 6, 8, 10 };
    Employee[] empArray =
        { new Employee(5), new Employee(7), new Employee(9) };


    Console.WriteLine("The int array...");
    foreach( int theInt in intArray )
    {
        Console.WriteLine(theInt.ToString());
    }

    Console.WriteLine("\nThe employee array...");
    foreach ( Employee e in empArray )
    {
        Console.WriteLine(e.ToString());
    }
}
```

Output:
```
The int array...
2
4
6
8
10

The employee array...
5
7
9
```

In Example 15-3, you created an Employee array by first allocating space for the array (which was filled with nulls).

```
empArray = new Employee[3];
```

You then filled the array by writing a for loop and adding a value for each member:

```
// populate the array
for (int i = 0;i<empArray.Length;i++)
{
    empArray[i] = new Employee(i+5);
}
```

In Example 15-4, you *initialized* the array by providing the values at the time you instantiated the array:

```
Employee[] empArray =
    { new Employee(5), new Employee(7), new Employee(9) };
```

This combines the steps of defining the array and populating the array.

The params Keyword

C# provides the keyword params.

```
public void DisplayVals(params int[] intVals)
```

This keyword indicates that the method treats all the parameters passed to it as an array, even if you pass in the parameters as individual values. This helps you solve the thorny programming problem of how you can define a method that takes a variable number of parameters (that is, when you can't know at compile time how many parameters you'll be passing into the method).

As far as the client (the calling method) is concerned, you pass in a variable number of parameters.

```
myObject.DisplayVals(5,7,9);         // display 3 values
myObject.DisplayVals(5,7,9,11,13);   // display 5 values
```

The implementing method (DisplayVals) treats the variable number of parameters *as an array* and can just iterate through the array to find each parameter!

```
public void DisplayVals(params int[] intVals)
{
    foreach (int i in intVals)
    {
        Console.WriteLine("DisplayVals {0}",i);
    }
}
```

In effect, even though you invoked DisplayVals() with this code:

```
myObject.DisplayVals(5,7,9,11,13);
```

the DisplayVals() method treats the invocation *exactly* as if you had written:

```
int [] explicitArray = new int[5] {5,7,9,11,13};
DisplayVals(explicitArray);
```

In fact, you can call that same DisplayVals() method and pass in an actual array. You are free to call it either way: with individual parameters that are treated as an array, or with an array. Example 15-5 demonstrates how to use the params keyword.

Example 15-5. The params keyword

```
using System;

namespace ParamsDemo
{
    class Tester
    {
        public void Run()
        {
            int a = 5;
            int b = 6;
            int c = 7;
            Console.WriteLine("Calling with three integers");
            DisplayVals(a,b,c);

            Console.WriteLine("\nCalling with four integers");
            DisplayVals(5,6,7,8);

            Console.WriteLine("\ncalling with an array of four integers");
            int [] explicitArray = new int[4] {5,6,7,8};
            DisplayVals(explicitArray);
        }

        // takes a variable number of integers
        public void DisplayVals(params int[] intVals)
        {
            foreach (int i in intVals)
            {
                Console.WriteLine("DisplayVals {0}",i);
            }
        }

        [STAThread]
        static void Main()
        {
            Tester t = new Tester();
            t.Run();
        }
    }
}
```

Output:
```
Calling with three integers
DisplayVals 5
DisplayVals 6
DisplayVals 7

Calling with four integers
DisplayVals 5
DisplayVals 6
DisplayVals 7
DisplayVals 8
```

Example 15-5. The params keyword (continued)

```
calling with an array of four integers
DisplayVals 5
DisplayVals 6
DisplayVals 7
DisplayVals 8
```

The first time you call DisplayVals(), you pass in three integer variables:

```
int a = 5;
int b = 6;
int c = 7;
DisplayVals(a,b,c);
```

The second time you call DisplayVals(), you pass in four literal constants:

```
DisplayVals(5,6,7,8);
```

In both cases, DisplayVals() treats the parameters as if they were declared in an array. In the final invocation, you explicitly create an array and pass that as the parameter to the method:

```
int [] explicitArray = new int[4] {5,6,7,8};
DisplayVals(explicitArray);
```

Thus, you can call DisplayVals() by passing in any number of variables (a,b,c), by passing in any number of literal constants (5,6,7,8), or by passing in an array (explicitArray) with any number of members.

Multidimensional Arrays

You can think of arrays as long rows of slots into which values can be placed. Once you have a picture of a row of slots, imagine five rows, one on top of another. This is the classic two-dimensional array of rows and columns. The rows run across the array and the columns run up and down the array, as illustrated in Figure 15-1.

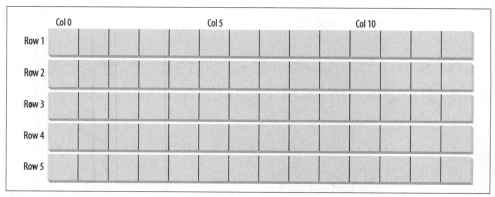

Figure 15-1. Rows and columns create a multidimensional array

A third dimension is possible but somewhat harder to picture. Imagine making your arrays three-dimensional, with new rows stacked atop the old two-dimensional array. OK, now imagine four dimensions. Now imagine ten.

Those of you who are not string-theory physicists have probably given up, as have I. Multidimensional arrays are useful, however, even if you can't quite picture what they would look like. You might, for example, use a four-dimensional array to track movement in three dimensions (x,y,z) over time.

C# supports two types of multidimensional arrays: rectangular and jagged. In a rectangular array, every row is the same length. In a jagged array, however, each row can be a different length. In fact, you can think of each row in a jagged array as an array unto itself. Thus, a jagged array is actually an array of arrays.

Rectangular Arrays

A rectangular array is an array of two (or more) dimensions. In the classic two-dimensional array, the first dimension is the number of rows and the second dimension is the number of columns.

To declare a two-dimensional array, use the following syntax:

```
type [,] array-name
```

For example, to declare and instantiate a two-dimensional rectangular array named myRectangularArray that contains two rows and three columns of integers, you would write:

```
int [,] myRectangularArray = new int[2,3];
```

In Example 15-6, you create a two-dimensional array of integers and populate the array using two for loops. The outer for loop iterates once for each row, and the inner for loop iterates once for each column in each row:

```
for (int i = 0;i < rows;i++)
{
    for (int j = 0;j<columns;j++)
    {
        rectangularArray[i,j] = i+j;
    }
}
```

Then use a second set of for loops to display the contents of the array:

```
for (int i = 0;i < rows;i++)
{
    for (int j = 0;j<columns;j++)
    {
        Console.WriteLine("rectangularArray[{0},{1}] = {2}",
            i,j,rectangularArray[i,j]);
    }
}
```

The complete listing is shown in Example 15-6, followed by analysis.

Example 15-6. Rectangular array

```
using System;

namespace MultiDimensionalArrays
{
    class Tester
    {
        public void Run()
        {
            const int rows = 4;
            const int columns = 3;

            // declare a 4x3 integer array
            int[,] rectangularArray = new int[rows, columns];

            // populate the array
            for (int i = 0;i < rows;i++)
            {
                for (int j = 0;j<columns;j++)
                {
                    rectangularArray[i,j] = i+j;
                }
            }

            // report the contents of the array
            for (int i = 0;i < rows;i++)
            {
                for (int j = 0;j<columns;j++)
                {
                    Console.WriteLine("rectangularArray[{0},{1}] = {2}",
                        i,j,rectangularArray[i,j]);
                }
            }
        }

        [STAThread]
        static void Main()
        {
            Tester t = new Tester();
            t.Run();
        }
    }
}
```
Output:
```
rectangularArray[0,0] = 0
rectangularArray[0,1] = 1
rectangularArray[0,2] = 2
rectangularArray[1,0] = 1
rectangularArray[1,1] = 2
rectangularArray[1,2] = 3
rectangularArray[2,0] = 2
rectangularArray[2,1] = 3
rectangularArray[2,2] = 4
```

Example 15-6. Rectangular array (continued)

```
rectangularArray[3,0] = 3
rectangularArray[3,1] = 4
rectangularArray[3,2] = 5
```

In Example 15-6, you declare a pair of constant values to be used to specify the number of rows (4) and the number of columns (3) in the two-dimensional array:

```
const int rows = 4;
const int columns = 3;
```

Creating these constants allows you to refer to the rows and columns by number throughout the program. If you decide later to change the value of either, you only have to make the change in one location in your code.

You use the numeric values for the rows and columns to specify the dimensions of the array in the combined declaration and instantiation statement:

```
int[,] rectangularArray = new int[rows, columns];
```

Notice the syntax. Everything up to and including the equal sign (=) is the declaration; everything following is the instantiation. The brackets in the int[,] declaration indicate that the type is an array of integers, and the single comma indicates the array has two dimensions; two commas would indicate three dimensions, and so on. The actual instantiation of rectangularArray:

```
new int[rows, columns]
```

sets the size of each dimension. Just as you can initialize a one-dimensional array using bracketed lists of values, you can initialize a two-dimensional array using a similar syntax.

```
int[,] rectangularArray =
{
  {0,1,2}, {3,4,5}, {6,7,8}, {9,10,11}
};
```

The outer braces mark the entire array initialization, and the inner braces mark each of the elements in the second dimension. Since this is a 4x3 array (four rows by three columns), you have four sets of three initialized values (12 in all). Writing the initialization as:

```
int[,]rectangularArray =
{
  {0,1,2,3}, {4,5,6,7}, {8,9,10,11}
};
```

would instead initialize a 3x4 array (three rows by four columns).

Example 15-7 rewrites the Run() method from Example 15-6 to create and initialize a two-dimensional array.

Example 15-7. Initializing a two-dimensional array

```
public void Run()
{
    const int rows = 4;
    const int columns = 3;

    // define and initialize the array
    int[,] rectangularArray =
    {
      {0,1,2}, {3,4,5}, {6,7,8}, {9,10,11}
    };

    // report the contents of the array
    for (int i = 0;i < rows;i++)
    {
        for (int j = 0;j<columns;j++)
        {
            Console.WriteLine("rectangularArray[{0},{1}] = {2}",
                i,j,rectangularArray[i,j]);
        }
    }
}
```
Output:
```
rectangularArray[0,0] = 0
rectangularArray[0,1] = 1
rectangularArray[0,2] = 2
rectangularArray[1,0] = 3
rectangularArray[1,1] = 4
rectangularArray[1,2] = 5
rectangularArray[2,0] = 6
rectangularArray[2,1] = 7
rectangularArray[2,2] = 8
rectangularArray[3,0] = 9
rectangularArray[3,1] = 10
rectangularArray[3,2] = 11
```

You might guess that you can access the element at rectangularArray[1,0] by referring to it as rectangularArray[0,3]. After all, element [1,0] is just the fourth element of twelve. That actually works in some languages, but not in C#. If you try, you will run right into an exception:

```
Exception occurred: System.IndexOutOfRangeException:
Index was outside the bounds of the array.
at Programming_CSharp.Tester.Main() in
csharp\programming csharp\listing0703.cs:line 23
```

C# arrays are smart and they keep track of their bounds. When you define a 4x3 array, you must treat it as such, and not as a 3x4 or a 12x1 array.

As the output illustrates, the C# compiler understands the syntax of your initialization; the objects are accessed with the appropriate offsets.

Jagged Arrays

A jagged array is an array of arrays. Specifically, a jagged array is a type of multi-dimensional array in which each row can be a different size from all the other rows. Thus, a graphical representation of the array has a "jagged" appearance, as in Figure 15-2.

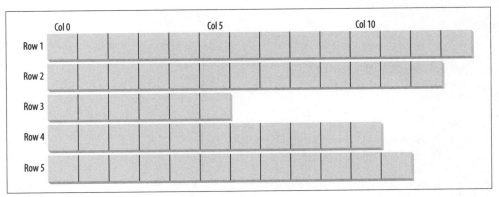

Figure 15-2. Jagged array

You can think of each row in a jagged array as a one-dimensional array unto itself. Thus, technically speaking, a jagged array is an array of arrays. When you create a jagged array, you declare the number of rows in your array. Each row holds a one-dimensional array, and each row can be of any length. To declare a jagged array, use the following syntax, where the number of brackets indicates the number of dimensions of the array:

```
type [] []...
```

For example, you would declare a two-dimensional jagged array of integers named myJaggedArray as follows:

```
int [] [] myJaggedArray;
```

Address the elements in the array as follows: the array name then the offset into the array of arrays (the row), and then the offset into the chosen array (the column within the chosen row). That is, to access the fifth element of the third array, write:

```
myJaggedArray[2][4]
```

Remember that all arrays are zero-based. The third element is at offset 2, and the fifth element is at offset 4.

Example 15-8 creates a jagged array named myJaggedArray, initializes its elements, and then prints their content. To save space, the program takes advantage of the fact that integer array elements are automatically initialized to zero, and it initializes the values of only some of the elements.

Notice that when you accessed the members of the rectangular array, you put the indexes all within one set of square brackets:

```
ArrayrectangularArray[row,column]
```

However, with a jagged array you need a pair of brackets:

```
jaggedArray[row][column]
```

You can keep this straight by thinking of the first as a single array of more than one dimension and the jagged array as an array of arrays.

Example 15-8. Jagged array

```
using System;

namespace JaggedArray
{
    class Tester
    {
        public void Run()
        {
            const int rows = 4;
            const int rowZero = 5;   // num elements
            const int rowOne = 2;
            const int rowTwo = 3;
            const int rowThree = 5;

            // declare the jagged array as 4 rows high
            int[][] jaggedArray = new int[rows][];

            // declare the rows of various lengths
            jaggedArray[0] = new int[rowZero];
            jaggedArray[1] = new int[rowOne];
            jaggedArray[2] = new int[rowTwo];
            jaggedArray[3] = new int[rowThree];

            // Fill some (but not all) elements of the rows
            jaggedArray[0][3] = 15;
            jaggedArray[1][1] = 12;
            jaggedArray[2][1] = 9;
            jaggedArray[2][2] = 99;
            jaggedArray[3][0] = 10;
            jaggedArray[3][1] = 11;
            jaggedArray[3][2] = 12;
            jaggedArray[3][3] = 13;
            jaggedArray[3][4] = 14;

            for (int i = 0;i < rowZero; i++)
            {
                Console.WriteLine("jaggedArray[0][{0}] = {1}",
                    i,jaggedArray[0][i]);
            }

            for (int i = 0;i < rowOne; i++)
            {
                Console.WriteLine("jaggedArray[1][{0}] = {1}",
```

Example 15-8. Jagged array (continued)

```
                     i,jaggedArray[1][i]);
        }

        for (int i = 0;i < rowTwo; i++)
        {
            Console.WriteLine("jaggedArray[2][{0}] = {1}",
                i,jaggedArray[2][i]);
        }
        for (int i = 0;i < rowThree; i++)
        {
            Console.WriteLine("jaggedArray[3][{0}] = {1}",
                i,jaggedArray[3][i]);
        }
    }

    [STAThread]
    static void Main()
    {
        Tester t = new Tester();
        t.Run();
    }
  }
}

output:
jaggedArray[0][0] = 0
jaggedArray[0][1] = 0
jaggedArray[0][2] = 0
jaggedArray[0][3] = 15
jaggedArray[0][4] = 0
jaggedArray[1][0] = 0
jaggedArray[1][1] = 12
jaggedArray[2][0] = 0
jaggedArray[2][1] = 9
jaggedArray[2][2] = 99
jaggedArray[3][0] = 10
jaggedArray[3][1] = 11
jaggedArray[3][2] = 12
jaggedArray[3][3] = 13
jaggedArray[3][4] = 14
```

Example 15-8 creates a jagged array with four rows:

```
int[][] jaggedArray = new int[rows][];
```

Notice that the size of the second dimension is not specified. The columns in a jagged array vary by row; thus they are set by creating a new array for each row. Each of these arrays can have a different size:

```
jaggedArray[0] = new int[rowZero];
jaggedArray[1] = new int[rowOne];
jaggedArray[2] = new int[rowTwo];
jaggedArray[3] = new int[rowThree];
```

If you look back at the values of the constants (rowZero through rowThree), you'll be able to figure out that there are 15 slots in this array.

Once an array size is specified for each row, you need to populate the various members of each array (row) and then print out their contents to ensure that all went as expected.

System.Array

C# implements arrays with the class System.Array. The Array class has a number of useful methods. Table 15-1 shows a few of the more important methods and properties of the System.Array class.

Table 15-1. Useful methods and properties of System.Array

Method or Property	Description
Clear()	Public static method that sets a range of elements in the array to zero or to a null reference
Copy()	Overloaded public static method that copies a section of one array to another array
IndexOf()	Overloaded public static method that returns the index (offset) of the first instance of a value in a one-dimensional array
LastIndexOf()	Overloaded public static method that returns the index of the last instance of a value in a one-dimensional array
Reverse()	Overloaded public static method that reverses the order of the elements in a one-dimensional array
Sort()	Overloaded public static method that sorts the values in a one-dimensional array
IsFixedSize	Public property that returns a value indicating whether the array has a fixed size
Length	Public property that returns the length of the array
Rank	Public property that returns the number of dimensions of the array

The Array class's static methods, Reverse() and Sort(), make manipulation of the objects within the array very easy. Note, however, that to reverse or sort the elements of the array, they must be of a type that implements the IComparable interface. (Chapter 16 describes the collection interfaces.) The .NET Framework includes the String class, which does implement this interface, so we'll demonstrate both Reverse() and Sort() with Strings. The complete listing is shown in Example 15-9, followed by the output and analysis.

Example 15-9. Reverse() and Sort() methods of Array

```
using System;

namespace ReverseAndSort
{
    class Tester
    {
```

Example 15-9. Reverse() and Sort() methods of Array (continued)

```csharp
    public static void DisplayArray(object[] theArray)
    {

        foreach (object obj in theArray)
        {
            Console.WriteLine("Value: {0}", obj);
        }
        Console.WriteLine("\n");
    }

    public void Run()
    {
        String[] myArray =
            {
                "Who", "is", "John", "Galt"
            };

        Console.WriteLine("Display myArray...");
        DisplayArray(myArray);

        Console.WriteLine("Reverse and display myArray...");
        Array.Reverse(myArray);
        DisplayArray(myArray);

        String[] myOtherArray =
            {
                "We", "Hold", "These", "Truths",
                "To", "Be", "Self", "Evident",
            };

        Console.WriteLine("Display myOtherArray...");
        DisplayArray(myOtherArray);

        Console.WriteLine("Sort and display myOtherArray...");
        Array.Sort(myOtherArray);
        DisplayArray(myOtherArray);
    }

    [STAThread]
    static void Main()
    {
        Tester t = new Tester();
        t.Run();
    }
  }
}
```

Output:
```
Display myArray...
Value: Who
Value: is
Value: John
Value: Galt
```

Example 15-9. Reverse() and Sort() methods of Array (continued)

```
Reverse and display myArray...
Value: Galt
Value: John
Value: is
Value: Who

Display myOtherArray...
Value: We
Value: Hold
Value: These
Value: Truths
Value: To
Value: Be
Value: Self
Value: Evident

Sort and display myOtherArray...
Value: Be
Value: Evident
Value: Hold
Value: Self
Value: These
Value: To
Value: Truths
Value: We
```

The example begins by creating myArray, an array of strings containing the words:

```
"Who", "is", "John", "Galt"
```

This array is displayed and then passed to the Array.Reverse() method, where it is displayed again to see that the array itself has been reversed:

```
Value: Galt
Value: John
Value: is
Value: Who
```

Similarly, the example creates a second array, myOtherArray, containing the words:

```
"We", "Hold", "These", "Truths",
"To", "Be", "Self", "Evident",
```

which is passed to the Array.Sort() method. Then Array.Sort() happily sorts them alphabetically:

```
Value: Be
Value: Evident
Value: Hold
Value: Self
Value: These
Value: To
Value: Truths
Value: We
```

The method to display the strings has been made somewhat generic by declaring the type passed in to be an array of objects:

```
public static void DisplayArray(object[] theArray)
```

The DisplayArray() method iterates through the array of objects, passing each to WriteLine().

```
foreach (object obj in theArray)
{
    Console.WriteLine("Value: {0}", obj);
}
```

Since WriteLine() calls ToString() on objects, and since every object (including String) supports ToString(), declaring the temporary variable obj to be of type Object works very well. Using objects has the advantage that you can reuse your DisplayArray() method with arrays of other types of objects, once you know how to implement the IComparable interface (shown in Chapter 17).

Indexers

Some classes act like collections. For example, a ListBox class might act as a collection of the strings it displays. You might write your own School class that would act as a collection of all the Students enrolled in the school.

An *indexer* is a C# construct that allows you to treat a class as if it were a collection, using the familiar [] syntax of arrays. This lets you write:

```
mySchool[5];
```

to obtain the sixth Student in your School object.

An indexer is actually a special kind of property that includes get() and set() methods to specify its behavior. Declare an indexer property within a class using the following syntax:

```
type this [type argument]{get; set;}
```

The *type* specifies the type of object that returns the indexer, while the *type argument* within the square brackets specifies what kind of argument is used to index into the collection that contains the target objects.

 The square brackets do not indicate that *type argument* is optional. The square brackets themselves are part of the syntax of the indexer.

Although it is common to use integers as index values, you can index a collection on other types as well, including strings. This lets you write:

```
mySchool["John Galt"];
```

to index into your School's internal collection and find the Student object whose name field (for example) matches the index string.

You can even provide an indexer with multiple parameters if you wish to provide the syntax for accessing into your class as if it were a multidimensional array!

The this keyword is a reference to the current object and stands in as the name of the indexer. As with a normal property, you must define get() and set() methods that determine how the requested object is retrieved from or assigned to its collection.

Let's look at an example of how you might use an indexer. Suppose you create a list-box control named myListBox that contains a list of strings stored in a one-dimensional array, a private member variable named myStrings.

A listbox control contains member properties and methods in addition to its array of strings. However, it would be convenient to be able to access the listbox object with an index, just as if the listbox itself were an array. For example, such a property would permit statements like the following:

```
string theFirstString = myListBox[0];
string theLastString = myListBox[LastElementOffset];
```

Example 15-10 declares a listbox control class called ListBoxTest that contains, as a private member variable, a simple array (myStrings). The listbox control also provides an indexer for accessing the contents of its internal array. To keep Example 15-10 simple, you'll strip the listbox control down to just a few features.

The example ignores everything having to do with listbox being a user control and focuses only on the array of strings the listbox maintains (and methods for manipulating them). In a real application, of course, these are a small fraction of the total methods of a listbox, whose principal job is to display the strings and enable user choice.

Example 15-10. Using an indexer

```
using System;

namespace Indexers
{
    // a simplified ListBox control
    public class ListBoxTest
    {
        private string[] strings;
        private int ctr = 0;

        // initialize the listbox with strings
        public ListBoxTest(params string[] initialStrings)
        {
            // allocate space for the strings
            strings = new String[256];

            // copy the strings passed in to the constructor
```

Example 15-10. Using an indexer (continued)

```
        foreach (string s in initialStrings)
        {
            strings[ctr++] = s;
        }
    }

    // add a single string to the end of the listbox
    public void Add(string theString)
    {
        if (ctr >= strings.Length)
        {
            // handle bad index
        }
        else
            strings[ctr++] = theString;
    }

    // allow array-like access
    public string this[int index]
    {
        get
        {
            if (index < 0 || index >= strings.Length)
            {
                // handle bad index
            }
            return strings[index];
        }
        set
        {
            // add only through the add method
            if (index >= ctr )
            {
                // handle error
            }
            else
                strings[index] = value;
        }
    }

    // publish how many strings you hold
    public int GetNumEntries()
    {
        return ctr;
    }

}

class Tester
{
    public void Run()
    {
```

Example 15-10. Using an indexer (continued)

```
            // create a new listbox and initialize
            ListBoxTest lbt =
                new ListBoxTest("Hello", "World");

            Console.WriteLine("After creation...");
            for (int i = 0;i<lbt.GetNumEntries();i++)
            {
                Console.WriteLine("lbt[{0}]: {1}",i,lbt[i]);
            }

            // add a few strings
            lbt.Add("Who");
            lbt.Add("Is");
            lbt.Add("John");
            lbt.Add("Galt");

            Console.WriteLine("\nAfter adding strings...");
            for (int i = 0;i<lbt.GetNumEntries();i++)
            {
                Console.WriteLine("lbt[{0}]: {1}",i,lbt[i]);
            }


            // test the access
            string subst = "Universe";
            lbt[1] = subst;

            // access all the strings
            Console.WriteLine("\nAfter editing strings...");
            for (int i = 0;i<lbt.GetNumEntries();i++)
            {
                Console.WriteLine("lbt[{0}]: {1}",i,lbt[i]);
            }
        }

        [STAThread]
        static void Main()
        {
            Tester t = new Tester();
            t.Run();
        }
    }
}
```
Output:
```
After creation...
lbt[0]: Hello
lbt[1]: World

After adding strings...
lbt[0]: Hello
lbt[1]: World
lbt[2]: Who
```

Example 15-10. Using an indexer (continued)

```
lbt[3]: Is
lbt[4]: John
lbt[5]: Galt

After editing strings...
lbt[0]: Hello
lbt[1]: Universe
lbt[2]: Who
lbt[3]: Is
lbt[4]: John
lbt[5]: Galt
```

Example 15-10 begins by creating two private members: an array of strings named (appropriately) strings and an integer named ctr (which is initialized to 0):

```
private string[] strings;
private int ctr = 0;
```

The member variable ctr keeps track of how many strings have been added to this array.

Initialize the array in the constructor with the following statement, which allots memory for 256 String objects:

```
strings = new String[256];
```

The remainder of the constructor adds the parameters to the array. Again, for simplicity, simply add new strings to the array in the order received in the constructor's parameter list:

```
// copy the strings passed in to the constructor
foreach (string s in initialStrings)
{
    strings[ctr++] = s;
}
```

Because you cannot know at compile time how many strings will be added, use the params keyword, as described earlier in this chapter. The Add() method of ListBox-Test does nothing more than append a new string to the internal array.

The key feature of ListBoxTest, however, is the indexer. Declare the indexer property with the this keyword:

```
public string this[int index]
```

The syntax of the indexer is very similar to that for properties. There needs to be a get() method, a set() method, or both. In Example 15-10, the get() method endeavors to implement rudimentary bounds checking, and, assuming the index requested is acceptable, it returns the value requested:

```
get
{
    if (index < 0 || index >= strings.Length)
    {
```

```
        // handle bad index
    }
    return strings[index];
}
```

The set() method checks to make sure that the index you are setting already has a value in the listbox. If not, it treats the set() as an error; new elements can only be added using Add() with this approach. The set accessor method takes advantage of the implicit parameter named value that represents whatever is assigned using the index operator:

```
set
{
if (index >= ctr )
 {
    // handle error
 }
 else
    strings[index] = value;
}
```

Thus, if you write:

```
lbt[5] = "Hello World"
```

the compiler calls the indexer set() method on your object and passes in the string Hello World as an implicit parameter named value. This is analogous to how set accessors work for other properties. Remember, if you have a property named Weight and you write:

```
myObject.Weight = 5;
```

the set accessor is called and the implicit parameter value evaluates to 5. Similarly, if you write:

```
myObject[3] = "hello";
```

the indexer property's set accessor is called and the implicit parameter value evaluates to "hello." The offset (3) is available to the set accessor as the index. You can thus write:

```
strings[index] = value
```

and index will be 3 and value will be "hello," and this code will assign the string hello to the fourth element in the member variable strings.

Indexers and Assignment

You cannot assign to an index that does not have a value. Thus, in Example 15-10, if you write:

```
lbt[10] = "wow!";
```

you would trigger the error handler in the set() method, which would note that the index you've used (10) is larger than the counter (6).

As an alternative, you might change the set() method to check the Length of the buffer rather than the current value of the counter. If a value was entered for an index that did not yet have a value, you would update ctr:

```
set
{
    // add only through the add method
    if (index >= strings.Length )
    {
        // handle error
    }
    else
    {
        strings[index] = value;
        if (ctr < index+1)
            ctr = index+1;
    }
}
```

This allows you to create a "sparse" array in which you can assign to offset 10 without ever having assigned to offset 9. Thus, if you now write:

```
lbt[10] = "wow!";
```

the output would be:

```
lbt[0]: Hello
lbt[1]: Universe
lbt[2]: Who
lbt[3]: Is
lbt[4]: John
lbt[5]: Galt
lbt[6]:
lbt[7]:
lbt[8]:
lbt[9]:
lbt[10]: wow!
```

Indexing on Other Values

C# does not require that you always use an integer value as the index to a collection. You are free to create indexers that index on strings and other types. In fact, the index value can be overloaded so that a given collection can be indexed, for example, by an integer value or by a string value, depending on the needs of the client. In the case of your listbox, you might want to be able to index into the listbox based on a string. Example 15-11 illustrates a string indexer. The indexer calls findString(), which is a helper method that returns a record based on the value of the string provided. Notice that the overloaded indexer and the indexer from Example 15-10 are able to coexist. The complete listing is shown, followed by the output and then a detailed analysis.

Example 15-11. String indexer

```
using System;

namespace Indexers
{
    // a simplified ListBox control
    public class ListBoxTest
    {
        private string[] strings;
        private int ctr = 0;

        // initialize the listbox with strings
        public ListBoxTest(params string[] initialStrings)
        {
            // allocate space for the strings
            strings = new String[256];

            // copy the strings passed in to the constructor
            foreach (string s in initialStrings)
            {
                strings[ctr++] = s;
            }
        }

        // add a single string to the end of the listbox
        public void Add(string theString)
        {
            strings[ctr] = theString;
            ctr++;
        }

        // allow array-like access
        public string this[int index]
        {
            get
            {
                if (index < 0 || index >= strings.Length)
                {
                    // handle bad index
                }
                return strings[index];
            }
            set
            {
                strings[index] = value;
            }
        }

        // helper method, given a string find
        // first matching record that starts with the target
        private int findString(string searchString)
        {
            for (int i = 0;i<strings.Length;i++)
```

Example 15-11. String indexer (continued)

```
        {
            if (strings[i].StartsWith(searchString))
            {
                return i;
            }
        }
        return -1;
    }

    // index on string
    public string this[string index]
    {
        get
        {
            if (index.Length == 0)
            {
                // handle bad index
            }

            return this[findString(index)];
        }
        set
        {
            strings[findString(index)] = value;
        }
    }

    // publish how many strings you hold
    public int GetNumEntries()
    {
        return ctr;
    }
}


class Tester
{
    public void Run()
    {
        // create a new listbox and initialize
        ListBoxTest lbt =
            new ListBoxTest("Hello", "World");

        // add a few strings
        lbt.Add("Who");
        lbt.Add("Is");
        lbt.Add("John");
        lbt.Add("Galt");

        // test the access
        string subst = "Universe";
```

Example 15-11. String indexer (continued)

```
            lbt[1] = subst;
            lbt["Hel"] = "GoodBye";
            // lbt["xyz"] = "oops";


            // access all the strings
            for (int i = 0; i<lbt.GetNumEntries(); i++)
            {
                Console.WriteLine("lbt[{0}]: {1}",i,lbt[i]);
            }


        }

        [STAThread]
        static void Main()
        {
            Tester t = new Tester();
            t.Run();
        }
    }
}
```
Output:
```
lbt[0]: GoodBye
lbt[1]: Universe
lbt[2]: Who
lbt[3]: Is
lbt[4]: John
lbt[5]: Galt
```

Example 15-11 is identical to Example 15-10 except for the addition of an over-loaded indexer that can match a string:

```
        public string this[string index]
```

To support the indexer that indexes on a string, you also create the method find-String():

```
        private int findString(string searchString)
```

The findString() method simply iterates through the strings held in the private member array myStrings until it finds a string that starts with the target string used in the index. If found, it returns the index of that string, otherwise it returns the value −1.

You see in Main() that the user first passes in an integer as the index value:

```
        string subst = "Universe";
        lbt[1] = subst;
```

The second time you index into the array, however, you pass in a string, rather than an integer:

```
        lbt["Hel"] = "GoodBye";
```

This calls the overloaded indexer's set accessor:

```csharp
public string this[string index]
{
    get
    {
        if (index.Length == 0)
        {
            // handle bad index
        }

        return this[findString(index)];
    }
    set
    {
        strings[findString(index)] = value;
    }
}
```

The set accessor assigns the value ("Goodbye") to the strings array. It needs to know what index to use, so it must translate the index it was given ("hel") into an integer index for the strings array. To do so, it calls the helper method findString(). The findString() method takes the string passed in to the set accessor ("Hel") and returns the index of the matching string in the strings array, or it returns –1 if that string is not found.

The set accessor then uses that returned value as an index into the strings array. If findString() returns –1 (the string was not found), the index into strings generates an exception (System.NullReferenceException), as you can see by un-commenting the following line in Main():

```csharp
lbt["xyz"] = "oops";
```

The proper handling of not finding a string is, as they say, left as an exercise for the reader. You might consider displaying an error message or otherwise allowing the user to recover from the error.

Exceptions are discussed in Chapter 18.

CHAPTER 16

Collection Interfaces and Types

A collection is a container that holds a group of objects. Collections are used to hold all the strings in a listbox, to hold all the employees in a company, to hold all the controls on a page, and so forth. You've already seen the simplest collection, the array (see Chapter 15). An array is a collection that provides an indexed list of elements, all of the same type.

The .NET Framework provides a number of already built and tested collection classes, including the ArrayList, Queue, and Stack. This chapter will explain how to use these collections and will provide examples of their use.

The Collection Interfaces

Every collection has certain shared characteristics, which are captured by the collection interfaces. The .NET Framework provides standard interfaces for enumerating, comparing, and creating collections.

 Chapter 14 introduced interfaces, which create a contract that a class can fulfill. Implementing an interface allows clients of the class to know exactly what to expect from the class.

By implementing the collection interfaces, your custom class provides the same semantics as the collection classes available through the .NET Framework. Table 16-1 lists the key collection interfaces and their uses.

Table 16-1. The collection interfaces

Interface	Purpose
IEnumerable	Enumerates through a collection using a foreach statement
IEnumerator	Iterates over a collection and supports the foreach loop
ICollection	Implemented by all collections
IComparer	Compares two objects; used for sorting

Table 16-1. The collection interfaces (continued)

Interface	Purpose
IList	Used by collections that can be indexed
IDictionary	For key/value-based collections such as Hashtable and SortedList
IDictionaryEnumerator	Allows enumeration with `foreach` of a collection that supports IDictionary

This chapter will focus on the IEnumerable interface, using it to demonstrate how you can implement the collection interfaces in your own classes to allow clients to treat your custom classes as if they were collections. For example, you might create a custom class named ListBoxTest. Your ListBoxTest will have a set of strings to be displayed. You can implement the collection interfaces in your ListBoxTest class to allow clients to treat your ListBoxTest as if it were a collection. This allows clients to add to the ListBoxTest using the index operator (e.g., `myListBox[5] = "New String"`), to sort the ListBoxTest, to enumerate the elements of the ListBoxTest, and so forth.

The IEnumerable Interface

In the previous chapter, you developed a simple ListBoxTest class that provided an indexer for array-like semantics. That is, your ListBoxTest implemented its own indexer so that you could treat the ListBoxTest object like it was an Array:

```
myListBoxTest[5] = "Hello world";
string theText = myListBoxTest[1];
```

Of course, ListBoxTest is not an array; it is just a custom class that can be treated like an array because you gave it this indexer. You can make your ListBoxTest class even more like a real array by providing support for iterating over the contents of the array using the foreach statement. To provide support for the foreach statement, you'll need to implement the IEnumerable interface.

When you iterate over an array you visit each member in turn. Programmers talk about iterating over an array, iterating the array, iterating through the array, and enumerating the array. All of these terms mean the same thing.

The foreach statement will work with any class that implements the IEnumerable interface. Classes that implement the IEnumerable interface have a single method, GetEnumerator(), that returns an object that implements a second interface, IEnumerator.

Note the subtle difference in the names of these two interfaces. IEnumer*able* vs. IEnumer*ator*. The former designates a class that can be enumerated, the latter designates a class that does the actual enumeraion.

The entire job of the IEnumerable interface is to define the GetEnumerator() method. The job of the GetEnumerator() method is to generate an enumerator—that is, an instance of a class that implements the IEnumerator interface.

By implementing the IEnumerable interface, your ListBoxTest class is saying "you can enumerate my members, just ask me for my enumerator." The client asks the ListBoxTest for its enumerator by calling the GetEnumerator() method. What it gets back is an instance of a class that knows how to iterate over a list box. That class, ListBoxEnumerator, will implement the IEnumerator interface.

This gets a bit confusing, so let's use an example. When you implement the IEnumerable interface for ListBoxTest, you are promising potential clients that ListBoxTest will support enumeration. That allows clients of your ListBoxTest class to write code like this:

```
foreach (string s in ListBoxTest) { //... }
```

You implement IEnumerable by providing the GetEnumerator() method, which returns an implementation of IEnumerator. In this case, you'll return an instance of ListBoxEnumerator, and ListBoxEnumerator will implement the IEnumerator interface:

```
public IEnumerator GetEnumerator()
{
    return (IEnumerator) new ListBoxEnumerator(this);
}
```

The ListBoxEnumerator is a specialized instance of IEnumerator that knows how to enumerate the contents of your ListBoxTest class. Notice two things about this implementation. First, the constructor for ListBoxEnumerator takes a single argument, and you pass in the this reference. Doing so passes in a reference to the current ListBoxTest object, which is the object that will be enumerated. Second, notice that the ListBoxEnumerator is cast to an IEnumerator before it is returned. This cast is safe because the ListBoxEnumerator class implements the IEnumerator interface.

 An alternative to creating a specialized class to implement IEnumerator is to have the enumerable class (ListBoxTest) implement IEnumerator itself. In that case, the IEnumerator returned by GetEnumerator would be the ListBoxTest object, cast to IEnumerator.

Putting the enumeration responsibility into a dedicated class that implements IEnumerator (ListBoxEnumerator) is generally preferred to the alternative of letting the collection class (ListBoxTest) know how to enumerate itself. The specialized enumeration class encapsulates the responsibility of enumeration and the collection class (ListBoxTest) is not cluttered with a lot of enumeration code.

Because ListBoxEnumerator is specialized to know only how to enumerate ListBoxTest objects (and not any other enumerable objects), make ListBoxEnumerator a private class, contained within the definition of ListBoxTest. The complete listing is shown in Example 16-1, followed by a detailed analysis.

Example 16-1. Enumeration

```
using System;

namespace Enumeration
{
    using System;
    using System.Collections;

    // implements IEnumerable
    public class ListBoxTest : IEnumerable
    {
        private string[] strings;
        private int ctr = 0;

        // private nested implementation of ListBoxEnumerator
        private class ListBoxEnumerator : IEnumerator
        {
            // member fields of the nested ListBoxEnumerator class
            private ListBoxTest currentListBox;
            private int index;

            // public within the private implementation
            // thus, private within ListBoxTest
            public ListBoxEnumerator(ListBoxTest currentListBox)
            {
                // a particular ListBoxTest instance is
                // passed in, hold a reference to it
                // in the member variable currentListBox.
                this.currentListBox = currentListBox;
                index = -1;
            }

            // Increment the index and make sure the
            // value is valid
            public bool MoveNext()
            {
                index++;
                if (index >= currentListBox.strings.Length)
                    return false;
                else
                    return true;
            }

            public void Reset()
            {
                index = -1;
            }

            // Current property defined as the
            // last string added to the listbox
            public object Current
            {
                get
                {
```

Example 16-1. Enumeration (continued)

```
                return(currentListBox[index]);
        }
    }
} // end nested class

// Enumerable classes can return an enumerator
public IEnumerator GetEnumerator()
{
    return (IEnumerator) new ListBoxEnumerator(this);
}

// initialize the listbox with strings
public ListBoxTest(params string[] initialStrings)
{
    // allocate space for the strings
    strings = new String[8];

    // copy the strings passed in to the constructor
    foreach (string s in initialStrings)
    {
        strings[ctr++] = s;
    }
}

// add a single string to the end of the listbox
public void Add(string theString)
{
    strings[ctr] = theString;
    ctr++;
}

// allow array-like access
public string this[int index]
{
    get
    {
        if (index < 0 || index >= strings.Length)
        {
            // handle bad index
        }
        return strings[index];
    }
    set
    {
        strings[index] = value;
    }
}

// publish how many strings you hold
public int GetNumEntries()
{
    return ctr;
}
```

Example 16-1. Enumeration (continued)

```
    }

  class Tester
  {
     public void Run()
     {
        // create a new listbox and initialize
        ListBoxTest currentListBox =
           new ListBoxTest("Hello", "World");

        // add a few strings
        currentListBox.Add("Who");
        currentListBox.Add("Is");
        currentListBox.Add("John");
        currentListBox.Add("Galt");

        // test the access
        string subst = "Universe";
        currentListBox[1] = subst;

        // access all the strings
        foreach (string s in currentListBox)
        {
           Console.WriteLine("Value: {0}", s);
        }
     }

     [STAThread]
     static void Main()
     {
        Tester t = new Tester();
        t.Run();
     }
  }
}
```

Output:
```
Value: Hello
Value: Universe
Value: Who
Value: Is
Value: John
Value: Galt
Value:
Value:
```

The definition of the ListBoxEnumerator class is the most interesting aspect of this code. Notice that this class is defined within the definition of ListBoxTest. It is a contained class. It is also marked private; the only method that will ever instantiate a ListBoxEnumerator object is the GetEnumerator() method of ListBoxTest.

```
    private class ListBoxEnumerator : IEnumerator
    {
```

ListBoxEnumerator is defined to implement the IEnumerator interface, which defines one property and two methods, as shown in Table 16-2.

Table 16-2. IEnumerator

Property or Method	Description
Current	Property that returns the current element
MoveNext()	Method that advances the enumerator to the next element
Reset()	Method that sets the enumerator to its initial position, *before* the first element

The ListBoxTest object to be enumerated is passed in as an argument to the ListBox-Enumerator constructor, where it is assigned to the member variable currentList-Box. The constructor also sets the member variable index to −1, indicating that you have not yet begun to enumerate the object:

```
public ListBoxEnumerator(ListBoxTest currentListBox)
{
    this.currentListBox = currentListBox;
    index = -1;
}
```

 −1 is used as a signal to indicate that the enumerator is not yet pointing to any of the elements in the ListBoxTest object. You can't use the value 0, because 0 is a valid offset into the collection.

The MoveNext() method increments the index and then checks the length property of the strings array to ensure that you have not run past the end of the strings array. If you have run past the end, you return false; otherwise you return true:

```
public bool MoveNext()
{
    index++;
    if (index >= currentListBox.strings.Length)
        return false;
    else
        return true;
}
```

The IEnumerator method Reset() does nothing but reset the index to −1. You can call Reset() any time you want to start over iterating the ListBoxTest object.

The Current property is implemented to return the string at the index. This is an arbitrary decision; in other classes, Current has whatever meaning the designer decides is appropriate. However defined, every enumerator must be able to return the current member, as accessing the current member is what enumerators are for. The interface defines the Current property to return an object. Since strings are derived from object, there is an implicit cast of the string to the more general object type.

```
public object Current
{
    get
    {
        return(currentListBox[index]);
    }
}
```

The call to foreach fetches the enumerator and uses it to enumerate over the array. Because foreach displays every string, whether or not you've added a meaningful value, in Example 16-1 the strings array is initialized to hold only eight strings.

Now that you've seen how ListBoxTest implements IEnumerable, let's examine how the ListBoxTest object is used. The program begins by creating a new ListBoxTest object and passing two strings to the constructor.

```
public void Run()
{
    ListBoxTest currentListBox =
        new ListBoxTest("Hello", "World");
```

When the ListBoxTest object (currentListBox) is created, an array of Strings is created with room for eight strings. The initial two strings passed in to the constructor are added to the array.

```
public ListBoxTest(params string[] initialStrings)
{
    // allocate space for the strings
    strings = new String[8];

    // copy the strings passed in to the constructor
    foreach (string s in initialStrings)
    {
        strings[ctr++] = s;
    }
}
..
```

Back in Run(), four more strings are added using the Add() method, and the second string is updated with the word "Universe," just as in Example 15-11.

```
currentListBox.Add("Who");
currentListBox.Add("Is");
currentListBox.Add("John");
currentListBox.Add("Galt");

string subst = "Universe";
currentListBox[1] = subst;
```

You iterate over the strings in currentListBox with a foreach loop, displaying each string in turn:

```
foreach (string s in currentListBox)
{
    Console.WriteLine("Value: {0}", s);
}
```

The foreach loop checks that your class implements IEnumerable (and throws an exception if it does not) and invokes GetEnumerator():

```
public IEnumerator GetEnumerator()
{
    return (IEnumerator) new ListBoxEnumerator(this);
}
```

GetEnumerator() calls the ListBoxEnumerator constructor, thus initializing the index to −1.

```
public ListBoxEnumerator(ListBoxTest currentListBox)
{
    this.currentListBox = currentListBox;
    index = -1;
}
```

The first time through the loop, the foreach loop automatically invokes Move-Next(), which immediately increments the index to 0 and returns true.

```
public bool MoveNext()
{
    index++;
    if (index >= currentListBox.strings.Length)
        return false;
    else
        return true;
}
```

The foreach loop then uses the Current property to get back the current string.

```
public object Current
{
    get
    {
        return(currentListBox[index]);
    }
}
```

The Current property invokes the ListBoxTest's indexer, getting back the string stored at index 0. This string is assigned to the variable s defined in the foreach loop, and that string is displayed on the console. The foreach loop repeats these steps (call MoveNext(), access the Current property, display the string) until all the strings in the ListBoxTest object have been displayed.

Walking Through foreach in a Debugger

The calls to MoveNext() and Current are done for you by the foreach construct; you will not see these invoked directly, though you can step into the methods in the debugger as you iterate through the foreach loop. The debugger makes the relationships among the foreach construct, the ListBoxTest class, and its enumerator explicit. To examine these relationships, put a breakpoint at the foreach loop, as shown in Figure 16-1.

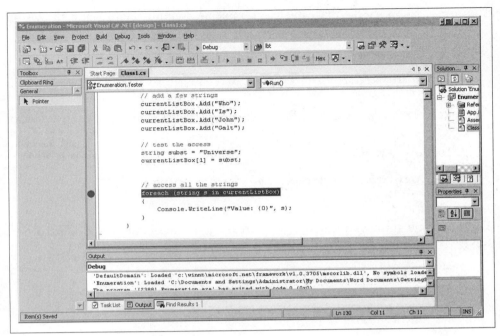

Figure 16-1. Setting a breakpoint on foreach

Run the application to the breakpoint by pressing the F5 key. Press F11 to step into the foreach loop, and you are in the MoveNext() method of the ListBoxEnumerator. (There is no explicit call to this method, but the method is invoked by the foreach construct itself.) Notice the Autos window shows the this reference and the index (currently –1), both circled and highlighted in Figure 16-2.

Now expand the this reference in the Autos window. You'll see the CurrentListBox as a property. Expand that property to see the strings as a property, as well as ctr, indicating that there are six strings so far, as shown in Figure 16-3.

Expand the strings member variable and see the six strings, nicely tucked away in the strings array, in the order you added them. This is shown in Figure 16-4.

Press the F11 key once. This increments the index property from –1 to zero. The index property is listed in red in the Autos window. (Each time a value changes, it is marked in red.)

The MoveNext() method tests whether the index (0) is greater than the Length of the array (8). Since at this point it is not, MoveNext() returns true, indicating that you have not exceeded the bounds of the array but instead have moved to the next valid value in the collection.

Press F11 repeatedly, until you return to the foreach loop. Pressing F11 again moves the highlight to the string in the foreach statement, and one more press of F11 steps you into the Current property's accessor. Continue pressing F11, and step into the

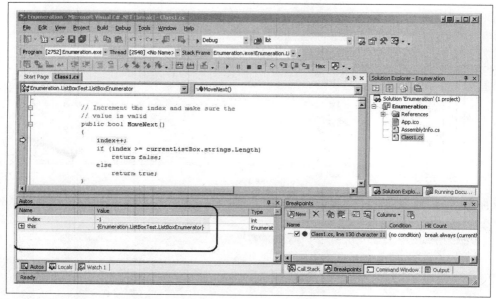

Figure 16-2. The Autos window in MoveNext()

Name	Value	Type
index	-1	int
☐ this	{Enumeration.ListBoxTest.ListBoxEnumerator}	Enumerat
— System.Object	{Enumeration.ListBoxTest.ListBoxEnumerator}	System.C
☐ currentListBox	{Enumeration.ListBoxTest}	Enumerat
— System.Object	{Enumeration.ListBoxTest}	System.C
☐ strings	{Length=8}	string[]
— ctr	6	int
— Item	<cannot view indexed property>	string
— index	-1	int
— Current	<error: an exception of type: {System.IndexOutOfRangeExceptic	System.C

Autos · Locals · Watch 1

Figure 16-3. The Autos window with this expanded

indexer of the ListBoxTest class, where the current index (0) is used as an index into the internal strings array, as shown in Figure 16-5.

If you continue pressing F11, you will exit the enumerator and return to the foreach loop where the string (Hello) is displayed.

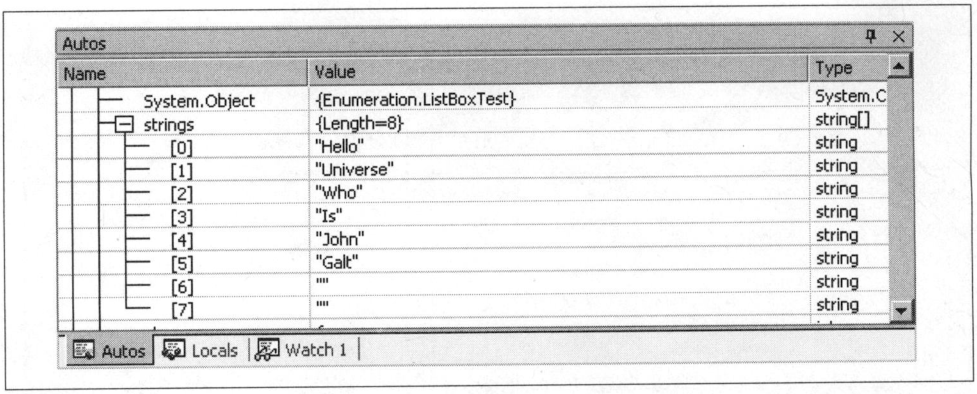

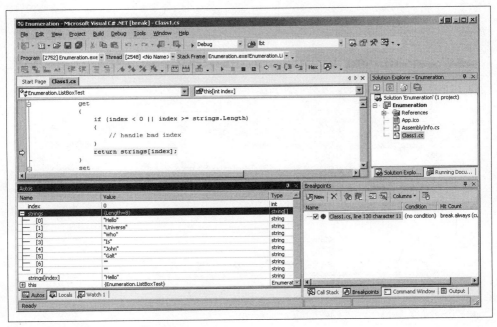

Figure 16-4. *The strings expanded*

Figure 16-5. *Indexing into the strings array*

Array Lists

Imagine that your program asks the user for input or gathers input from a web site. As it finds objects (strings, books, values, etc.), you would like to add them to an array, but you have no idea how many objects you'll collect in any given session.

It is difficult to use an array for such a purpose because you must declare the size of an Array object at compile time. If you try to add more objects than you've allocated memory for, the Array class throws an exception. If you do not know in advance how many objects your array will be required to hold, you run the risk of declaring either too small an array (and running out of room) or too large an array (and wasting memory).

The .NET Framework provides a class designed for just this situation. The ArrayList class is an array whose size is dynamically increased as required. The ArrayList class provides many useful methods and properties. Table 16-3 shows a few of the most important.

Table 16-3. ArrayList members

Method or property	Purpose
Capacity	Property containing the number of elements the array can currently hold
Count	Property to return the number of elements currently in the array
Item()	Method that gets or sets the element at the specified index. This is the indexer for the ArrayList class
Add()	Method to add an object to the ArrayList
Clear()	Method that removes all elements from the ArrayList
GetEnumerator()	Method that returns an enumerator to iterate an ArrayList
Insert()	Method that inserts an element into ArrayList
RemoveAt()	Method that removes the element at the specified index
Reverse()	Method that reverses the order of elements in the ArrayList
Sort()	Method that alphabetically sorts the ArrayList
ToArray()	Method that copies the elements of the ArrayList to a new array

When you create an ArrayList, you do not define how many objects it will contain. You add to the ArrayList using the Add() method, and the list takes care of its own internal bookkeeping, as illustrated in Example 16-2.

Example 16-2. Using an ArrayList

```
using System;
using System.Collections;

namespace ArrayListDemo
{
    // a class to hold in the array list
    public class Employee
    {
        private int empID;
        public Employee(int empID)
        {
            this.empID = empID;
        }
        public override  string ToString()
        {
            return empID.ToString();
        }
    }
```

Example 16-2. Using an ArrayList (continued)

```
    public int EmpID
    {
        get { return empID; }
        set { empID = value; }
    }
}

class Tester
{
    public void Run()
    {
        ArrayList empArray = new ArrayList();
        ArrayList intArray = new ArrayList();

        // populate the arraylists
        for (int i = 0;i<5;i++)
        {
            empArray.Add(new Employee(i+100));
            intArray.Add(i*5);
        }

        // print each member of the array
        foreach (int i in intArray)
        {
            Console.Write("{0} ", i.ToString());
        }

        Console.WriteLine("\n");

        // print each employee
        foreach(Employee e in empArray)
        {
            Console.Write("{0} ", e.ToString());
        }

        Console.WriteLine("\n");
        Console.WriteLine("empArray.Capacity: {0}",
            empArray.Capacity);
    }

    [STAThread]
    static void Main()
    {
        Tester t = new Tester();
        t.Run();
    }
}
}
```

Output:
```
0 5 10 15 20
100 101 102 103 104
empArray.Capacity: 16
```

Suppose you're defining two ArrayList objects, empArray to hold Employee objects and intArray to hold integers:

```
ArrayList empArray = new ArrayList();
ArrayList intArray = new ArrayList();
```

Each ArrayList object has a property, Capacity, which is the number of elements the ArrayList is capable of storing:

```
public int Capacity {virtual get; virtual set; }
```

 The default capacity for the ArrayList class is 16. You are free to set a different starting capacity for your ArrayList, but typically there is no need for you ever to do so.

Add elements to the ArrayList with the Add() method:

```
empArray.Add(new Employee(i+100));
intArray.Add(i*5);
```

When you add the 17th element, the capacity is automatically doubled to 32. If you change the for loop to:

```
for (int i = 0;i<17;i++)
```

the output looks like this:

```
0 5 10 15 20 25 30 35 40 45 50 55 60 65 70 75 80
5 6 7 8 9 10 11 12 13 14 15 16 17 18 19 20 21
empArray.Capacity: 32
```

Similarly, if you added a 33rd element, the capacity is doubled to 64. The 65th element increases the capacity to 128, the 129th element increases it to 256, and so forth.

Queues

A *queue* represents a first-in, first-out (FIFO) collection. The classic analogy is to a line (or queue if you are British) at a ticket window. The first person to join the line ought to be the first person to come off the line to buy a ticket.

The Queue class is a good collection to use when you are managing a limited resource. For example, you might want to send messages to a resource that can handle only one message at a time. You would then create a message queue so that you can say to your clients: "Your message is important to us. Messages are handled in the order in which they are received."

The Queue class has a number of member methods and properties, the most important of which are shown in Table 16-4.

Table 16-4. Queue members

Method or property	Purpose
Count	Public property that gets the number of elements in the Queue
Clear()	Method that removes all objects from the Queue
Contains()	Method that determines if an element is in the Queue
CopyTo()	Method that copies the Queue elements to an existing one-dimensional array
Dequeue()	Method that removes and returns the object at the beginning of the Queue
Enqueue()	Method that adds an object to the end of the Queue
GetEnumerator()	Method that returns an enumerator for the Queue
Peek()	Method that returns the object at the beginning of the Queue without removing it
ToArray()	Method that copies the elements to a new array

Add elements to your queue with the Enqueue() method, and take them off the queue with Dequeue() or by using an enumerator. Example 16-3 shows an example of using a Queue, followed by the output and a complete analysis.

Example 16-3. Implementing the Queue class

```
using System;
using System.Collections;

namespace QueueDemo
{
    class Tester
    {
        public void Run()
        {
            Queue intQueue = new Queue();

            // populate the array
            for (int i = 0;i<5;i++)
            {
                intQueue.Enqueue(i*5);
            }

            // Display the Queue.
            Console.Write( "intQueue values:\t" );
            DisplayValues( intQueue );

            // Remove an element from the Queue.
            Console.WriteLine(
                "\n(Dequeue)\t{0}", intQueue.Dequeue() );

            // Display the Queue.
            Console.Write( "intQueue values:\t" );
            DisplayValues( intQueue );

            // Remove another element from the queue.
            Console.WriteLine(
```

Example 16-3. Implementing the Queue class (continued)

```
                "\n(Dequeue)\t{0}", intQueue.Dequeue() );

        // Display the Queue.
        Console.Write( "intQueue values:\t" );
        DisplayValues( intQueue );

        // View the first element in the
        // Queue but do not remove.
        Console.WriteLine(
            "\n(Peek)    \t{0}", intQueue.Peek() );

        // Display the Queue.
        Console.Write( "intQueue values:\t" );
        DisplayValues( intQueue );
    }
    public static void DisplayValues( IEnumerable myCollection )
    {
        IEnumerator myEnumerator =
            myCollection.GetEnumerator();
        while ( myEnumerator.MoveNext() )
            Console.Write( "{0} ",myEnumerator.Current );
        Console.WriteLine();
    }

    [STAThread]
    static void Main()
    {
        Tester t = new Tester();
        t.Run();
    }
  }
}
```
Output:
```
intQueue values:        0 5 10 15 20

(Dequeue)       0
intQueue values:        5 10 15 20

(Dequeue)       5
intQueue values:        10 15 20

(Peek)          10
intQueue values:        10 15 20
```

In Example 16-3, the ArrayList from Example 16-2 is replaced by a Queue. I've dispensed with the Employee class and enqueued integers to save room in the book, but of course you can enqueue user-defined objects as well.

The program begins by creating an instance of a Queue, called intQueue:

```
    Queue intQueue = new Queue();
```

The queue is populated with integers:

```
for (int i = 0;i<5;i++)
{
    intQueue.Enqueue(i*5);
}
```

The contents of the queue are then displayed using the DisplayValues() method. This method takes a collection that implements the IEnumerable interface and asks that collection for its Enumerator.

 Each of the collections in the .NET Framework implements IEnumerable. It then explicitly iterates over the collection, displaying each element in turn.

```
public static void DisplayValues( IEnumerable myCollection )
{
    IEnumerator myEnumerator =
        myCollection.GetEnumerator();
    while ( myEnumerator.MoveNext() )
        Console.Write( "{0} ",myEnumerator.Current );
    Console.WriteLine();
}
```

You can avoid all the details of the Enumerator by using the foreach loop instead:

```
public static void DisplayValues( IEnumerable myCollection )
{
    foreach (object o in myCollection)
    {
        Console.WriteLine(o);
    }
}
```

Either version of DisplayValues() works equally well.

Display the first value in the queue without removing it by calling the Peek() method:

```
Console.WriteLine(
    "\n(Peek)   \t{0}", intQueue.Peek() );
```

Or, having displayed the values in the foreach loop, remove the current value by calling the Dequeue() method:

```
Console.WriteLine(
    "\n(Dequeue)\t{0}", intQueue.Dequeue() )
intQueue );
```

Stacks

A *stack* is a last-in, first-out (LIFO) collection, like a stack of dishes at a buffet table or a stack of coins on your desk. You add a dish on top, and that is the first dish you take off the stack.

The classic example of a stack is *the stack*, which is the portion of memory on which parameters and local variables are stored. See Chapter 8 for more about the stack.

The principal methods for adding to and removing from an instance of the Stack class are Push() and Pop(); Stack also offers a Peek() method, very much like Queue. Table 16-5 shows the most important methods and properties for Stack.

Table 16-5. Stack members

Method or Property	Purpose
Count	Public property that gets the number of elements in the Stack
Clear()	Method that removes all objects from the Stack
Contains()	Method that determines if an element is in the Stack
CopyTo()	Method that copies the Stack elements to an existing one-dimensional array
GetEnumerator()	Method that returns an enumerator for the Stack
Peek()	Method that returns the object at the top of the Stack without removing it
Pop()	Method that removes and returns the object at the top of the Stack
Push()	Method that inserts an object at the top of the Stack
ToArray()	Method that copies the elements to a new array

In Example 16-4, you rewrite Example 16-3 to use a Stack rather than a Queue. The logic is almost identical. The key difference is that a Stack is Last In, First Out, while a Queue is First In, First Out.

Example 16-4. Using a Stack

```
using System;
using System.Collections;
namespace StackDemo
{
    class Tester
    {
        public void Run()
        {
            Stack intStack = new Stack();

            // populate the array
            for (int i = 0;i<8;i++)
            {
                intStack.Push(i*5);
            }

            // Display the Stack.
            Console.Write( "intStack values:\t" );
            DisplayValues( intStack );
```

Example 16-4. Using a Stack (continued)

```
            // Remove an element from the stack.
            Console.WriteLine( "\n(Pop)\t{0}",
                intStack.Pop() );

            // Display the Stack.
            Console.Write( "intStack values:\t" );
            DisplayValues( intStack );

            // Remove another element from the stack.
            Console.WriteLine( "\n(Pop)\t{0}",
                intStack.Pop() );

            // Display the Stack.
            Console.Write( "intStack values:\t" );
            DisplayValues( intStack );

            // View the first element in the
            // Stack but do not remove.
            Console.WriteLine( "\n(Peek)    \t{0}",
                intStack.Peek() );

            // Display the Stack.
            Console.Write( "intStack values:\t" );
            DisplayValues( intStack );

        }
        public static void DisplayValues(
            IEnumerable myCollection )
        {
            foreach (object o in myCollection)
            {
                Console.WriteLine(o);
            }
        }

        [STAThread]
        static void Main()
        {
            Tester t = new Tester();
            t.Run();
        }
    }
}
```
Output:
```
(Pop)   35
intStack values:        30
25
20
15
10
5
0
```

Example 16-4. Using a Stack (continued)

```
(Pop)    30
intStack values:      25
20
15
10
5
0

(Peek)       25
intStack values:      25
20
15
10
5
```

You start Example 16-4 by creating a Stack object called intStack:

```
Stack intStack = new Stack();
```

Populate the stack with ints by calling the Push() method, which pushes the object onto the stack (i.e., adds it to the top of the stack); in this case, you push integers onto the stack.

```
for (int i = 0;i<8;i++)
{
    intStack.Push(i*5);
}
```

Remove an object from the stack by popping it off the stack with the Pop() method:

```
Console.WriteLine( "\n(Pop)\t{0}",
    intStack.Pop() );
```

Just as you could peek at the object at the beginning of the queue without dequeing it, you can Peek() at the object on top of the stack without popping it:

```
Console.WriteLine( "\n(Peek)    \t{0}",
    intStack.Peek() );
```

Copying from a Collection Type to an Array

The ArrayList, Queue, and Stack types contain overloaded CopyTo() and ToArray() methods for copying their elements to an array. The CopyTo() method copies its elements to an existing one-dimensional array, overwriting the contents of the array beginning at the index you specify. The ToArray() method returns a new array with the contents of the type's elements.

For example, in the case of a stack, ToArray() returns a new array containing the elements in the stack, and CopyTo() copies the stack over a pre-existing array. Example 16-5 modifies Example 16-4 to demonstrate both methods. The listing is followed by a complete analysis.

Example 16-5. Copying from a Stack type to an array

```csharp
using System;
using System.Collections;

namespace StackDemo
{
    class Tester
    {
        public void Run()
        {
            Stack intStack = new Stack();

            // populate the array
            for (int i = 1;i<5;i++)
            {
                intStack.Push(i*5);
            }

            // Display the Stack.
            Console.WriteLine( "intStack values:" );
            DisplayValues( intStack );


            const int arraySize = 10;
            int[] testArray = new int[arraySize];

            // populate the array
            for (int i = 1; i < arraySize; i++)
            {
                testArray[i] = i * 100;
            }
            Console.WriteLine("\nContents of the test array");
            DisplayValues( testArray );

            // Copy the intStack into the new array, start offset 3
            intStack.CopyTo( testArray, 3 );
            Console.WriteLine( "\nTestArray after copy:  " );
            DisplayValues( testArray );


            // Copy the entire source Stack
            // to a new standard array.
            Object[] myArray = intStack.ToArray();

            // Display the values of the new standard array.
            Console.WriteLine( "\nThe new  array:" );
            DisplayValues( myArray );

        }
        public static void DisplayValues(
            IEnumerable myCollection )
        {
            foreach (object o in myCollection)
            {
```

Example 16-5. Copying from a Stack type to an array (continued)

```
                Console.WriteLine(o);
            }
        }

    [STAThread]
    static void Main()
    {
        Tester t = new Tester();
        t.Run();
    }
  }
}
```

Output:
```
intStack values:
20
15
10
5

Contents of the test array
0
100
200
300
400
500
600
700
800
900

TestArray after copy:
0
100
200
20
15
10
5
700
800
900

The new array:
20
15
10
5
```

You begin again by creating the stack (intStack), populating it with integers and displaying its contents using WriteLine():

```
Stack intStack = new Stack();

for (int i = 1;i<5;i++)
{
    intStack.Push(i*5);
}

Console.WriteLine( "intStack values:" );
DisplayValues( intStack );
```

Next create an array and populate the array and display its values:

```
const int arraySize = 10;
int[] testArray = new int[arraySize];

for (int i = 1; i < arraySize; i++)
{
    testArray[i] = i * 100;
}
Console.WriteLine("\nContents of the test array");
DisplayValues( testArray );
```

You are ready to copy the stack over the array. You do so with the CopyTo() method, passing in the array name and the offset at which to begin the copy:

```
intStack.CopyTo( testArray, 3 );
```

This copies the four values from the stack over the array, starting at offset 3 (the fourth element in the array).

```
0
100
200
20
15
10
5
700
800
900
```

Rather than copying to an existing array, you are free to copy to a new array using the ToArray() method, which generates a properly sized new array to hold the contents of the stack:

```
Object[] myArray = intStack.ToArray();
```

CHAPTER 17

Strings

There was a time when people thought of computers as manipulating numeric values exclusively. Early computers were first used to calculate missile trajectories, and programming was taught in the math department of major universities.

Today, most programs are concerned more with strings of characters than with strings of numbers. Typically these strings are used for word processing, document manipulation, and creation of web pages.

C# provides built-in support for a fully functional string type. More importantly, C# treats strings as objects that encapsulate all the manipulation, sorting, and searching methods normally applied to strings of characters.

 The .NET Framework provides a *String* class (upper case S). The C# language offers an alias to the String class as the *string* class (lowercase s). These classes are interchangeable, and you are free to use either upper- or lowercase.

Complex string manipulation and pattern matching is aided by the use of *regular expressions*. C# combines the power and complexity of regular expression syntax, originally found only in string manipulation languages such as awk and Perl, with a fully object-oriented design.

In this chapter, you will learn to work with the C# string type and the .NET Framework System.String class that it aliases. You will see how to extract sub-strings, manipulate and concatenate strings, and build new strings with the StringBuilder class. In addition, you will find a short introduction to the RegEx class used to match strings based on regular expressions.

Creating Strings

C# treats strings as if they were built-in types. C# strings are flexible, powerful, and easy to use.

In .NET, each string object is an *immutable* sequence of Unicode characters. In other words, methods that appear to change the string actually return a modified copy; the original string remains intact.

The declaration of the System.String class is:

```
public sealed class String :
    IComparable, ICloneablee, IConvertible, IEnumerable
```

This declaration reveals that the class is sealed, meaning that it is not possible to derive from the String class. The class also implements four system interfaces—IComparable, ICloneable, IConvertible, and IEnumerable—which dictate functionality that System.String shares with other classes in the .NET Framework. Interfaces are introduced in Chapter 14.

The IComparable interface is implemented by types that can be sorted. Strings, for example, can be alphabetized; any given string can be compared with another string to determine which should come first in an ordered list. IComparable classes implement the CompareTo() method.

ICloneable objects can create new instances with the same value as the original instance. In this case, it is possible to clone a string to produce a new string with the same values (characters) as the original. ICloneable classes implement the Clone() method.

IConvertible classes provide methods to facilitate conversion to other primitive types; these methods include ToInt32(), ToDouble(), and ToDecimal().

IEnumerable, discussed in detail in Chapter 16, lets you use the foreach construct to enumerate a string as a collection of chars. That is, you can write:

```
string theString = "hello world";
foreach (char c in theString)
{
    Console.WriteLine(c);
}
```

The output is each letter of hello world on its own line.

String Literals

The most common way to create a string is to assign a quoted string of characters, known as a *string literal*, to a user-defined variable of type string. The following code declares a string called newString that contains the phrase *This is a string literal*.

```
string newString = "This is a string literal";
```

Escape Characters

Quoted strings can include *escape characters*, which begin with a backslash character (\). The two most common escape characters are "\n", which is used to create a new line, and "\t", which is used to insert a tab into a string.

In a quoted string a literal backslash must be preceded by another backslash ("\\"). Thus, if you were writing the string c:\myDirectory, you'd write:

```
"c:\\myDirectory"
```

Verbatim Strings

Strings can also be created using *verbatim string literals*, which start with the (@) symbol. This tells the String constructor that the string should be used verbatim, even if it spans multiple lines or includes escape characters. In a verbatim string literal, backslashes and the characters that follow them are simply considered additional characters of the string. Thus, the following two definitions are equivalent:

```
string literalOne = "\\\\MySystem\\MyDirectory\\ProgrammingC#.cs";
string verbatimLiteralOne = @"\\MySystem\MyDirectory\ProgrammingC#.cs";
```

In the first line, a nonverbatim string literal is used, and so the backslash character (\) must be *escaped*, which means it must be preceded by a second backslash character. In the second, a verbatim literal string is used, so the extra backslash is not needed. A second example illustrates two ways to specify multiline verbatim strings. The first definition uses a nonverbatim string with a newline escape character (\n) to signal the line break. The second definition uses a verbatim string literal:

```
string literalTwo = "Line One\nLine Two";
string verbatimLiteralTwo = @"Line One
Line Two";
```

Again, these declarations are interchangeable. Which one you use is a matter of convenience and personal style.

The ToString() Method

Another common way to create a string is to call the ToString() method on an object and assign the result to a string variable. All the built-in types override this method to simplify the task of converting a value (often a numeric value) to a string representation of that value. In the following example, the ToString() method of an integer type is called to store its value in a string:

```
int myInteger = 5;
string integerString = myInteger.ToString();
```

The call to myInteger.ToString() returns a string object that is then assigned to the string variable, integerString.

Manipulating Strings

The String class provides a host of methods for comparing, searching, and manipulating strings, the most important of which are shown in Table 17-1.

Table 17-1. String class methods

Method or property	Explanation
Chars	Property that returns the string indexer
Compare()	Overloaded public static method that compares two strings
Copy()	Public static method that creates a new string by copying another
Equals()	Overloaded public static and instance method that determines if two strings have the same value
Format()	Overloaded public static method that formats a string using a format specification
Length	Property that returns the number of characters in the instance
PadLeft()	Right-aligns the characters in the string, padding to the left with spaces or a specified character
PadRight()	Left-aligns the characters in the string, padding to the right with spaces or a specified character
Remove()	Deletes the specified number of characters
Split()	Divides a string, returning the substrings delimited by the specified characters
StartsWith()	Indicates if the string starts with the specified characters
Substring()	Retrieves a substring
ToCharArray()	Copies the characters from the string to a character array
ToLower()	Returns a copy of the string in lowercase
ToUpper()	Returns a copy of the string in uppercase
Trim()	Removes all occurrences of a set of specified characters from beginning and end of the string
TrimEnd()	Behaves like Trim(), but only at the end
TrimStart()	Behaves like Trim(), but only at the start

Comparing Strings

The Compare() method is overloaded. The first version takes two strings and returns a negative number if the first string is alphabetically before the second, a positive number if the first string is alphabetically after the second, and zero if they are equal. The second version works just like the first but is case-insensitive. Example 17-1 illustrates the use of Compare().

Example 17-1. Compare() method

```
using System;

namespace StringManipulation
{
   class Tester
   {
      public void Run()
      {
          // create some strings to work with
          string s1 = "abcd";
          string s2 = "ABCD";
          int result;  // hold the results of comparisons
```

Example 17-1. Compare() method (continued)

```
        // compare two strings, case sensitive
        result = string.Compare(s1, s2);
        Console.WriteLine(
            "compare s1: {0}, s2: {1}, result: {2}\n",
            s1, s2, result);

        // overloaded compare, takes boolean "ignore case"
        //(true = ignore case)
        result = string.Compare(s1,s2, true);
        Console.WriteLine("Compare insensitive. result: {0}\n",
            result);

    }

    [STAThread]
    static void Main()
    {
        Tester t = new Tester();
        t.Run();
    }
  }
}
```

Output:
```
compare s1: abcd, s2: ABCD, result: -1
Compare insensitive. result: 0
```

Example 17-1 begins by declaring two strings, s1 and s2, and initializing them with string literals:

```
string s1 = "abcd";
string s2 = "ABCD";
```

Compare() is used with many types. A negative return value indicates that the first parameter is less than the second, a positive result indicates the first parameter is greater than the second, and a zero indicates they are equal. In Unicode (as in ASCII), a lowercase letter has a smaller value than an uppercase letter; with strings identical except for case, lowercase comes first alphabetically. Thus, the output properly indicates that s1 (abcd) is "less than" s2 (ABCD):

```
compare s1: abcd, s2: ABCD, result: -1
```

The second comparison uses an overloaded version of Compare(), which takes a third Boolean parameter, the value of which determines whether case should be ignored in the comparison. If the value of this "ignore case" parameter is true, the comparison is made without regard to case. This time the result is 0, indicating that the two strings are identical:

```
Compare insensitive. result: 0
```

Concatenating Strings

There are a couple of ways to concatenate strings in C#. You can use the Concat()
method, which is a static public method of the String class:

```
string s3 = string.Concat(s1,s2);
```

or you can simply use the overloaded concatenation (+) operator:

```
string s4 = s1 + s2;
```

Example 17-2 demonstrates both of these methods.

Example 17-2. Concatenation

```
using System;

namespace StringManipulation
{
    class Tester
    {
        public void Run()
        {
            string s1 = "abcd";
            string s2 = "ABCD";

            // concatenation method
            string s3 = string.Concat(s1,s2);
            Console.WriteLine(
                "s3 concatenated from s1 and s2: {0}", s3);

            // use the overloaded operator
            string s4 = s1 + s2;
            Console.WriteLine(
                "s4 concatenated from s1 + s2: {0}", s4);

        }

        static void Main()
        {
            Tester t = new Tester();
            t.Run();
        }
    }
}
```
Output:
```
s3 concatenated from s1 and s2: abcdABCD
s4 concatenated from s1 + s2: abcdABCD
```

In Example 17-2, the new string s3 is created by calling the static Concat() method
and passing in s1 and s2, while the string s4 is created by using the overloaded concatenation operator (+) that concatenates two strings and returns a string as a result.

Copying Strings

Similarly, you can create a new copy of a string in two ways. First, you can use the static Copy() method:

```
string s5 = string.Copy(s2);
```

or, for convenience, you might instead use the overloaded assignment operator (=), which implicitly makes a copy:

```
string s6 = s5;
```

Example 17-3 demonstrates string copying.

Example 17-3. Copying strings

```
using System;

namespace StringManipulation
{
    class Tester
    {
        public void Run()
        {
            string s1 = "abcd";
            string s2 = "ABCD";

            // the string copy method
            string s5 = string.Copy(s2);
            Console.WriteLine(
                "s5 copied from s2: {0}", s5);

            // use the overloaded operator
            string s6 = s5;
            Console.WriteLine("s6 = s5: {0}", s6);
        }

        static void Main()
        {
            Tester t = new Tester();
            t.Run();
        }
    }
}
```
Output:
```
s5 copied from s2: ABCD
s6 = s5: ABCD
```

Testing for Equality

The .NET String class provides three ways to test for the equality of two strings. First, you can use the overloaded Equals() method and ask one string (say, s6) directly whether another string (s5) is of equal value:

```
Console.WriteLine(
    "\nDoes s6.Equals(s5)?: {0}",
    s6.Equals(s5));
```

You can also pass both strings to String's static method Equals():

```
Console.WriteLine(
    "Does Equals(s6,s5)?: {0}"
    string.Equals(s6,s5));
```

Or you can use the String class' overloaded equality operator (==):

```
Console.WriteLine(
    "Does s6==s5?: {0}", s6 == s5);
```

In each of these cases, the returned result is a Boolean value (true for equal and false
for unequal). Example 17-4 demonstrates these techniques.

Example 17-4. Are all strings created equal?

```
using System;

namespace StringManipulation
{
    class Tester
    {
        public void Run()
        {
            string s1 = "abcd";
            string s2 = "ABCD";

            // the string copy method
            string s5 = string.Copy(s2);
            Console.WriteLine(
                "s5 copied from s2: {0}", s5);

            // copy with the overloaded operator
            string s6 = s5;
            Console.WriteLine("s6 = s5: {0}", s6);

            // member method
            Console.WriteLine(
                "\nDoes s6.Equals(s5)?: {0}",
                s6.Equals(s5));

            // static method
            Console.WriteLine(
                "Does Equals(s6,s5)?: {0}",
                string.Equals(s6,s5));

            // overloaded operator
            Console.WriteLine(
                "Does s6==s5?: {0}", s6 == s5);
        }

        static void Main()
```

Example 17-4. Are all strings created equal? (continued)

```
        {
            Tester t = new Tester();
            t.Run();
        }
    }
}
```

Output:
```
s5 copied from s2: ABCD
s6 = s5: ABCD

Does s6.Equals(s5)?: True
Does Equals(s6,s5)?: True
Does s6==s5?: True
```

The equality operator is the most natural of the three methods to use when you have two string objects. However, some languages, such as VB.NET, do not support operator overloading, so be sure to override the Equals() instance method as well.

Other Useful String Methods

The String class includes a number of useful methods and properties for finding specific characters or substrings within a string, as well as for manipulating the contents of the string. Example 17-5 demonstrates a few such methods. Following the output is a complete analysis.

Example 17-5. Useful methods of the String class

```
using System;

namespace StringManipulation
{
    class Tester
    {
        public void Run()
        {
            string s1 = "abcd";
            string s2 = "ABCD";
            string s3 = @"Liberty Associates, Inc.
                provides custom .NET development,
                on-site Training and Consulting";

            // the string copy method
            string s5 = string.Copy(s2);
            Console.WriteLine(
                "s5 copied from s2: {0}", s5);

            // Two useful properties: the index and the length
            Console.WriteLine(
                "\nString s3 is {0} characters long. ",
                s5.Length);
```

Example 17-5. Useful methods of the String class (continued)

```
            Console.WriteLine(
                "The 5th character is {0}\n", s3[4]);

            // test whether a string ends with a set of characters
            Console.WriteLine("s3:{0}\nEnds with Training?: {1}\n",
                s3,
                s3.EndsWith("Training") );
            Console.WriteLine(
                "Ends with Consulting?: {0}",
                s3.EndsWith("Consulting"));

            // return the index of the substring
            Console.WriteLine(
                "\nThe first occurrence of Training ");
            Console.WriteLine ("in s3 is {0}\n",
                s3.IndexOf("Training"));

            // insert the word excellent before "training"
            string s10 = s3.Insert(101,"excellent ");
            Console.WriteLine("s10: {0}\n",s10);

            // you can combine the two as follows:
            string s11 = s3.Insert(s3.IndexOf("Training"),
                "excellent ");
            Console.WriteLine("s11: {0}\n",s11);
        }

        [STAThread]
        static void Main()
        {
            Tester t = new Tester();
            t.Run();
        }
    }
}
```

Output:
```
s5 copied from s2: ABCD

String s3 is 4 characters long.
The 5th character is r

s3:Liberty Associates, Inc.
            provides custom .NET development,
            on-site Training and Consulting
Ends with Training?: False

Ends with Consulting?: True

The first occurrence of Training
in s3 is 103

s10: Liberty Associates, Inc.
```

Example 17-5. Useful methods of the String class (continued)

```
            provides custom .NET development,
            on-sitexcellent e Training and Consulting

s11: Liberty Associates, Inc.
            provides custom .NET development,
            on-sitexcellent e Training and Consulting
```

The Length property returns the length of the entire string, and the index operator ([ ]) is used to find a particular character within a string:

```
Console.WriteLine(
    "\nString s3 is {0} characters long. ",
    s5.Length);

Console.WriteLine(
    "The 5th character is {0}\n", s3[4]);
```

Here's the output:

```
String s3 is 4 characters long.
The 5th character is r
```

The EndsWith() method asks a string whether a substring is found at the end of the string. Thus, you might first ask s3 if it ends with "Training" (which it does not) and then if it ends with "Consulting" (which it does):

```
Console.WriteLine("s3:{0}\nEnds with Training?: {1}\n",
    s3,
    s3.EndsWith("Training") );
Console.WriteLine(
    "Ends with Consulting?: {0}",
    s3.EndsWith("Consulting"));
```

The output reflects that the first test fails and the second succeeds:

```
Ends with Training?: False
Ends with Consulting?: True
```

The IndexOf() method locates a substring within a string, and the Insert() method inserts a new substring into a copy of the original string. The following code locates the first occurrence of "Training" in s3:

```
Console.WriteLine("\nThe first occurrence of Training ");
Console.WriteLine ("in s3 is {0}\n",
    s3.IndexOf("Training"));
```

The output indicates that the offset is 101:

```
The first occurrence of Training
in s3 is 101
```

Then use that value to insert the word "excellent", followed by a space, into that string. Actually the insertion is into a copy of the string returned by the Insert() method and assigned to s10:

```
string s10 = s3.Insert(101,"excellent ");
Console.WriteLine("s10: {0}\n",s10);
```

Here's the output:

```
s10: Liberty Associates, Inc.
            provides custom .NET development,
            on-site excellent Training and Consulting
```

Finally, combine these operations to make a more efficient insertion statement:

```
string s11 = s3.Insert(s3.IndexOf("Training"),"excellent ");
Console.WriteLine("s11: {0}\n",s11);
```

with the identical result:

```
s11: Liberty Associates, Inc.
            provides custom .NET development,
            on-site excellent Training and Consulting
```

Finding Substrings

The String class has methods for finding and extracting substrings. For example, the IndexOf() method returns the index of the *first* occurrence of a string (or one or more characters) within a target string. For example, given the definition of the string s1 as:

```
string s1 = "One Two Three Four";
```

you can find the first instance of the characters "hre" by writing:

```
int index = s1.IndexOf("hre");
```

This code sets the int variable index to 9, which is the offset of the letters "hre" in the string s1.

Similarly, the LastIndexOf() method returns the index of the *last* occurrence of a string or substring. While the following code:

```
s1.IndexOf("o");
```

returns the value 6 (the first occurrence of the lowercase letter o is at the end of the word Two), the method call:

```
s1.LastIndexOf("o");
```

returns the value 15 (the last occurrence of o is in the word Four).

The Substring() method returns a series of characters. You can ask it for all the characters starting at a particular offset and ending either with the end of the string or with an offset you (optionally) provide. Example 17-6 illustrates the Substring() method.

Example 17-6. Finding substrings by index

```
using System;

namespace StringSearch
```

Example 17-6. Finding substrings by index (continued)

```
{
    class Tester
    {
        public void Run()
        {
            // create some strings to work with
            string s1 = "One Two Three Four";

            int index;

            // get the index of the last space
            index=s1.LastIndexOf(" ");

            // get the last word.
            string s2 = s1.Substring(index+1);

            // set s1 to the substring starting at 0
            // and ending at index (the start of the last word
            // thus s1 has one two three
            s1 = s1.Substring(0,index);

            // find the last space in s1 (after two)
            index = s1.LastIndexOf(" ");

            // set s3 to the substring starting at
            // index, the space after "two" plus one more
            // thus s3 = "three"
            string s3 = s1.Substring(index+1);

            // reset s1 to the substring starting at 0
            // and ending at index, thus the string "one two"
            s1 = s1.Substring(0,index);

            // reset index to the space between
            // "one" and "two"
            index = s1.LastIndexOf(" ");

            // set s4 to the substring starting one
            // space after index, thus the substring "two"
            string s4 = s1.Substring(index+1);

            // reset s1 to the substring starting at 0
            // and ending at index, thus "one"
            s1 = s1.Substring(0,index);

            // set index to the last space, but there is
            // none so index now = -1
            index = s1.LastIndexOf(" ");

            // set s5 to the substring at one past
            // the last space. there was no last space
            // so this sets s5 to the substring starting
            // at zero
```

Example 17-6. Finding substrings by index (continued)

```
        string s5 = s1.Substring(index+1);

        Console.WriteLine ("s2: {0}\ns3: {1}",s2,s3);
        Console.WriteLine ("s4: {0}\ns5: {1}\n",s4,s5);
        Console.WriteLine ("s1: {0}\n",s1);
    }

    static void Main()
    {
        Tester t = new Tester();
        t.Run();
    }
  }
}
```
Output:
```
s2: Four
s3: Three
s4: Two
s5: One

s1: One
```

Example 17-6 is not the most elegant solution possible to the problem of extracting words from a string, but it is a good first approximation, and it illustrates a useful technique. The example begins by creating a string, s1:

```
string s1 = "One Two Three Four";
```

The local variable index is assigned the value of the last literal space in the string (which comes before the word Four):

```
index=s1.LastIndexOf(" ");
```

The substring that begins one position later is assigned to the new string, s2:

```
string s2 = s1.Substring(index+1);
```

This extracts the characters from index +1 to the end of the line (i.e., the string Four) and assigns the value Four to s2.

The next step is to remove the word Four from s1; assign to s1 the substring of s1 that begins at 0 and ends at the index:

```
s1 = s1.Substring(0,index);
```

After this line executes, the variable s1 will point to a new string object that will contain the appropriate substring of the string s1 used to point to. That original string will be destroyed by the garbage collector since no variable now references it.

You reassign index to the last (remaining) space, which points you to the beginning of the word Three. You then extract the characters "Three" into string s3. Continue like this until you've populated s4 and s5. Finally, display the results:

```
s2: Four
s3: Three
s4: Two
s5: One
s1: One
```

Splitting Strings

A more effective solution to the problem illustrated in Example 17-1 would be to use the String class's Split() method, which parses a string into substrings. To use Split(), pass in an array of delimiters (characters that indicate where to divide the words). The method returns an array of substrings (which Example 17-7 illustrates). The complete analysis follows the code.

Example 17-7. The Split() method

```
using System;

namespace StringSearch
{
    class Tester
    {
        public void Run()
        {
            // create some strings to work with
            string s1 = "One,Two,Three Liberty Associates, Inc. ";

            // constants for the space and comma characters
            const char Space = ' ';
            const char Comma = ',';

            // array of delimiters to split the sentence with
            char[] delimiters = new char[]
            {
                Space,
                Comma
            };

            string output = "";
            int ctr = 1;

            // split the string and then iterate over the
            // resulting array of strings

            String[] resultArray = s1.Split(delimiters);

            foreach (String subString in resultArray)
            {
```

Example 17-7. The Split() method (continued)

```
                output += ctr++;
                output += ": ";
                output += subString;
                output += "\n";
            }
            Console.WriteLine(output);

        }

        static void Main()
        {
            Tester t = new Tester();
            t.Run();
        }
    }
}
```
Output:
```
1: One
2: Two
3: Three
4: Liberty
5: Associates
6:
7: Inc.
```

Example 17-7 starts by creating a string to parse:

```
string s1 = "One,Two,Three Liberty Associates, Inc.";
```

The delimiters are set to the space and comma characters. Then call Split() on the string, passing in the delimiters:

```
String[] resultArray = s1.Split(delimiters);
```

Split() returns an array of the substrings that you can then iterate over using the foreach loop as explained in Chapter 6.

```
foreach (String subString in resultArray)
```

> You can, of course, combine the call to split with the iteration, as in the following:
>
> ```
> foreach (string subString in s1.Split(delimiters))
> ```
>
> C# programmers are fond of combining statements like this. The advantage of splitting the statement into two, however, and of using an interim variable like resultArray is that you can examine the contents of resultArray in the debugger.

Start the foreach loop by initializing output to an empty string, and then build up the output string in four steps. Start by concatenating the incremented value of ctr to the output string, using the += operator.

```
output += ctr++;
```

Next add the colon, then the substring returned by Split(), and then the newline.

```
output += ": ";
output += subString;
output += "\n";
```

With each concatenation, a new copy of the string is made, and all four steps are repeated for each substring found by Split().

This repeated copying of string is terribly inefficient. The problem is that the string type is not designed for this kind of operation. What you want is to create a new string by appending a formatted string each time through the loop. The class you need is StringBuilder.

The StringBuilder Class

You can use the System.Text.StringBuilder class for creating and modifying strings. Semantically, it is the encapsulation of a constructor for a string. Table 17-2 summarizes the important members of StringBuilder.

Table 17-2. StringBuilder members

Method or property	Explanation
Append()	Overloaded public method that appends a typed object to the end of the current StringBuilder
AppendFormat()	Overloaded public method that replaces format specifiers with the formatted value of an object
EnsureCapacity()	Ensures that the current StringBuilder has a capacity at least as large as the specified value
Capacity	Property that retrieves or assigns the number of characters the StringBuilder is capable of holding
Chars	Property that contains the indexer
Insert()	Overloaded public method that inserts an object at the specified position
Length	Property that retrieves or assigns the length of the StringBuilder
MaxCapacity	Property that retrieves the maximum capacity of the StringBuilder
Remove()	Removes the specified characters
Replace()	Overloaded public method that replaces all instances of specified characters with new characters

Unlike String, StringBuilder is mutable; when you modify an instance of the StringBuilder class, you modify the actual string, not a copy.

Example 17-8 replaces the String object in Example 17-7 with a StringBuilder object.

Example 17-8. The StringBuilder class

```
using System;
using System.Text;

namespace StringSearch
{
   class Tester
   {
```

Example 17-8. The StringBuilder class (continued)

```csharp
    public void Run()
    {
        // create some strings to work with
        string s1 = "One,Two,Three Liberty Associates, Inc.";

        // constants for the space and comma characters
        const char Space = ' ';
        const char Comma = ',';

        // array of delimiters to split the sentence with
        char[] delimiters = new char[]
        {
            Space,
            Comma
        };

        // use a StringBuilder class to build the
        // output string
        StringBuilder output = new StringBuilder();
        int ctr = 1;

        // split the string and then iterate over the
        // resulting array of strings
        foreach (string subString in s1.Split(delimiters))
        {
            // AppendFormat appends a formatted string
            output.AppendFormat("{0}: {1}\n",ctr++,subString);
        }
        Console.WriteLine(output);

    }

    [STAThread]
    static void Main()
    {
        Tester t = new Tester();
        t.Run();
    }
  }
}
```

Only the last part of the program is modified. Rather than using the concatenation operator to modify the string, use the AppendFormat() method of StringBuilder to append new formatted strings as you create them. This is much easier and far more efficient. The output is identical:

```
1: One
2: Two
3: Three
4: Liberty
5: Associates
6:
7: Inc.
```

Because you passed in delimiters of both comma and space, the space after the comma between "Associates" and "Inc." is returned as a word, numbered 6 in the previous code. That is not what you want. To eliminate this, you need to tell Split() to match a comma (as between One, Two, and Three), a space (as between Liberty and Associates), or a comma followed by a space. It is that last bit that is tricky and requires that you use a regular expression.

Regular Expressions

Regular expressions are a powerful language for describing and manipulating text. Underlying regular expressions is a technique called *pattern matching*, which involves comparing one string to another, or comparing a series of wildcards that represent a type of string to a literal string. A regular expression is *applied* to a string—that is, to a set of characters. Often that string is an entire text document.

The result of applying a regular expression to a string is either to return a substring or to return a new string representing a modification of some part of the original string. (Remember that string objects are immutable and so cannot be changed by the regular expression.)

By applying a properly constructed regular expression to the following string:

```
One,Two,Three Liberty Associates, Inc.
```

you can return any or all of its substrings (e.g., Liberty or One) or modified versions of its substrings (e.g., LIBeRtY or OnE). What the regular expression does is determined by the syntax of the regular expression itself.

A regular expression consists of two types of characters: *literals* and *metacharacters*. A literal is a character you want to match in the target string. A metacharacter is a special symbol that acts as a command to the regular expression parser. The parser is the engine responsible for understanding the regular expression. For example, if you create a regular expression:

```
^(From|To|Subject|Date):
```

this will match any substring with the letters "From", "To", "Subject", or "Date" so long as those letters start a new line (^) and end with a colon (:).

The caret (^) indicates to the regular expression parser that the string you're searching for must begin a new line. The letters "From" and "To" are literals, and the metacharacters left and right parentheses ((,)) and vertical bar (|) are all used to group sets of literals and indicate that any of the choices should match. Thus you would read the following line as "match any string that begins a new line, followed by any of the four literal strings From, To, Subject, or Date, and followed by a colon":

```
^(From|To|Subject|Date):
```

A full explanation of regular expressions is beyond the scope of this book, but all the regular expressions used in the examples are explained. For a complete understanding of regular expressions, I highly recommend *Mastering Regular Expressions*, Second Edition, by Jeffrey E. F. Friedl (O'Reilly).

The Regex Class

The .NET Framework provides an object-oriented approach to regular expression pattern matching and replacement.

The Framework Class Library namespace System.Text.RegularExpressions is the home to all the .NET Framework objects associated with regular expressions. The central class for regular expression support is Regex, which provides methods and properties for working with regular expressions, the most important of which are shown in Table 17-3.

Table 17-3. Regex members

Method or property	Explanation
Regex constructor	Overloaded; creates an instance of Regex
Options	Property that returns the options passed in to the constructor
IsMatch()	Method that indicates whether a match is found in the input string
Match	Searches an input string and returns a match for a regular expression
Matches	Searches an input string and returns all successful matches for a regular expression
Replace	Replace all occurrences of a pattern with a replacement string
Split	Splits an input string into an array of substrings based on a regular expression

Example 17-9 rewrites Example 17-8 to use regular expressions and thus solve the problem of searching for more than one type of delimiter.

Example 17-9. Regular expressions

```
using System;
using System.Text;
using System.Text.RegularExpressions;

namespace RegularExpressions
{
    class Tester
    {
        public void Run()
        {
            string s1 =
                "One,Two,Three Liberty Associates, Inc.";
            Regex theRegex = new Regex(" |, |,");
            StringBuilder sBuilder = new StringBuilder();
            int id = 1;
```

Example 17-9. Regular expressions (continued)

```
        foreach (string subString in theRegex.Split(s1))
        {
            sBuilder.AppendFormat(
                "{0}: {1}\n", id++, subString);
        }
        Console.WriteLine("{0}", sBuilder);
    }

    [STAThread]
    static void Main()
    {
        Tester t = new Tester();
        t.Run();
    }
}
}
```

Output:

```
1: One
2: Two
3: Three
4: Liberty
5: Associates
6: Inc.
```

Example 17-9 begins by creating a string, s1, identical to the string used in Example 17-8:

```
string s1 = "One,Two,Three Liberty Associates, Inc.";
```

and a regular expression that is used to search the string:

```
Regex theRegex = new Regex(" |,|, ");
```

One of the overloaded constructors for Regex takes a regular expression string as its parameter.

This can be a bit confusing. In the context of a C# program, which is the regular expression: the text passed in to the constructor or the Regex object itself? It is true that the text string passed to the constructor is a regular expression in the traditional sense of the term. From a C# (i.e., object-oriented) point of view, however, the argument to the constructor is just a string of characters; it is the object called theRegex that is the regular expression object.

The rest of the program proceeds like Example 17-8, except that rather than calling the Split() method of String on string s1, the Split() method of Regex is called. TheRegex.Split() acts in much the same way as String.Split(), returning an array of strings as a result of matching the regular expression pattern within theRegex. Because it matches a regular expression, rather than using a set of delimiters, you have much greater control over how the string is split.

CHAPTER 18
Throwing and Catching Exceptions

C# handles errors and abnormal conditions with *exceptions*. An exception is an object that encapsulates information about an unusual program occurrence, such as running out of memory or losing a network connection. When an exceptional circumstance arises, an exception is thrown. You might throw an exception in your own methods (for example, if you realize that an invalid parameter has been provided), or an exception might be thrown in a class provided by the Framework Class Library (for example, if you try to write to a read-only file). Many exceptions are thrown by the runtime when the program can no longer continue due to an operating system problem (such as a security violation).

Throwing an exception is sometimes called *raising* an exception.

You provide for the possibility of exceptions by adding try/catch blocks in your program. The catch blocks are also called *exception handlers*. The idea is that you *try* potentially dangerous code, and if an exception is thrown you *catch* the exception in your catch block.

Catching an exception is sometimes referred to as *handling* the exception.

Ideally, after the exception is caught the program can fix the problem and continue. Even if your program can't continue, by catching the exception you have an opportunity to print a meaningful error message and terminate gracefully.

It is important to distinguish exceptions from *bugs* and *errors*. A bug is a programmer mistake that should be fixed before the code is shipped. An exception is not the result of a programmer mistake (though such mistakes can also raise exceptions). Rather, exceptions are raised as a result of predictable but unpreventable problems that arise while your program is running (e.g., a network connection is dropped or you run out of disk space).

An error is caused by user action. For example, the user might enter a number where a letter is expected. Once again, an error might cause an exception, but you can prevent that by implementing code to validate user input. Whenever possible, user errors should be anticipated and prevented.

Even if you remove all bugs and anticipate all user errors, you will still run into predictable but unpreventable problems, such as running out of memory or attempting to open a file that no longer exists. These are exceptions. You cannot prevent exceptions, but you can handle them so that they do not bring down your program.

Throwing Exceptions

All exceptions are either of type System.Exception or of types derived from System. Exception. The CLR System namespace includes a number of exception types that can be used by your program. These exception types include ArgumentNullException, InvalidCastException, and OverflowException, as well as many others. You can guess their use based on their name. For example, ArgumentNull exception is thrown when an argument to a method is null when that is not an expected (or acceptable) value.

This chapter describes how to write your programs to catch and handle exceptions. This chapter also shows you how to use the properties of the Exception class to provide information to the user about what went wrong, and it shows you how to create and use your own custom exception types.

Searching for an Exception Handler

When your program encounters an exceptional circumstance, such as running out of memory, it throws (or raises) an exception. Exceptions must be handled before the program can continue.

The search for an exception handler can unwind the stack. This means that if the currently running function does not handle the exception, the current function terminates and the calling function gets a chance to handle the exception. If none of the calling functions handles it, the exception ultimately is handled by the Common Language Runtime (CLR), which abruptly terminates your program.

If function A calls function B and function B calls function C, these function calls are all placed on the stack. When a programmer talks about "unwinding the stack" what is meant is that you back up from C to B to A, as illustrated in Figure 18-1.

If you must unwind the stack from C to B to A to handle the exception, when you are done, you are in A; there is no automatic return to C.

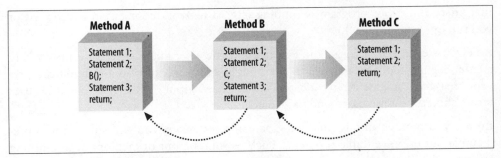

Figure 18-1. Unwinding the stack

If you return all the way to the first method (Main) and no exception handler is found, the default exception handler (provided by the compiler) is invoked. The default exception handler just terminates the program.

The throw Statement

To signal an abnormal condition in a C# program, throw an exception by using the throw keyword. The following line of code creates a new instance of System.Exception and then throws it:

```
throw new System.Exception();
```

Example 18-1 illustrates what happens if you throw an exception and there is no try/catch block to catch and handle the exception. In this example, you'll throw an exception even though nothing has actually gone wrong, just to illustrate how an exception can bring your program to a halt.

Example 18-1. Unhandled exception

```
using System;

namespace ExceptionHandling
{
    class Tester
    {

        static void Main()
        {
            Console.WriteLine("Enter Main...");
            Tester t = new Tester();
            t.Run();
            Console.WriteLine("Exit Main...");
        }
        public void Run()
        {
            Console.WriteLine("Enter Run...");
            Func1();
            Console.WriteLine("Exit Run...");
        }
```

Example 18-1. Unhandled exception (continued)

```
    public void Func1()
    {
        Console.WriteLine("Enter Func1...");
        Func2();
        Console.WriteLine("Exit Func1...");
    }

    public void Func2()
    {
        Console.WriteLine("Enter Func2...");
        throw new System.Exception();
        Console.WriteLine("Exit Func2...");
    }

    }
}
```
Output:
```
Enter Main...
Enter Run...
Enter Func1...
Enter Func2...
```

```
Unhandled Exception: System.Exception: Exception of type System.Exception was thrown. at
ExceptionHandling.Tester.Func2() in source\exceptions\exceptionhandling\class1.cs:line 34
    at ExceptionHandling.Tester.Func1() in source\exceptions\exceptionhandling\class1.cs:
line 27
    at ExceptionHandling.Tester.Run() in source\exceptions\exceptionhandling\class1.cs:line
19
    at ExceptionHandling.Tester.Main() in source\exceptions\exceptionhandling\class1.cs:
line 13
```

This simple example writes to the console as it enters and exits each method. Main()
calls Run(), which in turn calls Func1(). After printing out the Enter Func1 message,
Func1() immediately calls Func2(). Func2() prints out the first message and throws
an object of type System.Exception.

Execution immediately stops, and the CLR looks to see if there is a handler in
Func2(). There is not, and so the runtime unwinds the stack (never printing the exit
statement) to Func1(). Again, there is no handler, and the runtime unwinds the stack
back to Main(). With no exception handler there, the default handler is called, which
prints the error message, and terminates the program.

The try and catch Statements

To handle exceptions, take the following steps:

1. Execute any code that you suspect might throw an exception (such as code that
   opens a file or allocates memory) within a try block.
2. Catch any exceptions that are thrown in a catch block.

A try block is created using the keyword try and is enclosed in braces. A catch block is created using the keyword catch and is also enclosed in braces. Example 18-2 illustrates these constructs. Note that Example 18-2 is identical to Example 18-1 except that now the program includes a try/catch block.

Example 18-2. Try and catch blocks

```
using System;

namespace ExceptionHandling
{
    class Tester
    {
        static void Main()
        {
            Console.WriteLine("Enter Main...");
            Tester t = new Tester();
            t.Run();
            Console.WriteLine("Exit Main...");
        }
        public void Run()
        {
            Console.WriteLine("Enter Run...");
            Func1();
            Console.WriteLine("Exit Run...");
        }


        public void Func1()
        {
            Console.WriteLine("Enter Func1...");
            Func2();
            Console.WriteLine("Exit Func1...");
        }

        public void Func2()
        {
            Console.WriteLine("Enter Func2...");
            try
            {
                Console.WriteLine("Entering try block...");
                throw new System.Exception();
                Console.WriteLine("Exiting try block...");
            }
            catch
            {
                Console.WriteLine("Exception caught and handled!");
            }
            Console.WriteLine("Exit Func2...");
        }
    }
}
```

Example 18-2. Try and catch blocks (continued)

Output:
```
Enter Main...
Enter Run...
Enter Func1...
Enter Func2...
Entering try block...
Exception caught and handled!
Exit Func2...
Exit Func1...
Exit Run...
Exit Main...
```

Following the try statement is the catch statement. In a real catch statement, you might silently fix the problem (e.g., retry a database connection), or you might interact with the user to solve the problem (e.g., offer the user the opportunity to close other applications and free up memory). In Example 18-2, the catch statement simply reports that the exception has been caught and handled.

Notice that the exit statements are now written. With the exception handled, execution resumes immediately after the catch block.

How the Call Stack Works

Examine the output of Example 18-2 carefully. You see the code enter Main(), Func1(), Func2(), and the try block. You never see it exit the try block, though it does exit Func2(), Func1(), and Main(). What happened?

When the exception is thrown, execution halts immediately and is handed to the catch block. It *never* returns to the original code path. It never gets to the line that prints the exit statement for the try block. The catch block handles the error, and then execution falls through to the code following the catch block.

Because there is a catch block, the stack does not need to unwind. The exception is now handled, there are no more problems, and the program continues. This becomes a bit clearer if you move the try/catch blocks up to Func1(), as Example 18-3 shows.

Example 18-3. Unwinding the stack by one level
```
using System;

namespace ExceptionHandling
{
    class Tester
    {

        static void Main()
        {
            Console.WriteLine("Enter Main...");
```

Example 18-3. Unwinding the stack by one level (continued)

```
            Tester t = new Tester();
            t.Run();
            Console.WriteLine("Exit Main...");
    }
    public void Run()
    {
        Console.WriteLine("Enter Run...");
        Func1();
        Console.WriteLine("Exit Run...");
    }


    public void Func1()
    {
        Console.WriteLine("Enter Func1...");
        try
        {
            Console.WriteLine("Entering try block...");
            Func2();
            Console.WriteLine("Exiting try block...");
        }
        catch
        {
            Console.WriteLine("Exception caught and handled!");
        }
        Console.WriteLine("Exit Func1...");
    }

    public void Func2()
    {
        Console.WriteLine("Enter Func2...");
        throw new System.Exception();
        Console.WriteLine("Exit Func2...");
    }
  }
}
Output:
Enter Main...
Enter Run...
Enter Func1...
Entering try block...
Enter Func2...
Exception caught and handled!
Exit Func1...
Exit Run...
Exit Main...
```

This time the exception is not handled in Func2(); it is handled in Func1(). When Func2() is called, it uses Console.WriteLine() to display its first milestone:

```
    Enter Func2...
```

Then Func2() throws an exception and execution halts. The runtime looks for a handler in Func2(), but there isn't one. Then the stack begins to unwind, and the runtime looks for a handler in the calling function: Func1(). There is a catch block in Func1(), so its code is executed. Execution then resumes immediately following the catch statement, printing the exit statement for Func1() and then for Main().

If you're not entirely sure why the "Exiting Try Block" statement and the "Exit Func2" statement are not printed, try putting the code into a debugger and then stepping through it.

Creating Dedicated catch Statements

So far, you've been working with generic catch statements only. You can create dedicated catch statements that handle only some exceptions and not others, based on the type of exception thrown. Example 18-4 illustrates how to specify which exception you'd like to handle.

Example 18-4. Three dedicated catch statements

```
using System;

namespace ExceptionHandling
{
    class Tester
    {

        public void Run()
        {
            try
            {
                double a = 5;
                double b = 0;
                Console.WriteLine("Dividing {0} by {1}...",a,b);
                Console.WriteLine ("{0} / {1} = {2}",
                    a, b, DoDivide(a,b));
            }

            // most derived exception type first
            catch (System.DivideByZeroException)
            {
                Console.WriteLine(
                    "DivideByZeroException caught!");
            }

            catch (System.ArithmeticException)
            {
                Console.WriteLine(
                    "ArithmeticException caught!");
            }
```

Example 18-4. Three dedicated catch statements (continued)

```csharp
            // generic exception type last
        catch
        {
            Console.WriteLine(
                "Unknown exception caught");
        }
    }

    // do the division if legal
    public double DoDivide(double a, double b)
    {
        if (b == 0)
            throw new System.DivideByZeroException();
        if (a == 0)
            throw new System.ArithmeticException();
        return a/b;
    }

    static void Main()
    {
        Console.WriteLine("Enter Main...");
        Tester t = new Tester();
        t.Run();
        Console.WriteLine("Exit Main...");
    }


    }
}
```

Output:
```
Enter Main...
Dividing 5 by 0...
DivideByZeroException caught!
Exit Main...
```

In Example 18-4, the DoDivide() method does not let you divide zero by another number, nor does it let you divide a number by zero. If you try to divide by zero, it throws an instance of DivideByZeroException. If you try to divide zero by another number, there is no appropriate exception; dividing zero by another number is a legal mathematical operation and shouldn't throw an exception at all. However, for the sake of this example, assume you don't want to allow division of zero by any number; you will throw an ArithmeticException.

When the exception is thrown, the runtime examines each exception handler in the order in which they appear in the code and matches the first one it can. When you run this program with a=5 and b=7, the output is:

```
5 / 7 = 0.7142857142857143
```

As you'd expect, no exception is thrown. However, when you change the value of a to 0, the output is:

```
ArithmeticException caught!
```

The exception is thrown, and the runtime examines the first exception: Divide-ByZeroException. Because this does not match, it goes on to the next handler, ArithmeticException, which does match.

In a final pass through, suppose you change a to 7 and b to 0. This throws the DivideByZeroException.

 You have to be particularly careful with the order of the catch statements in this case because the DivideByZeroException is derived from ArithmeticException. If you reverse the catch statements, the DivideByZeroException matches the ArithmeticException handler and the exception never gets to the DivideByZeroException handler. In fact, if their order is reversed, it is impossible for *any* exception to reach the DivideByZeroException handler. Then the compiler recognizes that the DivideByZeroException handler cannot be reached and reports a compile error!

Typically, a method catches every exception it can anticipate for the code it is running. However, it is possible to distribute your try/catch statements, catching some specific exceptions in one function and more generic exceptions in higher calling functions. Your design goals should dictate the exact design.

Assume you have a Method A that calls another Method B, which in turn calls Method C, which calls Method D, which then calls Method E. Method E is deep in your code, while methods B and A are higher up. If you anticipate that Method E might throw an exception, you should create a try/catch block deep in your code to catch that exception as close as possible to the place where the problem arises. You might also want to create more general exception handlers higher up in the code in case unanticipated exceptions slip by.

The finally Statement

In some instances, throwing an exception and unwinding the stack can create a problem. For example, if you opened a file or otherwise committed a resource, you might need an opportunity to close the file or flush the buffer.

If there is some action you *must* take regardless of whether an exception is thrown, such as closing a file, you have two strategies to choose from. One approach is to enclose the dangerous action in a try block and then to perform the necessary action (close the file) in both the catch and try blocks. However, this is an ugly duplication of code, and it's error prone. C# provides a better alternative in the finally block.

You create a finally block with the keyword finally, and you enclose the block in braces. The code in the finally block is guaranteed to be executed regardless of whether an exception is thrown. The TestFunc() method in the next listing, Example 18-5, simulates opening a file as its first action. The method then undertakes some mathematical operations, and then the file is closed.

 A finally block can be created with or without catch blocks, but a finally block requires a try block to execute. It is an error to exit a finally block with break, continue, return, or goto.

It is possible that sometime between opening and closing the file an exception will be thrown. If this were to occur, it would be possible for the file to remain open. The developer knows that no matter what happens, at the end of this method the file should be closed, so the file close function call is moved to a finally block, where it is executed regardless of whether an exception is thrown. Example 18-5 uses a finally block.

Example 18-5. Using a finally block

```
using System;

namespace ExceptionHandling
{
    class Tester
    {
        public void Run()
        {
            try
            {
                Console.WriteLine("Open file here");
                double a = 5;
                double b = 0;
                Console.WriteLine ("{0} / {1} = {2}",
                    a, b, DoDivide(a,b));
                Console.WriteLine (
                    "This line may or may not print");
            }

                // most derived exception type first
            catch (System.DivideByZeroException)
            {
                Console.WriteLine(
                    "DivideByZeroException caught!");
            }
            catch
            {
                Console.WriteLine("Unknown exception caught");
            }
            finally
            {
```

Example 18-5. Using a finally block (continued)

```
                Console.WriteLine ("Close file here.");
            }
        }

    // do the division if legal
    public double DoDivide(double a, double b)
    {
        if (b == 0)
            throw new System.DivideByZeroException();
        if (a == 0)
            throw new System.ArithmeticException();
        return a/b;
    }

    static void Main()
    {
        Console.WriteLine("Enter Main...");
        Tester t = new Tester();
        t.Run();
        Console.WriteLine("Exit Main...");
    }
    }
}
```

Output:
```
Enter Main...
Open file here
DivideByZeroException caught!
Close file here.
Exit Main...
```

In Example 18-5, one of the catch blocks from Example 18-4 has been eliminated to save space and a finally block has been added. Whether or not an exception is thrown, the finally block is executed; thus, in both examples the following message is output:

```
    Close file here.
```

Of course, in a real application you would actually open the file in the try block, and you'd actually close the file in the finally block. The details of file manipulation have been eliminated to keep the example simple.

Exception Class Methods and Properties

So far you've been using the exception as a sentinel—that is, the presence of the exception signals the errors—but you haven't touched or examined the Exception object itself. The System.Exception class provides a number of useful methods and properties.

The Message property provides information about the exception, such as why it was thrown. The Message property is read-only; the code throwing the exception can pass in the message as an argument to the exception constructor, but the Message property cannot be modified by any method once set in the constructor.

The HelpLink property provides a link to a help file associated with the exception. This property is read/write. In Example 18-6, the Exception.HelpLink property is set and retrieved to provide information to the user about the DivideByZeroException. It is generally a good idea to provide a help file link for any exceptions you create, so that the user can learn how to correct the exceptional circumstance.

The read-only StackTrace property is set by the CLR. This property is used to provide a *stack trace* for the error statement. A stack trace is used to display the call stack: the series of method calls that lead to the method in which the exception was thrown.

Example 18-6. Inside the Exception class

```
using System;

namespace ExceptionHandling
{
   class Tester
   {
      public void Run()
      {
         try
         {
            Console.WriteLine("Open file here");
            double a = 12;
            double b = 0;
            Console.WriteLine ("{0} / {1} = {2}",
               a, b, DoDivide(a,b));
            Console.WriteLine (
               "This line may or may not print");
         }

         // most derived exception type first
         catch (System.DivideByZeroException e)
         {
            Console.WriteLine(
               "\nDivideByZeroException! Msg: {0}",
               e.Message);
            Console.WriteLine(
               "\nHelpLink: {0}", e.HelpLink);
            Console.WriteLine(
               "\nHere's a stack trace: {0}\n",
               e.StackTrace);
         }
         catch
         {
            Console.WriteLine(
```

Example 18-6. Inside the Exception class (continued)

```
                "Unknown exception caught");
        }
        finally
        {
            Console.WriteLine (
                "Close file here.");
        }

    }

    // do the division if legal
    public double DoDivide(double a, double b)
    {
        if (b == 0)
        {
            DivideByZeroException e =
                new DivideByZeroException();
            e.HelpLink =
                "http://www.libertyassociates.com";
            throw e;
        }
        if (a == 0)
            throw new ArithmeticException();
        return a/b;
    }

    static void Main()
    {
        Console.WriteLine("Enter Main...");
        Tester t = new Tester();
        t.Run();
        Console.WriteLine("Exit Main...");
    }
  }
}
```

Output:
```
Enter Main...
Open file here

DivideByZeroException! Msg: Attempted to divide by zero.

HelpLink: http://www.libertyassociates.com

Here's a stack trace:
  at ExceptionHandling.Tester.DoDivide(Double a, Double b) in class1.cs:line 54
   at ExceptionHandling.Tester.Run() in class1.cs:line 14

Close file here.
Exit Main...
```

In the output of Example 18-6, the stack trace lists the methods in the reverse order in which they were called; by reviewing this order, you can infer that the error occurred in DoDivide(), which was called by Run(). When methods are deeply nested, the stack trace can help you understand the order of method calls and thus track down the point at which the exception occurred.

In this example, rather than simply throwing a DivideByZeroException, you create a new instance of the exception:

```
DivideByZeroException e = new DivideByZeroException();
```

You do not pass in a custom message, and so the default message is printed:

```
DivideByZeroException! Msg: Attempted to divide by zero.
```

The designer of each Exception class has the option to provide a default message for that exception type. All the standard exceptions provide a default message, and it is a good idea to add a default message to your custom exceptions as well (see the section "Custom Exceptions," later in this chapter).

If you want, you can modify this line of code to pass in a custom message:

```
new DivideByZeroException(
    "You tried to divide by zero which is not meaningful");
```

In this case, the output message reflects the custom message:

```
DivideByZeroException! Msg:
You tried to divide by zero which is not meaningful
```

Before throwing the exception, set the HelpLink property:

```
e.HelpLink = "http://www.libertyassociates.com";
```

When this exception is caught, Console.WriteLine prints both the Message and the HelpLink:

```
catch (System.DivideByZeroException e)
{
    Console.WriteLine("\nDivideByZeroException! Msg: {0}",
        e.Message);
    Console.WriteLine("\nHelpLink: {0}", e.HelpLink);
```

The Message and HelpLink properties allow you to provide useful information to the user. The exception handler also prints the StackTrace by getting the StackTrace property of the Exception object:

```
Console.WriteLine("\nHere's a stack trace: {0}\n",
    e.StackTrace);
```

The output of this call reflects a full StackTrace leading to the moment the exception was thrown. In this case, only two methods were executed before the exception, DoDivide() and Run():

```
Here's a stack trace:
    at ExceptionHandling.Tester.DoDivide(Double a, Double b) in class1.cs:line 54
    at ExceptionHandling.Tester.Run() in class1.cs:line 14
```

Note that I've shortened the pathnames, so your printout might look a little different.

Custom Exceptions

The intrinsic exception types the CLR provides, coupled with the custom messages shown in the previous example, will often be all you need to provide extensive information to a catch block when an exception is thrown.

There will be times, however, when you want to provide more extensive information or need special capabilities in your exception. It is a trivial matter to create your own *custom exception* class; the only restriction is that it must derive (directly or indirectly) from System.ApplicationException. Example 18-7 illustrates the creation of a custom exception.

Example 18-7. A custom exception

```csharp
using System;

namespace ExceptionHandling
{
    // custom exception class
    public class MyCustomException :
        System.ApplicationException
    {
        public MyCustomException(string message):
            base(message) // pass the message up to the base class
        {

        }
    }

    class Tester
    {
        public void Run()
        {
            try
            {
                Console.WriteLine("Open file here");
                double a = 0;
                double b = 5;
                Console.WriteLine ("{0} / {1} = {2}",
                    a, b, DoDivide(a,b));
                Console.WriteLine (
                    "This line may or may not print");
            }

            // most derived exception type first
```

Example 18-7. A custom exception (continued)

```
                catch (System.DivideByZeroException e)
                {
                    Console.WriteLine(
                        "\nDivideByZeroException! Msg: {0}",
                        e.Message);
                    Console.WriteLine(
                        "\nHelpLink: {0}\n", e.HelpLink);
                }

                // catch custom exception
                catch (MyCustomException e)
                {
                    Console.WriteLine(
                        "\nMyCustomException! Msg: {0}",
                        e.Message);
                    Console.WriteLine(
                        "\nHelpLink: {0}\n", e.HelpLink);
                }
                catch       // catch any uncaught exceptions
                {
                    Console.WriteLine(
                        "Unknown exception caught");
                }
                finally
                {
                    Console.WriteLine ("Close file here.");
                }
        }

        // do the division if legal
        public double DoDivide(double a, double b)
        {
            if (b == 0)
            {
                DivideByZeroException e =
                    new DivideByZeroException();
                e.HelpLink=
                    "http://www.libertyassociates.com";
                throw e;
            }
            if (a == 0)
            {
                // create a custom exception instance
                MyCustomException e =
                    new MyCustomException(
                    "Can't have zero divisor");
                e.HelpLink =
                    "http://www.libertyassociates.com/NoZeroDivisor.htm";
                throw e;
            }
            return a/b;
        }
```

Example 18-7. A custom exception (continued)

```
    static void Main()
    {
        Console.WriteLine("Enter Main...");
        Tester t = new Tester();
        t.Run();
        Console.WriteLine("Exit Main...");
    }
  }
}
```
Output:
```
Enter Main...
Open file here

MyCustomException! Msg: Can't have zero divisor

HelpLink: http://www.libertyassociates.com/NoZeroDivisor.htm

Close file here.
Exit Main...
```

MyCustomException is derived from System.ApplicationException and consists of nothing more than a constructor that takes a string message that it passes to its base class.

The advantage of creating this custom exception class is that it better reflects the particular design of the Test class, in which it is not legal to have a zero divisor. Using the ArithmeticException rather than a custom exception would work as well, but it might confuse other programmers because a zero divisor wouldn't normally be considered an arithmetic error.

CHAPTER 19

Delegates and Events

When a head of state dies, the president of the United States typically does not have time to attend the funeral personally. Instead, he dispatches a delegate. Often this delegate is the vice president, but sometimes the VP is unavailable and the president must send someone else, such as the secretary of state or even the first lady. He does not want to "hardwire" his delegated authority to a single person; he might delegate this responsibility to anyone who is able to execute the correct international protocol.

The president defines in advance what authority will be delegated (attend the funeral), what parameters will be passed (condolences, kind words), and what value he hopes to get back (good will). He then assigns a particular person to that delegated responsibility at "runtime," as the course of his presidency progresses.

In programming, you are often faced with situations where you need to execute a particular action, but you don't know in advance which method you'll want to call to execute that action. You might not even know which object you'll perform the action with. For example, a button might know that it must notify *some* object when it is pushed, but it might not know which object or objects need to be notified. Rather than wiring the button to a particular object, you will connect the button to a *delegate* and then resolve that delegate to a particular method when the program executes.

Today's Graphical User Interface (GUI) programming model requires *event-driven programming*. A GUI program waits for the user to take an action, such as choosing among menu selections, pushing buttons, updating text fields, and clicking icons. Each action causes an event to be raised. Other events can be raised without direct user action, such as events that correspond to timer ticks of the internal clock, email being received, and file-copy operations completing.

An event is the encapsulation of the idea that "something happened," to which the program must respond. Events and delegates are tightly coupled concepts because flexible event handling requires that the response to the event be dispatched to the appropriate event handler. An event handler is typically implemented in C# as a delegate.

Delegates

In C#, a delegate is a reference type that encapsulates methods with a specified parameter list and return type.

A delegate is created with the delegate keyword, followed by a return type and the parameter list of the methods that can be delegated to it, as in the following:

```
public delegate int WhichIsFirst(object obj1, object obj2);
```

This declaration defines a delegate named WhichIsFirst that encapsulates any method that takes two objects as parameters and that returns an int.

Once the delegate is defined, you can encapsulate a member method with that delegate by instantiating the delegate and passing in as a parameter the name of a method that matches the return type and parameter list.

Using Delegates to Specify Methods at Runtime

Suppose, for example, that you want to create a simple collection class called Pair that can hold and sort any two objects passed to it. You can't know in advance what kind of objects a Pair will hold, but by creating methods within those objects to which the sorting task can be delegated, you can delegate responsibility for determining their order to the objects themselves.

Different objects will sort differently; for example, a Pair of Counter objects might sort in numeric order, while a Pair of Buttons might sort alphabetically by their name.

What a nightmare this could be for the creator of the Pair class. The class must know how each type of object sorts. If you add a Button, the Pair class must know to ask the Buttons for their names and sort them alphabetically. If you then add a Pair of Employees, the Pair class must know to ask the Employees for their date of hire, and sort by date. There must be a better way!

The answer is to delegate this responsibility to the objects themselves. If the Button objects know which Button comes first and the Employee objects know which Employee comes first, then the Pair class can become *much* more flexible. This is the essence of good object-oriented design: delegate responsibility to the class that is in the best position to have the knowledge required for the task at hand.

Delegating the responsibility for knowing how the objects are sorted to the objects themselves decouples the Pair class from the types contained in the Pair. The Pair no longer needs to know how the objects are sorted; it just needs to know that they *can* be sorted.

Of course, the objects you put in the Pair container must know how to tell the Pair which object comes first. The Pair container must specify the method these objects need to implement. Rather than specifying a particular method, however, the Pair will just specify the signature and return type of the method. That is, the Pair will say, in essence, "I can hold any type of object that offers a method that takes two objects and returns an int signifying which comes first."

Define the method you require by creating a delegate that specifies the parameter list and return type of the method the object (e.g., Button) must provide to allow the Pair to determine which object should be first and which should be second.

The Pair class defines a delegate, WhichIsFirst. The Sort() method takes as a parameter an instance of the WhichIsFirst delegate. When the Pair needs to know how to order its objects, it invokes the delegate, passing in its two objects as parameters. The responsibility for deciding which of the two objects comes first is delegated to the method encapsulated by the delegate.

To test the delegate, create two classes, a Dog class and a Student class. Dogs and Students have little in common, except that they both implement methods that can be encapsulated by WhichComesFirst, and thus both Dog objects and Student objects are eligible to be held within Pair objects.

In Example 19-1, you will create a couple of Students and a couple of Dogs and store them in Pairs. You will then create delegate objects to encapsulate their respective methods that match the delegate signature and return type, and you'll ask the Pair objects to sort the Dog and Student objects. Example 19-1 shows a complete program illustrating the use of delegates. This is a long and somewhat complicated program that will be analyzed in detail following the output.

Example 19-1. Delegates

```
using System;

namespace DelegatesAndEvents
{
    public enum comparison
    {
        theFirstComesFirst = 1,
        theSecondComesFirst = 2
    }

    // A simple collection to hold two items
    public class Pair
    {
        // Private array to hold the two objects
        private object[] thePair = new object[2];

        // The delegate declaration
        public delegate comparison
            WhichIsFirst(object obj1, object obj2);
```

Example 19-1. Delegates (continued)

```
        // Passed in constructor takes two objects,
        // added in order received
        public Pair(
            object firstObject,
            object secondObject)
        {
            thePair[0] = firstObject;
            thePair[1] = secondObject;
        }

        // Public method that orders the
        // two objects by whatever criteria the objects like!
        public void Sort(
            WhichIsFirst theDelegatedFunc)
        {
            if (theDelegatedFunc(thePair[0],thePair[1])
                == comparison.theSecondComesFirst)
            {
                object temp = thePair[0];
                thePair[0] = thePair[1];
                thePair[1] = temp;
            }
        }

        // Public method that orders the
        // two objects by the reverse of whatever criteria the
        // objects likes!
        public void ReverseSort(
            WhichIsFirst theDelegatedFunc)
        {
            if (theDelegatedFunc(thePair[0],thePair[1]) ==
                comparison.theFirstComesFirst)
            {
                object temp = thePair[0];
                thePair[0] = thePair[1];
                thePair[1] = temp;
            }
        }

        // Ask the two objects to give their string value
        public override string ToString()
        {
            return thePair[0].ToString() + ", "
                + thePair[1].ToString();
        }
    }

    public class Dog
    {
        private int weight;

        public Dog(int weight)
```

Example 19-1. Delegates (continued)

```
        {
            this.weight=weight;
        }

        // dogs are sorted by weight
        public static comparison WhichDogComesFirst(
            Object o1, Object o2)
        {
            Dog d1 = (Dog) o1;
            Dog d2 = (Dog) o2;
            return d1.weight > d2.weight ?
                comparison.theSecondComesFirst :
                comparison.theFirstComesFirst;
        }
        public override string ToString()
        {
            return weight.ToString();
        }
    }

    public class Student
    {
        private string name;
        public Student(string name)
        {
            this.name = name;
        }

        // Students are sorted alphabetically
        public static comparison
            WhichStudentComesFirst(Object o1, Object o2)
        {
            Student s1 = (Student) o1;
            Student s2 = (Student) o2;
            return (String.Compare(s1.name, s2.name) < 0 ?
                comparison.theFirstComesFirst :
                comparison.theSecondComesFirst);
        }

        public override string ToString()
        {
            return name;
        }
    }

    class Tester
    {
        public void Run()
        {
            // Create two students and two dogs
            // and add them to Pair objects
            Student Jesse = new Student("Jesse");
```

Example 19-1. Delegates (continued)

```
            Student Stacey = new Student ("Stacey");
            Dog Milo = new Dog(65);
            Dog Fred = new Dog(12);

            Pair studentPair = new Pair(Jesse,Stacey);
            Pair dogPair = new Pair(Milo, Fred);
            Console.WriteLine("studentPair\t\t\t: {0}",
                studentPair.ToString());
            Console.WriteLine("dogPair\t\t\t: {0}",
                dogPair.ToString());

            // Instantiate the delegates
            Pair.WhichIsFirst  theStudentDelegate =
                new Pair.WhichIsFirst(
                Student.WhichStudentComesFirst);

            Pair.WhichIsFirst theDogDelegate =
                new Pair.WhichIsFirst(
                Dog.WhichDogComesFirst);

            // Sort using the delegates
            studentPair.Sort(theStudentDelegate);
            Console.WriteLine("After Sort studentPair\t: {0}",
                studentPair.ToString());
            studentPair.ReverseSort(theStudentDelegate);
            Console.WriteLine("After ReverseSort studentPair\t: {0}",
                studentPair.ToString());

            dogPair.Sort(theDogDelegate);
            Console.WriteLine("After Sort dogPair\t\t: {0}",
                dogPair.ToString());
            dogPair.ReverseSort(theDogDelegate);
            Console.WriteLine("After ReverseSort dogPair\t: {0}",
                dogPair.ToString());
        }

    static void Main()
    {
        Tester t = new Tester();
        t.Run();
    }
  }
}
```

Output:

```
studentPair                  : Jesse, Stacey
dogPair                      : 65, 12
After Sort studentPair       : Jesse, Stacey
After ReverseSort studentPair : Stacey, Jesse
After Sort dogPair           : 12, 65
After ReverseSort dogPair    : 65, 12
```

Let's consider Example 19-1, step by step. You begin by creating a Pair constructor that takes two objects and stashes them away in a private array (thePair):

```
public class Pair
{
    private object[] thePair = new object[2];

    public Pair(object firstObject, object secondObject)
    {
        thePair[0] = firstObject;
        thePair[1] = secondObject;
    }
```

Override ToString() to obtain the string value of the two objects:

```
public override string ToString()
{
    return thePair [0].ToString() + ", " + thePair[1].ToString();
}
```

You now have two objects in your Pair and you can display their values. You're ready to sort them and display the results of the sort.

Create the delegate WhichIsFirst that defines the signature for the sorting method.

```
public delegate comparison
    WhichIsFirst(object obj1, object obj2);
```

This delegate definition can be a bit confusing. Figure 19-1 illustrates the various parts of the definition.

Figure 19-1. A delegate definition

The return value is of type comparison, which is the enumeration defined earlier in the file:

```
public enum comparison
{
    theFirstComesFirst = 1,
    theSecondComesFirst = 2
}
```

Any method that takes two objects and returns a comparison can be encapsulated by this delegate at runtime.

Now define the Sort() method for the Pair class:

```
public void Sort(WhichIsFirst theDelegatedFunc)
{
```

```
    if (theDelegatedFunc(thePair[0],thePair[1]) ==
        comparison.theSecondComesFirst)
    {
        object temp = thePair[0];
        thePair[0] = thePair[1];
        thePair[1] = temp;
    }
}
```

This method takes a parameter: a delegate of type WhichIsFirst named the-DelegatedFunc. The Sort() method delegates responsibility for deciding which of the two objects in the Pair comes first to the method encapsulated by that delegate. In the body of the Sort() method it invokes the delegated method and examines the return value, which is one of the two enumerated values of comparison.

If the value returned is theSecondComesFirst, the objects within the pair are swapped; otherwise no action is taken.

Notice that theDelegatedFunc is the name of the parameter to represent the method encapsulated by the delegate. You can assign any method (with the appropriate return value and signature) to this parameter. It is as if you had a method that took an int as a parameter:

```
    int SomeMethod (int myParam){//...}
```

The parameter name is myParam, but you can pass in any int value or variable. Similarly the parameter name in the delegate example is theDelegatedFunc, but you can pass in any method that meets the return value and signature defined by the delegate WhichIsFirst.

Imagine you are sorting students by name. You write a method that returns theFirstComesFirst if the first student's name comes first and theSecondComesFirst if the second student's name does. If you pass in "Amy, Beth", the method returns theFirstComesFirst, and if you pass in "Beth, Amy", it returns theSecondComesFirst. If you get back theSecondComesFirst, the Sort() method reverses the items in its array, setting Amy to the first position and Beth to the second.

Now add one more method, ReverseSort(), which puts the items into the array in reverse order:

```
    public void ReverseSort(WhichIsFirst theDelegatedFunc)
    {
        if (theDelegatedFunc(thePair[0], thePair[1]) ==
                comparison.theFirstComesFirst)
        {
            object temp = thePair[0];
            thePair[0] = thePair[1];
            thePair[1] = temp;
        }
    }
```

The logic of the ReverseSort() method is the same as that of the Sort() method, except that ReverseSort() performs the swap of the items if the delegated method says that the *first* item comes first. In Example 19-1, because the delegated function thinks the first item comes first, and this is a reverse sort, the result you want is for the second item to come first.

This time if you pass in "Amy, Beth," the delegated function returns theFirstComes-First (i.e., Amy should come first), but because this is a *reverse* sort it swaps the values, setting Beth first. This allows you to use the same delegated function that you used with Sort(), without forcing the object to support a function that returns the reverse sorted value.

Now all you need are some objects to sort. Create two absurdly simple classes: Student and Dog. Assign Student objects a name at creation:

```
public class Student
{
    public Student(string name)
    {
        this.name = name;
    }
}
```

The Student class requires two methods: one to override ToString() and the other to be encapsulated as the delegated method.

Student must override ToString() so that the ToString() method in Pair, which invokes ToString() on the contained objects, works properly; the implementation does nothing more than return the student's name (which is already a string object):

```
public override string ToString()
{
    return name;
}
```

It must also implement a method to which Pair.Sort() can delegate the responsibility of determining which of two objects comes first:

```
return (String.Compare(s1.name, s2.name) < 0 ?
    comparison.theFirstComesFirst :
    comparison.theSecondComesFirst);
```

As you saw in Chapter 17, String.Compare() is a .NET Framework method on the String class that compares two strings and returns less than zero if the first is smaller, greater than zero if the second is smaller, and zero if they are the same.

Notice also that the logic here returns theFirstComesFirst only if the first string is smaller; if they are the same or the second is larger, this method returns theSecond-ComesFirst.

Notice that the WhichStudentComesFirst() method takes two objects as parameters and returns a comparison. This qualifies it to be a Pair.WhichIsFirst delegated method, whose signature and return value it matches.

The second class is Dog. For our purposes, Dog objects will be sorted by weight, with lighter dogs before heavier. Here's the complete declaration of Dog:

```
public class Dog
{
    private int weight;

    public Dog(int weight)
    {
        this.weight=weight;
    }

    // dogs are ordered by weight
    public static comparison WhichDogComesFirst(
        Object o1, Object o2)
    {
        Dog d1 = (Dog) o1;
        Dog d2 = (Dog) o2;
        return d1.weight > d2.weight ?
            comparison.theSecondComesFirst :
            comparison.theFirstComesFirst;
    }
    public override string ToString()
    {
        return weight.ToString();
    }
}
```

Notice that the Dog class also overrides ToString() and implements a static method with the correct signature for the delegate. Notice also that the Dog and Student delegate methods do not have the same name. They do not need to have the same name because they will be assigned to the delegate dynamically at runtime. You can call your delegated method names anything you like, but creating parallel names (e.g., WhichDogComesFirst and WhichStudentComesFirst) makes the code easier to understand and maintain.

The Run() method creates two Student objects and two Dog objects and then adds them to Pair containers. The student constructor takes a string for the student's name, and the dog constructor takes an int for the dog's weight.

```
public void Run()
{
    Student Jesse = new Student("Jesse");
    Student Stacey = new Student ("Stacey");
    Dog Milo = new Dog(65);
    Dog Fred = new Dog(12);
Pair studentPair = new Pair(Jesse,Stacey);
Pair dogPair = new Pair(Milo, Fred);
Console.WriteLine("studentPair\t\t\t: {0}",
    studentPair.ToString());
Console.WriteLine("dogPair\t\t\t\t: {0}",
    dogPair.ToString());
```

Display the contents of the two Pair containers to see the order of the objects. The output looks like this:

```
studentPair          : Jesse, Stacey
dogPair              : 65, 12
```

As expected, the objects are in the order in which they were added to the Pair containers. Next, instantiate two delegate objects:

```
Pair.WhichIsFirst  theStudentDelegate =
    new Pair.WhichIsFirst(
    Student.WhichStudentComesFirst);

Pair.WhichIsFirst theDogDelegate =
    new Pair.WhichIsFirst(
    Dog.WhichDogComesFirst);
```

The first delegate, theStudentDelegate, is created by passing in the appropriate method from the Student class. The second delegate, theDogDelegate, is passed a method from the Dog class.

The delegates are now objects that can be passed to methods. Pass the delegates first to the Sort() method and then to the ReverseSort() method of the Pair object:

```
studentPair.Sort(theStudentDelegate);
studentPair.ReverseSort(theStudentDelegate);

dogPair.Sort(theDogDelegate);
dogPair.ReverseSort(theDogDelegate);
```

The results are displayed on the console:

```
After Sort studentPair          : Jesse, Stacey
After ReverseSort studentPair   : Stacey, Jesse
After Sort dogPair              : 12, 65
After ReverseSort dogPair       : 65, 12
```

Static Methods Versus Instance Methods

In Example 19-1, the methods you encapsulated with the delegates were static methods of the Student and Dog classes:

```
public static comparison
    WhichStudentComesFirst(Object o1, Object o2)
```

You could declare the WhichStudentComesFirst() method to be an instance method instead:

```
public comparison
    WhichStudentComesFirst(Object o1, Object o2)
```

You can still encapsulate it as a delegate, but you must refer to it through an instance, rather than through the class:

```
Pair.WhichIsFirst  theStudentDelegate =
    new Pair.WhichIsFirst(
    Jesse.WhichStudentComesFirst);
```

You decide whether to use instance or static methods. The advantage of static methods is that you don't need an instance of the class to create the delegate, but instance methods can be slightly more efficient when you are calling them many times.

Static Delegates

A disadvantage of Example 19-1 is that it forces the calling class, in this case Tester, to instantiate the delegates it needs in order to sort the objects in a Pair. Notice that in Example 19-1, within the Run() method of Tester, you see this code:

```
Pair.WhichIsFirst  theStudentDelegate =
    new Pair.WhichIsFirst(
    Student.WhichStudentComesFirst);
```

What is going on here is that the Tester class needs to know that it must instantiate an instance of the WhichIsFirst delegate (declared in Pair) and that it must pass in the WhichStudentComesFirst method of the Student class. Once it has created this delegate, it can invoke the sort by passing in the delegate it just created:

```
studentPair.Sort(theStudentDelegate);
```

Tester then goes on to instantiate a second delegate, passing in the WhichDog-ComesFirst() method to create the delegate for the Dog objects and invoking Sort() with that delegate as well:

```
Pair.WhichIsFirst theDogDelegate =
    new Pair.WhichIsFirst(
    Dog.WhichDogComesFirst);
dogPair.Sort(theDogDelegate);
```

Rather than forcing Tester to know which method Student and Dog must use to accomplish the sort, it would be better to get the delegate from the Student or Dog classes themselves. You can give the implementing classes (Student and Dog) the responsibility for instantiating the delegate by giving each implementing class its own static delegate. In that case, rather than knowing which method implements the sort for the Student, Tester would only need to know that the Student class has a static delegate named, for example, OrderStudents, and the author of the Tester class could then write:

```
studentPair.Sort(Student.OrderStudents);
```

Thus, you can modify Student to add this definition, which creates a static, read-only delegate named OrderStudents:

```
public static readonly Pair.WhichIsFirst OrderStudents =
    new Pair.WhichIsFirst(Student.WhichStudentComesFirst);
```

 Marking OrderStudents read-only denotes that once this static field is created, it will not be modified.

You can create a similar delegate within Dog:

```
public static readonly Pair.WhichIsFirst OrderDogs =
    new Pair.WhichIsFirst(Dog. WhichDogComesFirst);
```

These are now static fields of their respective classes. Each is pre-wired to the appropriate method within the class. You can invoke delegates without declaring a local delegate instance. You just pass in the static delegate of the class:

```
studentPair.Sort(Student.OrderStudents);
studentPair.ReverseSort(Student.OrderStudents);
```

Example 19-2 shows the complete listing. Note that after these changes, the output is identical to that of the previous example.

Example 19-2. Static delegate members

```
using System;

namespace DelegatesAndEvents
{
    public enum comparison
    {
        theFirstComesFirst = 1,
        theSecondComesFirst = 2
    }

    // A simple collection to hold two items.
    public class Pair
    {
        // Private array to hold the two objects.
        private object[] thePair = new object[2];

        // The delegate declaration.
        public delegate comparison
            WhichIsFirst(object obj1, object obj2);

        // Passed in constructor takes two objects,
        // added in order received.
        public Pair(
            object firstObject,
            object secondObject)
        {
            thePair[0] = firstObject;
            thePair[1] = secondObject;
        }

        // Public method that orders
        // the two objects by whatever criteria the objects like!
        public void Sort(
            WhichIsFirst theDelegatedFunc)
        {
            if (theDelegatedFunc(thePair[0],thePair[1])
                == comparison.theSecondComesFirst)
            {
```

Example 19-2. Static delegate members (continued)

```
                object temp = thePair[0];
                thePair[0] = thePair[1];
                thePair[1] = temp;
            }
        }

        // Public method that orders
        // the two objects by the reverse of whatever criteria
        // the objects like!
        public void ReverseSort(
            WhichIsFirst theDelegatedFunc)
        {
            if (theDelegatedFunc(thePair[0],thePair[1]) ==
                comparison.theFirstComesFirst)
            {
                object temp = thePair[0];
                thePair[0] = thePair[1];
                thePair[1] = temp;
            }
        }

        // Ask the two objects to give their string value.
        public override string ToString()
        {
            return thePair[0].ToString() + ", "
                + thePair[1].ToString();
        }
    }

    public class Dog
    {
        private int weight;

        // A static delegate.
        public static readonly Pair.WhichIsFirst OrderDogs =
            new Pair.WhichIsFirst(Dog. WhichDogComesFirst);

        public Dog(int weight)
        {
            this.weight=weight;
        }

        // Dogs are sorted by weight.
        public static comparison WhichDogComesFirst(
            Object o1, Object o2)
        {
            Dog d1 = (Dog) o1;
            Dog d2 = (Dog) o2;
            return d1.weight > d2.weight ?
                comparison.theSecondComesFirst :
                comparison.theFirstComesFirst;
        }
```

Example 19-2. Static delegate members (continued)

```
        public override string ToString()
        {
            return weight.ToString();
        }
    }

    public class Student
    {
        private string name;

        // A static delegate.
        public static readonly Pair.WhichIsFirst OrderStudents =
            new Pair.WhichIsFirst(Student.WhichStudentComesFirst);

        public Student(string name)
        {
            this.name = name;
        }

        // Students are sorted alphabetically.
        public static comparison
            WhichStudentComesFirst(Object o1, Object o2)
        {
            Student s1 = (Student) o1;
            Student s2 = (Student) o2;
            return (String.Compare(s1.name, s2.name) < 0 ?
                comparison.theFirstComesFirst :
                comparison.theSecondComesFirst);
        }

        public override string ToString()
        {
            return name;
        }
    }

    class Tester
    {
        public void Run()
        {
            // Create two students and two dogs
            // and add them to Pair objects.
            Student Jesse = new Student("Jesse");
            Student Stacey = new Student ("Stacey");
            Dog Milo = new Dog(65);
            Dog Fred = new Dog(12);

            // Create the Pair object.
            Pair studentPair = new Pair(Jesse,Stacey);
            Pair dogPair = new Pair(Milo, Fred);
            Console.WriteLine("studentPair\t\t\t: {0}",
                studentPair.ToString());
```

Example 19-2. Static delegate members (continued)

```
        Console.WriteLine("dogPair\t\t\t\t: {0}",
            dogPair.ToString());

        // Tell the student Pair to sort itself,
        // passing in the Student delegate.
        studentPair.Sort(Student.OrderStudents);
        Console.WriteLine("After Sort studentPair\t\t: {0}",
            studentPair.ToString());
        studentPair.ReverseSort(Student.OrderStudents);
        Console.WriteLine("After ReverseSort studentPair\t: {0}",
            studentPair.ToString());

        // Tell the Dog pair to sort itself,
        // passing in the Dog delegate.
        dogPair.Sort(Dog.OrderDogs);
        Console.WriteLine("After Sort dogPair\t\t: {0}",
            dogPair.ToString());
        dogPair.ReverseSort(Dog.OrderDogs);
        Console.WriteLine("After ReverseSort dogPair\t: {0}",
            dogPair.ToString());

    }

    [STAThread]
    static void Main()
    {
        Tester t = new Tester();
        t.Run();
    }
  }
}
```

Delegates as Properties

The problem with static delegates is that they must be instantiated, whether or not
they are ever used, as with Student and Dog in Example 19-2. You can improve these
classes by changing the static delegate fields to properties.

For Student, take out the declaration:

```
public static readonly Pair.WhichIsFirst OrderStudents =
    new Pair.WhichIsFirst(Student.WhichStudentComesFirst);
```

and replace it with:

```
public static Pair.WhichIsFirst OrderStudents
{
    get { return new Pair.WhichIsFirst(WhichStudentComesFirst); }
}
```

Similarly, replace the Dog static field with:

```
public static Pair.WhichIsFirst OrderDogs
{
```

```
        get { return new Pair.WhichIsFirst(WhichDogComesFirst); }
    }
```

The assignment of the delegates is unchanged:

```
studentPair.Sort(Student.OrderStudents);
dogPair.Sort(Dog.OrderDogs);
```

When the OrderStudent property is accessed, the delegate is created:

```
return new Pair.WhichIsFirst(WhichStudentComesFirst);
```

The key advantage is that the delegate is not created until it is requested. This allows the Tester class to determine when it needs a delegate but still allows the details of the creation of the delegate to be the responsibility of the Student (or Dog) class.

Multicasting

At times it is desirable to *multicast*: to call two implementing methods through a single delegate. This becomes particularly important when handling events (discussed later in this chapter).

With multicasting, you create a single delegate that calls multiple encapsulated methods. For example, when a button is pressed, you might want to take more than one action. You could implement this by giving the button a collection of delegates, but it is cleaner and easier to create a single multicast delegate.

Two delegates can be combined with the addition operator (+). The result is a new multicast delegate that invokes both of the original implementing methods. For example, assuming Writer and Logger are delegates, the following line will combine them and produce a new multicast delegate named myMulticastDelegate:

```
myMulticastDelegate = Writer + Logger;
```

You can add delegates to a multicast delegate using the plus-equals (+=) operator. This operator adds the delegate on the right side of the operator to the multicast delegate on the left. For example, assuming Transmitter and myMulticastDelegate are delegates, the following line adds Transmitter to myMulticastDelegate:

```
myMulticastDelegate += Transmitter;
```

To see how multicast delegates are created and used, let's walk through a complete example. Example 19-3 is followed by a complete analysis.

Example 19-3. Multicast delegates

```
using System;

namespace DelegatesAndEvents
{
    public class MyClassWithDelegate
    {
```

Example 19-3. Multicast delegates (continued)

```
        // The delegate declaration.
        public delegate void StringDelegate(string s);

    }

    public class MyImplementingClass
    {
        public static void WriteString(string s)
        {
            Console.WriteLine("Writing string {0}", s);
        }

        public static void LogString(string s)
        {
            Console.WriteLine("Logging string {0}", s);
        }

        public static void TransmitString(string s)
        {
            Console.WriteLine("Transmitting string {0}", s);
        }

    }

    class Tester
    {
        public void Run()
        {
            // Define three StringDelegate objects.
            MyClassWithDelegate.StringDelegate
                Writer, Logger, Transmitter;

            // Define another StringDelegate
            // to act as the multicast delegate.
            MyClassWithDelegate.StringDelegate
                myMulticastDelegate;

            // Instantiate the first three delegates,
            // passing in methods to encapsulate.
            Writer = new MyClassWithDelegate.StringDelegate(
                MyImplementingClass.WriteString);
            Logger = new MyClassWithDelegate.StringDelegate(
                MyImplementingClass.LogString);
            Transmitter =
                new MyClassWithDelegate.StringDelegate(
                MyImplementingClass.TransmitString);

            // Invoke the Writer delegate method.
            Writer("String passed to Writer\n");

            // Invoke the Logger delegate method.
            Logger("String passed to Logger\n");
```

Example 19-3. Multicast delegates (continued)

```
        // Invoke the Transmitter delegate method.
        Transmitter("String passed to Transmitter\n");

        // Tell the user you are about to combine
        // two delegates into the multicast delegate.
        Console.WriteLine(
            "myMulticastDelegate = Writer + Logger");

        // Combine the two delegates;  assign the result
        // to myMulticastDelegate
        myMulticastDelegate = Writer + Logger;

        // Call the delegated methods; two methods
        // will be invoked.
        myMulticastDelegate(
            "First string passed to Collector");

        // Tell the user you are about to add
        // a third delegate to the multicast.
        Console.WriteLine(
            "\nmyMulticastDelegate += Transmitter");

        // Add the third delegate.
        myMulticastDelegate += Transmitter;

        // Invoke the three delegated methods.
        myMulticastDelegate(
            "Second string passed to Collector");

        // Tell the user you are about to remove
        // the Logger delegate.
        Console.WriteLine(
            "\nmyMulticastDelegate -= Logger");

        // Remove the Logger delegate.
        myMulticastDelegate -= Logger;

        // Invoke the two remaining delegated methods.

        myMulticastDelegate(
            "Third string passed to Collector");
    }

    [STAThread]
    static void Main()
    {
        Tester t = new Tester();
        t.Run();
    }
  }
}
```

Example 19-3. Multicast delegates (continued)

Output:
```
Writing string String passed to Writer

Logging string String passed to Logger

Transmitting string String passed to Transmitter

myMulticastDelegate = Writer + Logger
Writing string First string passed to Collector
Logging string First string passed to Collector

myMulticastDelegate += Transmitter
Writing string Second string passed to Collector
Logging string Second string passed to Collector
Transmitting string Second string passed to Collector

myMulticastDelegate -= Logger
Writing string Third string passed to Collector
Transmitting string Third string passed to Collector
```

In Example 19-3, you create a class called MyClassWithDelegate, which defines a delegate that takes a string as a parameter and returns void:

```
public delegate void StringDelegate(string s);
```

You then define a class called MyImplementingClass that has three methods, all of which return void and take a string as a parameter: WriteString(), LogString(), and TransmitString(). The first writes the string to standard output, the second simulates writing to a log file, and the third simulates transmitting the string across the Internet. You instantiate the delegates to invoke the appropriate methods:

```
Writer("String passed to Writer\n");
Logger("String passed to Logger\n");
Transmitter("String passed to Transmitter\n");
```

To see how to combine delegates, create another Delegate instance:

```
MyClassWithDelegate.StringDelegate myMulticastDelegate;
```

and assign to it the result of "adding" two existing delegates:

```
myMulticastDelegate = Writer + Logger;
```

Add to this delegate an additional delegate using the += operator:

```
myMulticastDelegate += Transmitter;
```

Finally, selectively remove delegates using the -= operator:

```
DelegateCollector -= Logger;
```

In the Run() method, the delegates are declared:

```
MyClassWithDelegate.StringDelegate
    Writer, Logger, Transmitter;
```

```
MyClassWithDelegate.StringDelegate
    myMulticastDelegate;
```

The three instance delegates are defined:

```
Writer = new MyClassWithDelegate.StringDelegate(
    MyImplementingClass.WriteString);
Logger = new MyClassWithDelegate.StringDelegate(
    MyImplementingClass.LogString);
Transmitter =
    new MyClassWithDelegate.StringDelegate(
    MyImplementingClass.TransmitString);
```

and invoked:

```
Writer("String passed to Writer\n");
Logger("String passed to Logger\n");
Transmitter("String passed to Transmitter\n");
```

The fourth delegate, myMulticastDelegate, is then assigned the combination of the first two and is invoked, causing both delegated methods to be called:

```
myMulticastDelegate = Writer + Logger;
myMulticastDelegate(
    "First string passed to Collector");
```

The third delegate is added, and when myMulticastDelegate is invoked, all three delegated methods are called:

```
myMulticastDelegate += Transmitter;
myMulticastDelegate(
    "Second string passed to Collector");
```

Finally, Logger is removed, and when myMulticastDelegate is invoked, only the two remaining methods are called:

```
myMulticastDelegate -= Logger;
myMulticastDelegate(
    "Third string passed to Collector");
```

The power of multicast delegates is best understood in terms of events, discussed in the next section. When an event such as a button press occurs, an associated multicast delegate can invoke a series of event handler methods that will respond to the event.

Events

Graphical User Interfaces (GUIs) require that programs respond to events. An event might be a button push, a menu selection, the completion of a file transfer, or a similar occurrence. In a GUI environment, any number of widgets can raise an event. For example, when you click a Button, it might raise the Click event. When you add to a drop-down list, it might raise a ListChanged event.

Whenever something happens in relation to the program (whenever an event is raised), the code must provide a way to respond to it. You cannot predict the order in which events will arise. The system is quiescent until the event, and then it springs into action to handle the event.

Other classes will be interested in responding to these events. How they respond is not of interest to the class raising the event. The button says "I was clicked," and the responding classes react appropriately.

Publishing and Subscribing

In C#, any object can *publish* a set of events to which other classes can *subscribe*. When the publishing class raises an event, all the subscribed classes are notified.

> This design implements the publish/subscribe (also know as the observer) pattern described in the seminal work *Design Patterns* by Gamma et al. (Addison Wesley). Gamma et al. describe the intent of this pattern: "Define a one to many dependency between objects so that when one object changes state, all its dependents are notified and updated automatically."

With this mechanism, your object can say "Here are things I can notify you about," and other classes might sign up, saying "Yes, let me know when that happens." For example, a button might notify any number of interested observers when it is clicked. The button is called the *publisher* because the button publishes the Click event, and the other classes are the *subscribers* because they subscribe to the Click event.

Events and Delegates

In C#, you use delegates to implement events. The publishing class defines a delegate that the subscribing classes must implement. When the event is raised, the subscribing class's methods are invoked through the delegate.

As explained previously, a method that handles an event is called an event handler. You can declare your event handlers as you would any other delegate.

By convention, event handlers in the .NET Framework return void and take two parameters. The first parameter is the "source" of the event—that is, the publishing object. The second parameter is an object derived from EventArgs. The EventArgs class contains information about the event that can be of use to the event handler method. It is recommended that your event handlers follow this design pattern.

Events are properties of the class publishing the event. The event keyword controls how the event property is accessed by the subscribing classes. The keyword is designed to maintain the publish/subscribe idiom.

Suppose you want to create a Clock class that uses events to notify potential subscribers whenever the local time changes value by one second. Example 19-4 shows the complete source for this example, followed by the output and a detailed analysis.

Example 19-4. Events to update the time for the Clock class

```
using System;
using System.Threading;

namespace DelegatesAndEvents
{
    // A class to hold the information about the event;
    // in this case it will hold only information
    // available in the Clock class, but could hold
    // additional state information.
    public class TimeInfoEventArgs : EventArgs
    {
        public TimeInfoEventArgs(int hour, int minute, int second)
        {
            this.hour = hour;
            this.minute = minute;
            this.second = second;
        }
        public readonly int hour;
        public readonly int minute;
        public readonly int second;
    }

    // Our subject class; it is this class that other classes
    // will observe. This class publishes one event:
    // OnSecondChange. The observers subscribe to that event.
    public class Clock
    {
        // The delegate the subscribers must implement
        public delegate void SecondChangeHandler
            (
            object clock,
            TimeInfoEventArgs timeInformation
            );

        // The event we publish
        public event SecondChangeHandler OnSecondChange;

        // Set the clock running;
        // it will raise an event for each new second.
        public void Run()
        {
            for(;;)
            {
                // Sleep 10 milliseconds.
                Thread.Sleep(10);

                // Get the current time.
                System.DateTime dt = System.DateTime.Now;
```

Example 19-4. Events to update the time for the Clock class (continued)

```
            // If the second has changed,
            // notify the subscribers.
            if (dt.Second != second)
            {
                // Create the TimeInfoEventArgs object
                // to pass to the subscriber.
                TimeInfoEventArgs timeInformation =
                    new TimeInfoEventArgs(
                    dt.Hour,dt.Minute,dt.Second);

                // If anyone has subscribed, notify them.
                if (OnSecondChange != null)
                {
                    OnSecondChange(
                        this,timeInformation);
                }
            }

            // Update the state.
            this.second = dt.Second;
            this.minute = dt.Minute;
            this.hour = dt.Hour;


        }
    }
    private int hour;
    private int minute;
    private int second;
}

// Declares an observer class, DisplayClock, which subscribes to the
// Clock object's events. The job of DisplayClock is
// to display the current time.
public class DisplayClock
{
    // Given a Clock object, subscribe to
    // its SecondChangeHandler event.
    public void Subscribe(Clock theClock)
    {
        theClock.OnSecondChange +=
            new Clock.SecondChangeHandler(TimeHasChanged);
    }

    // The method that implements the
    // delegated functionality.
    public void TimeHasChanged(
        object theClock, TimeInfoEventArgs ti)
    {
        Console.WriteLine("Current Time: {0}:{1}:{2}",
            ti.hour.ToString(),
            ti.minute.ToString(),
            ti.second.ToString());
```

Example 19-4. Events to update the time for the Clock class (continued)

```
        }
    }

    // A second subscriber whose job is to write to a file.
    public class LogCurrentTime
    {
        public void Subscribe(Clock theClock)
        {
            theClock.OnSecondChange +=
                new Clock.SecondChangeHandler(WriteLogEntry);
        }

        // This method should write to a file, but
        // we write to the console to see the effect.
        // Note that this object keeps no state.
        public void WriteLogEntry(
            object theClock, TimeInfoEventArgs ti)
        {
            Console.WriteLine("Logging to file: {0}:{1}:{2}",
                ti.hour.ToString(),
                ti.minute.ToString(),
                ti.second.ToString());
        }
    }
    class Tester
    {
        public void Run()
        {
            // Create a new Clock object.
            Clock theClock = new Clock();

            // Create the DisplayClock object and tell it to
            // subscribe to the Clock just created.
            DisplayClock dc = new DisplayClock();
            dc.Subscribe(theClock);

            // Create a Log object and tell it
            // to subscribe to the Clock object.
            LogCurrentTime lct = new LogCurrentTime();
            lct.Subscribe(theClock);

            // Get the clock started.
            theClock.Run();

        }

        [STAThread]
        static void Main()
        {
            Tester t = new Tester();
            t.Run();
        }
    }
}
```

Example 19-4. Events to update the time for the Clock class (continued)

Output:
```
Current Time: 9:16:36
Logging to file: 9:16:36
Current Time: 9:16:37
Logging to file: 9:16:37
Current Time: 9:16:38
Logging to file: 9:16:38
Current Time: 9:16:39
Logging to file: 9:16:39
```

In Example 19-4, you create an event, OnSecondChange:

```
public event SecondChangeHandler OnSecondChange;
```

The general declaration of an event type is as follows:

```
[attributes] [modifiers] event type
        member-name
```

The optional attributes are an advanced topic that is not covered in this book. See *Programming C#*, Second Edition (O'Reilly) for more information. The optional modifier can be abstract, new, override, static, virtual, or one of the four standard access modifiers (public, private, etc.); access modifiers are discussed in Chapter 8. The modifier is followed by the event keyword.

The type is the delegate to which you want to associate the event (in this case SecondChangeHandler).

The member name is the name of the event (in this case OnSecondChange). It is customary to begin events with the word On.

Altogether, this declaration states that OnSecondChange is an event that is implemented by a delegate of type SecondChangeHandler.

The declaration for the SecondChangeHandler delegate is:

```
public delegate void SecondChangeHandler(
    object clock,
    TimeInfoEventArgs timeInformation
    );
```

As stated earlier, by convention an event handler returns void and takes two parameters: the source of the event (clock) and an object derived from EventArgs (TimeInfoEventArgs). TimeInfoEventArgs is a class designed for this book, defined as follows:

```
public class TimeInfoEventArgs : EventArgs
{
    public readonly int hour;
    public readonly int minute;
    public readonly int second;
    public TimeInfoEventArgs(int hour, int minute, int second)
    {
```

```
        this.hour = hour;
        this.minute = minute;
        this.second = second;
    }
}
```

The TimeInfoEventArgs object has information about the current hour, minute, and second. It defines a constructor and three public read-only integer variables.

In addition to a delegate and an event, a Clock has three member variables (hour, minute, and second), as well as a single method, Run():

```
public void Run()
{
    for(;;)
    {
        // Sleep ten milliseconds.
        Thread.Sleep(10);

        // Get the current time.
        System.DateTime dt = System.DateTime.Now;

        // If the second has changed,
        // notify the subscribers.
        if (dt.Second != second)
        {
            // Create the TimeInfoEventArgs object
            // to pass to the subscriber.
            TimeInfoEventArgs timeInformation =
                new TimeInfoEventArgs(dt.Hour,dt.Minute,dt.Second);

            // If anyone has subscribed, notify them.
            if (OnSecondChange != null)
            {
                OnSecondChange(this,timeInformation);
            }
        }

        // Update the state.
        this.second = dt.Second;
        this.minute = dt.Minute;
        this.hour = dt.Hour;

    }
}
```

Run() creates an infinite for loop that periodically checks the system time. If the time has changed from the Clock object's current time, it notifies all its subscribers and then updates its own state.

The first step is to sleep for ten milliseconds:

```
Thread.Sleep(10);
```

This makes use of Sleep(), which is a static method of the Thread class from the System.Threading namespace. The call to Sleep() causes a 10 second pause in execution, preventing the loop from running so tightly that little else on the computer gets done.

After sleeping for 10 milliseconds, the Run() method checks the current time:

```
System.DateTime dt = System.DateTime.Now;
```

About every 100 times that the Run() method checks the time, the second will have incremented. The Run() method notices that change and notifies its subscribers. To do so, it first creates a new TimeInfoEventArgs object:

```
if (dt.Second != second)
{
    // create the TimeInfoEventArgs object
    // to pass to the subscriber
    TimeInfoEventArgs timeInformation =
        new TimeInfoEventArgs(dt.Hour,dt.Minute,dt.Second);
```

It then notifies the subscribers by firing the OnSecondChange event:

```
    // if anyone has subscribed, notify them
    if (OnSecondChange != null)
    {
        OnSecondChange(this,timeInformation);
    }
}
```

If an event has no subscribers registered, it evaluates to null. The preceding test checks that the value is not null, ensuring that there are subscribers before calling OnSecondChange.

You will remember that OnSecondChange takes two arguments: the source of the event and the object derived from EventArgs. In Example 19-4, the Clock object's this reference is passed because the clock is the source of the event. The second parameter is the TimeInfoEventArgs object timeInformation created on the preceding line.

Raising the event invokes whatever methods have been registered with the Clock class through the delegate. More about this in a moment.

Once the event is raised, update the state of the Clock class:

```
this.second = dt.Second;
this.minute = dt.Minute;
this.hour = dt.Hour;
```

All that is left is to create classes that can subscribe to this event. You'll create two. Your first will be the DisplayClock class. The job of DisplayClock is not to keep track of time but rather to display the current time to the console.

Example 19-4 simplifies this class down to two methods. The first is a helper method named Subscribe(), which subscribes to the Clock object's OnSecondChange event. The second method is the event handler TimeHasChanged():

```
public class DisplayClock
{
    public void Subscribe(Clock theClock)
    {
        theClock.OnSecondChange +=
            new Clock.SecondChangeHandler(TimeHasChanged);
    }

    public void TimeHasChanged(
        object theClock, TimeInfoEventArgs ti)
    {
        Console.WriteLine("Current Time: {0}:{1}:{2}",
            ti.hour.ToString(),
            ti.minute.ToString(),
            ti.second.ToString());
    }
}
```

When the first method, Subscribe(), is invoked, it creates a new SecondChangeHandler delegate, passing in its event handler method TimeHasChanged(). It then registers the SecondChangeHandler delegate with the OnSecondChange event of Clock.

Create a second class, LogCurrentTime, that will also respond to this event. This class would normally log the event to a file, but for our demonstration purposes, it will log to the standard console:

```
public class LogCurrentTime
{
    public void Subscribe(Clock theClock)
    {
        theClock.OnSecondChange +=
            new Clock.SecondChangeHandler(WriteLogEntry);
    }

    // This method should write to a file, but
    // we write to the console to see the effect.
    // This object keeps no state.
    public void WriteLogEntry(
        object theClock, TimeInfoEventArgs ti)
    {
        Console.WriteLine("Logging to file: {0}:{1}:{2}",
            ti.hour.ToString(),
            ti.minute.ToString(),
            ti.second.ToString());
    }
}
```

Although in this example these two classes are very similar, in a production program any number of disparate classes might subscribe to an event.

Decoupling Publishers from Subscribers

The Clock class could simply print the time rather than raise an event, so why bother with the indirection of using delegates? The advantage of the publish/subscribe idiom is that any number of classes can be notified when an event is raised. The subscribing classes do not need to know how the Clock works, and the Clock does not need to know what subscribers are going to do in response to the event. Similarly, a Button can publish an OnClick event, and any number of unrelated objects can subscribe to that event, receiving notification when the Button is clicked.

The publisher and the subscribers are decoupled by the delegate. This is highly desirable; it makes for more flexible and robust code. The Clock can change how it detects time without breaking any of the subscribing classes, and the subscribing classes can change how they respond to time changes without breaking the Clock. The two classes spin independently of one another, and that makes for code that is easier to maintain.

Notice that events are added using the += operator. This allows new events to be added to the Clock object's OnSecondChange event without destroying the events already registered. When LogCurrentTime subscribes to the OnSecondChange event, you do not want the event to lose track of the fact that DisplayClock has already subscribed.

All that remains is to create a Clock class, create the DisplayClock class, and tell the DisplayClock object to subscribe to the event. Then create a LogCurrentTime class and tell it to subscribe as well. Finally, tell the Clock to run.

The net effect of this code is to create two classes, DisplayClock and LogCurrentTime, both of which subscribe to a third class's event (Clock.OnSecondChange).

CHAPTER 20
Afterword

Congratulations! If you've worked your way to this point in the book, you are now a C# programmer. You should be very proud. Of course, no primer can cover everything there is to know about .NET programming, and you are not at the end, but rather at the beginning of your education. Nonetheless, you've made a very good start.

Where to Go from Here

I intentionally kept this book short to provide you with the fundamentals without letting more difficult topics distract you from the core elements of the language. Now that you've completed the book, however, you may be wondering where to go from here in your pursuit of .NET.

There is a wealth of information available, both in books and online. The first task is to decide what you are interested in. Potential topics include:

- Advanced topics in C# programming
- Web (ASP.NET) programming
- Windows (Windows Forms) programming

Sooner or later you'll probably decide to read extensively on all three topics; the only question is which you tackle first. In the next sections, I'll recommend some more advanced books to help you find your way through these topics.

Advanced Topics in C#

If you decide that you want to understand all the nooks and crannies of C# before going on to create applications, you might consider reading a more advanced guide or a reference work on the language.

O'Reilly offers two choices: *Programming C#*, Second Edition, is my more advanced book, and *C# in a Nutshell*, by Peter Drayton, Ben Albahari, and Ted Neward, is a comprehensive reference work. The difference between *Programming C#*, Second Edition, and *Learning C#* is that *Programming C#* was written for experienced object-oriented programmers and does not spend as much time on the fundamentals. In exchange, this somewhat longer book does go into more detail and actually gets into the process of developing applications for the .NET platform.

You'll find that all of the material covered in *Learning C#* is also covered in the first twelve chapters of *Programming C#*, Second Edition. You may want to skim these chapters anyway, both for review and because some advanced topics do appear in these early chapters.

The next four chapters of *Programming C#* provide an overview of both ASP.NET and Windows Forms, as well as ADO.NET. ASP.NET is used for programming web applications and web services, while the Windows Forms technology is used to program Windows applications. ADO.NET is the .NET technology for interacting with databases.

The final part of *Programming C#* covers advanced topics in .NET programming such as assemblies, versioning, attributes and reflection, marshaling and remoting, threads and synchronization, streams, and interoperating with COM.

Assemblies are the basic unit of compilation. The chapter on assemblies and versioning addresses issues that arise when you create large commercial applications. You'll find information about private and shared assemblies, as well as an overview of how you manage the release of multiple versions of your program.

Attributes are metadata (data about your program). There is no coverage of attributes in *Learning C#* because this is an advanced topic. However, attributes and custom attributes allow you to control how your program is processed by the tools available in .NET. Reflection is the process of a program examining itself (or another program), and it allows you to discover, at runtime, the methods and properties of an object that was not known at compile time.

Threads are created when you want a program to do two things at once. When you have more than one thread operating in your program, you must control synchronization (making sure that access to your data is mediated so that one thread does not corrupt the data created in a second thread). The chapter on threading teaches you how to take control of this powerful aspect of .NET and create programs that are highly efficient.

Marshaling is the process of sending an object from one process or computer to another, which allows you to share objects across program boundaries. Remoting is the process of calling a method in a different program. These very advanced topics allow you to build highly distributed programs.

Streams allow you to read and write data both from a file and across the network. The .NET Framework provides extensive stream support, including support for reading and writing data across the standard web protocols such as HTTP.

Finally, many companies have extensive libraries of objects created in COM, the earlier Microsoft technology for building classes and controls. The chapter on COM in *Programming C#*, Second Edition, teaches you how to import these controls and DLL files into your .NET application (or export .NET controls to COM) to preserve your investment.

If you decide that you want to develop expertise in integrating COM with .NET, take a look at Adam Nathan's *.NET and Com* (Sams). I can't think of a more definitive book on this difficult topic.

There are a couple of other excellent books that provide an overview of .NET programming as well. Certainly take a look at Jeff Prosise's *Programming Microsoft .NET* (Microsoft Press) and also *Developing Applications with Visual Studio .NET* by Richard Grimes (Addison Wesley). Prosise and Grimes are two of the best writers in the field, and their books are very valuable.

If you want to go beyond the basics of .NET programming and get deep into the internals, there is no better book than *Applied Microsoft .NET Framework Programming* by Jeffrey Richter (Microsoft Press). Richter is a phenomenal writer, and his chapter on delegates alone is worth the cost of the book.

Another key topic in .NET programming is security. For the definitive word on .NET security, you'll want to buy *.NET Framework Security* by LaMacchia et al. (Addison Wesley).

Web (ASP.NET) Programming

Rather than diving deeper into the recesses of C#, you might decide to get started with building ASP.NET applications. ASP.NET applications can be interactive web sites, portals, or complete applications running on and distributed through the Web. For example, Microsoft offers a free sample application, *IBuySpy Store* (*http://ibuyspystore.com*), that demonstrates how you can build a full online store using ASP.NET technology.

Visual Studio .NET provides extensive support for building ASP.NET applications, and C# is the language of choice for this development. With what you've learned already, you are well prepared to move on to creating web applications.

I wrote *Programming ASP.NET* with Dan Hurwitz (O'Reilly) as a comprehensive guide to ASP.NET technology. You'll find extensive coverage of Web Form controls and event handling. You'll also find coverage of advanced programming technique, error handling, and validation. *Programming ASP.NET* devotes more than 150 pages to working with data in your web applications and also provides extensive coverage of web services. Finally, *Programming ASP.NET* offers coverage of such advanced topics as custom controls, security, caching and performance, and deployment related issues.

Windows Forms Programming

Another alternative is to focus on building rich-client Windows applications, using the new Windows Forms technology. Windows applications allow you to take advantage of the full resources of the operating system and yet still distribute aspects of your application over the Web.

A good starting point for more information on building rich-client applications is an article called "Return of the Rich Client" in the June 2002 MSDN Magazine by Jason Clark. You can read this article online at *http://msdn.microsoft.com/msdnmag/issues/02/06/rich/rich.asp*.

An excellent source of material on the details of Windows Forms and the underlying technology of building native Windows applications with .NET is *Programming Microsoft Windows with C#* by Charles Petzold (Microsoft Press). Petzold is the acknowledged master of Windows, and many of us learned Windows programming from his previous excellent book *Programming Windows, The Definitive Guide to the Win32 API* (Microsoft Press).

I am currently writing the O'Reilly book *Programming .NET Windows Applications*, again with Dan Hurwitz, to be published in the spring of 2003. Again we are targeting the book at programmers with a working knowledge of C# or VB.NET, as you now have.

Programming .NET Windows Applications will be a comprehensive guide to writing Windows applications that includes extensive coverage of Windows Form controls and event handling. As in *Programming ASP.NET*, you'll find coverage of advanced programming techniques, error handling, and validation.

The coverage of data handling will be extensive, and we will also provide complete coverage of advanced topics such as custom controls, security, performance, and deployment-related issues.

Other Resources

There are extensive resources available to the aspiring C# programmer. The most powerful, of course, is the MSDN library available from Microsoft (*http://www.msdn.microsoft.com*), which includes a number of different subscription levels, depending on your needs and resources.

Microsoft also hosts the gotdotnet forum (*http://www.gotdotnet.com*), which provides sample programs, extensive documentation, and articles on .NET programming. There are also dozens of excellent web sites devoted to .NET programming, not least of which is the O'Reilly site, *http://dotnet.oreilly.com*.

One of the most powerful resources available to C# programmers is the set of extensive mailing lists and newsgroups that have sprung up so quickly. I find the dotnet mailing lists from Developmentor (*http://discuss.develop.com*) and the ASP Friends lists (*http://www.aspfriends.com/aspfriends*) to be particularly useful.

Finally, I provide a FAQ, source code, and related material on my web site: *http://www.LibertyAssociates.com*, where you can also sign up for a private support discussion forum.

Best of luck with C#, and please do keep in touch.

C# Keywords

abstract
> A class modifier that specifies that the class must be derived from to be instantiated.

as
> A binary operator type that casts the left operand to the type specified by the right operand and that returns null rather than throwing an exception if the cast fails.

base
> A variable with the same meaning as this, except it accesses a base class implementation of a member.

bool
> A logical datatype that can be true or false.

break
> A jump statement that exits a loop or switch statement block.

byte
> A one-byte unsigned integral datatype.

case
> A selection statement that defines a particular choice in a switch statement.

catch
> The part of a try statement that catches exceptions of a specific type defined in the catch clause.

char
> A two-byte Unicode character datatype.

checked
> A statement or operator that enforces arithmetic bounds checking on an expression or statement block.

class
> An extendable reference type that combines data and functionality into one unit.

const
> A modifier for a local variable or field declaration that indicates the value is a constant. A const is evaluated at compile time and can only be a predefined type.

continue
> A jump statement that skips the remaining statements in a statement block and continues to the next iteration in a loop.

decimal
> A 16-byte precise decimal datatype.

default
> A marker in a switch statement specifying the action to take when no case statements match the switch expression.

delegate
> A type for defining a method signature so that delegate instances can hold and invoke a method or list of methods that match its signature.

do
> A loop statement to iterate a statement block until an expression at the end of the loop evaluates to false.

double
> An eight-byte floating-point datatype.

else
> A conditional statement that defines the action to take when a preceding if expression evaluates to false.

enum

A value type that defines a group of named numeric constants.

event

A member modifier for a delegate field or property that indicates only the += and −= methods of the delegate can be accessed.

explicit

An operator that defines an explicit conversion.

extern

A method modifier that indicates the method is implemented with unmanaged code.

false

A Boolean literal.

finally

The part of a try statement that is always executed when control leaves the scope of the try block.

fixed

A statement to pin down a reference type so that the garbage collector won't move it during pointer arithmetic operations.

float

A four-byte floating-point datatype.

for

A loop statement that combines an initialization statement, stopping condition, and iterative statement into one statement.

foreach

A loop statement that iterates over collections that implement IEnumerable.

get

The name of the accessor that returns the value of a property.

goto

A jump statement that jumps to a label within the same method and same scope as the jump point.

if

A conditional statement that executes its statement block if its expression evaluates to true.

implicit

An operator that defines an implicit conversion.

in

The operator between a type and an IEnumerable in a foreach statement.

int

A four-byte signed integral datatype.

interface

A contract that specifies the members a class or struct can implement to receive generic services for that type.

internal

An access modifier that indicates a type or type member is accessible only to other types in the same assembly.

is

A relational operator that evaluates to true if the left operand's type matches, is derived from, or implements the type specified by the right operand.

lock

A statement that acquires a lock on a reference-type object to help multiple threads cooperate.

long

An eight-byte signed integral datatype.

namespace

Maps a set of types to a common name.

new

An operator that calls a constructor on a type, allocating a new object on the heap if the type is a reference type, or initializing the object if the type is a value type. The keyword is overloaded to hide an inherited member.

null

A reference-type literal that indicates no object is referenced.

object

The type all other types derive from.

operator

A method modifier that overloads operators.

out

A parameter modifier that specifies the parameter is passed by reference and must be assigned by the method being called.

override

A method modifier that indicates that a method of a class overrides a virtual method of a class or interface.

params

A parameter modifier that specifies that the last parameter of a method can accept multiple parameters of the same type.

private

An access modifier that indicates that only the containing type can access the member.

protected

An access modifier that indicates that only the containing type or derived types can access the member.

public

An access modifier that indicates that a type or type member is accessible to all other types.

readonly

A field modifier specifying that a field can be assigned only once, in either its declaration or its containing type's constructor.

ref

A parameter modifier that specifies that the parameter is passed by reference and is assigned before being passed to the method.

return

A jump statement that exits a method, specifying a return value when the method is nonvoid.

sbyte

A one-byte signed integral datatype.

sealed

A class modifier that indicates a class cannot be derived from.

set

The name of the accessor that sets the value of a property.

short

A two-byte signed integral datatype.

sizeof

An operator that returns the size in bytes of a struct.

stackalloc

An operator that returns a pointer to a specified number of value types allocated on the stack.

static

A type member modifier that indicates that the member applies to the type rather than an instance of the type.

string

A predefined reference type that represents an immutable sequence of Unicode characters.

struct

A value type that combines data and functionality in one unit.

switch

A selection statement that allows a selection of choices to be made based on the value of a predefined type.

this

A variable that references the current instance of a class or struct.

throw

A jump statement that throws an exception when an abnormal condition has occurred.

true

A Boolean literal.

try

A statement that provides a way to handle an exception or a premature exit in a statement block.

typeof

An operator that returns the type of an object as a System.Type object.

uint

A four-byte unsigned integral datatype.

ulong

An eight-byte unsigned integral datatype.

unchecked

A statement or operator that prevents arithmetic bounds from checking on an expression.

unsafe

A method modifier or statement that permits pointer arithmetic to be performed within a particular block.

ushort

A two-byte unsigned integral datatype.

using

Specifies that types in a particular namespace can be referred to without requiring their fully qualified type names. The using statement defines a scope. At the end of the scope, the object is disposed.

value

The name of the implicit variable set by the set accessor of a property.

virtual

A class method modifier that indicates that a method can be overridden by a derived class.

void

A keyword used in place of a type for methods that don't have a return value.

volatile

Indicates that a field may be modified by the operating system or another thread.

while

A loop statement to iterate a statement block until an expression at the start of each iteration evaluates to false.

Index

Symbols

/* */ (comment delimeters), 11
+ (addition operator), 74
   combining delegates, 318
+= (addition self-assignment operator), 78
   adding events, 331
   adding to multicast delegates, 318, 321
&& (and operator), 81
= (assignment operator), 40, 73, 77
   copying strings, 269
\ (backslash), beginning escape
    characters, 264
{} (braces)
   enclosing block of statements, 50, 52–54
   enclosing class body, 11, 87
   enclosing initial array elements, 213
   enclosing namespaces, 10
^ (caret), indicating new line in regular
    expressions, 281
: (colon)
   creating a derived class, 137
   following labels, 62
   implementing interfaces, 180
   invoking constructor of base class, 139
+ (concatenation operator), 268
-- (decrement operator), 78
/ (division operator), 74
/= (division self-assignment operator), 78
. (dot operator), in object names, 10
== (equals operator), 57, 80, 270
> (greater than operator), 80
>= (greater than or equal to operator), 80
++ (increment operator), 64, 78

< (less than operator), 80
<= (less than or equal to operator), 57, 80
% (modulus operator), 75–77
%= (modulus self-assignment operator), 78
* (multiplication operator), 74
*= (multiplication self-assignment
    operator), 78
!= (not equals operator), 80, 164
! (not operator), 81
|| (or operator), 81
() (parentheses)
   changing order of evaluation, 83
   grouping in regular expressions, 281
+ (plus sign), in Autos window, 128
; (semicolon), ending statements with, 44, 46
/// (slashes, three), beginning comments, 12
// (slashes, two), beginning comments, 11
[] (square brackets)
   in array declarations, 207
   array index operator, 210
   in indexer declarations, 228
   in jagged array declaration, 222
   string index operator, 273
   in syntax specification, 42
- (subtraction operator), 74
-= (subtraction self-assignment operator), 78
   removing from multicast delegates, 321
? (ternary operator), 81
@ (verbatim string literals), 265
| (vertical bar), grouping in regular
    expressions, 281

We'd like to hear your suggestions for improving our indexes. Send email to *index@oreilly.com*.

A

abstract classes, 147–150, 337
  instantiating, 147
  interfaces compared to, 179
  (see also interfaces)
abstract keyword, 148
abstract methods, 147–150
  not used with explicitly implemented
    methods, 203
access modifiers, 95
  for class members, 17, 92, 140
  for classes, 87, 140
  not used in interface methods, 182
  not used with explicitly implemented
    methods, 203
accessors
  get accessors, 117, 182
  set accessors, 117, 182
Add() method, ArrayList class, 251, 253
Add QuickWatch item, VS.NET
    debugger, 131
Add Watch item, VS.NET debugger, 131
addition operator (+), 74
  combining delegates, 318
addition self-assignment operator (+=), 78
ADO.NET, books about, 333
aggregation of classes, 18
algorithm, 68
ampersand, two (&&), and operator, 81
analysis, object-oriented, 21
and operator (&&), 81
Append() method, StringBuilder class, 279
AppendFormat() method, StringBuilder
    class, 279
applications, 3
  creating from source code, 9
  running from VS.NET, 30
  types of, 2, 5
  (see also debugger; executable files;
    projects; source code)
arguments (see parameters)
arithmetical operators (see mathematical
    operators)
Array class (see System.Array class)
array lists, 250–253
  copying to arrays, 259–262
ArrayList class, 251–253
arrays, 142, 206
  accessing elements of, 210
  clearing, 225
  collections copying to, 259–262
  copying, 225

  declaring, 207
  default values of elements in, 208
  dimensions, number of, 225
  elements as value types, 207
  first instance of, determining, 225
  fixed size, determining if it has, 225
  index of, 210
  initializing (populating), 208, 213–215
  instantiating, 207
  iterating through with foreach
    statement, 212
  jagged, 206, 222–225
  last instance of, determining, 225
  length of, 210, 225
  for methods with variable number of
    parameters, 215–217
  multidimensional, 206, 217–225
  rectangular, 206, 218–221
  as reference types, 207
  reversing order of elements in, 225–227
  sorting elements in, 225–227
  System.Array class
    implementing, 225–228
  zero-based, 210
  (see also array lists)
as operator, 191–193, 337
ASP.NET, 5, 7, 333
assemblies, 333
assignment, definite, 38, 123
assignment operator (=), 40, 73, 77
  copying strings, 269
  (see also equals operator)
association among classes, 18
asterisk (*) as multiplication operator, 74
asterisk, equals sign (*=), multiplication
    self-assignment operator, 78
at sign (@) beginning verbatim string
    literals, 265
attributes, 87, 333
AutoHide property of window, 29
Autos window, VS.NET debugger, 128

B

backslash (\) beginning escape
    characters, 264
base class, 20, 137, 337
behavior of classes or objects (see methods)
bool type, 32, 35, 337
Boolean expression, 50
Boolean values, types for, 32, 35
boxing
  arrays, 207

Q

question mark (?), ternary operator, 81
Queue class, 253–256
queues, 253–256
    copying to arrays, 259–262
QuickWatch window, VS.NET
        debugger, 131

R

Rank property, System.Array class, 225
rational numbers, types for, 34
readonly keyword, 339
read-only properties, 118
reassignment operator, 77
rectangular arrays, 206, 218–221
red dot and red highlighting, in VS.NET
        debugger, 124
ref keyword, 120, 339
reference types, 120
    arrays as, 207
    classes as, 89–93
    value types being treated as, 152–154
ReferenceEquals() method, Object class, 151
Regex class, 282–283
Regex constructor, 282
regular expressions, 281–283
    book about, 282
    literals in, 281
    metacharacters in, 281
relational operators, 80–83
remainder in division, finding, 75–77
Remove() method
    StringBuilder class, 279
    System.String class, 266
RemoveAt() method, ArrayList class, 251
Replace() method
    Regex class, 282
    StringBuilder class, 279
Reset() method, IEnumerator interface, 245
responsibilities of an object, 15
return statement, 339
Reverse() method
    ArrayList class, 251
    System.Array class, 225–227
root class, 150–152
rows, in two-dimensional array, 218
Run() method, 104, 106–109
runtime, 35

S

sbyte type, 32, 33, 339
scope, local, 89
sealed classes, 150, 339
sealed structs, 176
self-assignment operators, 78, 84
semantics, 1, 8, 22
semicolon (;) at end of statements, 44, 46
server, 19
set accessors, 117, 182, 339
set() method, 182, 228, 232, 234
Shift-F11 keyboard shortcut, 126
short type, 32, 33, 339
signature of a method, 112, 114
signed numeric types, 33
sizeof operator, 339
slashes
    and asterisks (/* */), enclosing
        comments, 11
    and equals sign (/=), division
        self-assignment operator, 78
    one (/), division operator, 74
    three (///), beginning comments, 12
    two (//), beginning comments, 11
.sln extension, 26
Solution Explorer window in IDE, 28
solutions, VS.NET, 26
Sort() method
    ArrayList class, 251
    System.Array class, 225–227
source code, 3, 7
    compiling, 9
    .cs extension for, 25
    maintenance of, 52
    (see also applications; debugger)
spaces in code, 45
"spaghetti code", 62
specialization, 19, 134–136
    (see also inheritance)
Split() method
    Regex class, 282
    System.String class, 266, 277–279
square brackets ([])
    in array declarations, 207
    array index operator, 210
    in indexer declarations, 228
    in jagged array declaration, 222
    string index operator, 273
    in syntax specification, 42
stack, call (see call stack)
Stack class, 257–259

T

\t (tab escape character), 264
tab escape character (\t), 264
tabs in code, 45
TANSTAAFL, 24
task list in IDE, 28
technical support, for this book, x
templates for projects, 26
ternary operator (?), 81
text editor, 3
this keyword, 102, 229, 339
threads, 333
throw statement, 286, 339
titlebar in VS.NET, 28
ToArray() method
    ArrayList class, 251, 259–262
    Queue class, 254, 259–262
    Stack class, 257, 259–262
ToCharArray() method, System.String
    class, 266
ToLower() method, System.String class, 266
toolbars in VS.NET, 29
ToString() method, Object class, 151, 265
ToUpper() method, System.String class, 266
Trim() method, System.String class, 266
TrimEnd() method, System.String class, 266
TrimStart() method, System.String class, 266
true keyword, 339
try statement, 154, 287, 339
two-dimensional arrays (see
    multidimensional arrays)
typeof operator, 339
types, 32
    Boolean, 32, 35
    boxing, 152–154
    character, 32, 35
    checking compatibility of, 161
    compiler warnings and errors about, 35
    conversion (casting), 44, 167
        explicit conversion of, 167
        implicit conversion of, 167
        operators for, 167–171
        to string, 265
    default values if not initialized, 98
    intrinsic, 32, 89
    non-numeric, 35
    numeric, 33
    polymorphic, 141
    reference, 89–93, 120, 152–154
    unboxing, 152–154
    value, 89–93, 120, 152–154

U

uint type, 32, 33, 339
ulong type, 33, 339
UML (Unified Modeling Language), 135
unboxing value types, 152–154
unchecked operator, 339
unconditional branching, 48
    break statement, 57, 66
    continue statement, 67
    goto statement, 59
    method calls as, 48
    throw statement, 286
Unified Modeling Language (UML), 135
unmanaged resources, 109
unsafe keyword, 340
unsigned numeric types, 33
ushort type, 32, 33, 340
using declaration, 13
using statement, 110, 340

V

value keyword, 340
value types, 89–93, 120
    array elements as, 207
    intrinsic types as, 89
    structs as, 172
    treating as reference types, 152–154
variables, 33, 36–39
    assigning a value to, 36, 38, 73
    decrementing, 77–79
    displaying in debugger, 128, 129
    identifier for, 36
    incrementing, 77–79
    initializing, 36, 38
    local, 89
    naming, 36, 40
    reassigning values to, 77
    (see also member variables)
verbatim string literals, 265
versioning, 145
vertical bar (|), grouping in regular
    expressions, 281
vertical bar, two (||), or operator, 81
virtual keyword, 141, 145, 340
    marking interface methods with, 197, 201
    not used with explicity implemented
        methods, 203
Visual Basic .NET, 2
Visual Studio .NET (see VS.NET)
void keyword, 12, 340
volatile keyword, 340

VS.NET (Visual Studio .NET), 4, 23–31
   books about, 334
   Call Stack window, 131
   code completion feature of, 29
   compiling with, 9
   customizing to create Run()
      method, 106–109
   debugger, 124–132, 247–249
   editing window, 28
   help window, 28
   IntelliSense technology used by, 29, 36,
      104
   as MDI application, 27
   New Project dialog, 26
   online help files for, 31
   projects, 25–27
   Pushpin icon, 29
   running applications with, 30
   Solution Explorer window, 28
   solutions, 26
   Start icon, 30
   Start Page, 25
   task list, 28
   titlebar, 28
   toolbars, 29
   window behavior in, 28, 29
   X icon, 29

W

warnings, compiler, 35
Watch window, VS.NET debugger, 130
web applications, 2, 5, 7
web programming, books about, 334
web sites
   about this book, x
   ASP Friends lists, 336
   dotnet mailing list, 336
   for this book, x
   gotdotnet forum, 336
   MSDN library, 336
   .NET discussion lists, x
   O'Reilly & Associates, xi
while statement, 63, 71, 340
whitespace in programs, 45
whole numbers, types for, 34
Windows applications, 2, 6, 336
windows, behavior in VS.NET, 28, 29
Windows Forms, 5, 335
Write() method, Console class, 152
WriteLine() method, Console class, 37, 152,
   170

X

X icon, VS.NET, 29

4861

About the Author

Jesse Liberty is the author of a dozen books, including *Programming ASP.NET* and *Programming C#* from O'Reilly. Jesse is the president of Liberty Associates, Inc. (*http://www.LibertyAssociates.com*), where he provides .NET training, contract programming, and consulting. He is a former Vice President of electronic delivery for Citibank, and a former Distinguished Software Engineer and architect for AT&T, Ziff Davis, Xerox, and PBS.

Colophon

Our look is the result of reader comments, our own experimentation, and feedback from distribution channels. Distinctive covers complement our distinctive approach to technical topics, breathing personality and life into potentially dry subjects.

The animal on the cover of *Learning C#* is a goldfish. Goldfish are freshwater fish popular in aquariums and ponds. Though they are native to China, goldfish are one of the most common household pets all over the world. They were first domesticated centuries ago when it was discovered that carp, which are usually olive-colored, can have color mutations causing some of their scales to be red or gold. These mutated fish were bred to create many different varieties of goldfish, including the oranda, ryukin, lionhead, pearlscale, telescoped eye, and bubble eye types.

Most commercial goldfish are scaled and have metallic red, gold, white, silver, or black sheens. But the more rare "scaleless" fish have transparent scales, making them appear bright red, blue, purple, or calico-patterned. Though the wild carp from which goldfish are bred can measure up to 16 inches in length, most commercial goldfish are between 1 and 4 inches long.

Darren Kelly was the production editor, Catherine Morris was the copyeditor, and Sheryl Avruch was the proofreader for *Learning C#*. Tatiana Apandi Diaz and Claire Cloutier provided quality control. Interior composition was done by Philip Dangler and Genevieve d'Entremont. Angela Howard wrote the index.

Hanna Dyer designed the cover of this book, based on a series design by Edie Freedman. The cover image is a 19th-century engraving from the Dover Pictorial Archive. Emma Colby produced the cover layout with QuarkXPress 4.1 using Adobe's ITC Garamond font.

David Futato designed the interior layout. This book was converted to FrameMaker 5.5.6 with a format conversion tool created by Erik Ray, Jason McIntosh, Neil Walls, and Mike Sierra that uses Perl and XML technologies. The text font is Linotype Birka; the heading font is Adobe Myriad Condensed; and the code font is Lucas-Font's TheSans Mono Condensed. The illustrations that appear in the book were produced by Robert Romano and Jessamyn Read using Macromedia FreeHand 9 and Adobe Photoshop 6. The tip and warning icons were drawn by Christopher Bing. This colophon was written by Linley Dolby.